THE PETROGRAD WORKERS AND THE
FALL OF THE OLD REGIME

This is a study of the first months of the Russian Revolution as seen from the factory districts of Petrograd, the "red capital." Starting from a description of political culture in the different strata of the working class, the author proceeds to analyze the workers' conception of the revolution both in the Russian state and in the factory system. Making systematic use of the vast published and archival material now available, he shows that the workers greeted February as a national democratic revolution, albeit one with certain social goals that alone made political freedom meaningful. But these social demands posed no direct threat to capitalism, nor were they intended to. In this light, the radicalization that followed, culminating in the July demonstrations aimed at forcing the moderate Soviet leaders to take power, appears as an essentially defensive reaction based upon the growing realization by the workers that the propertied classes and their liberal representatives in the coalition were hostile to their aspirations and had turned against the revolution.

An attempt at understanding the revolution "from below," this book is intended to fill a gap in the Western literature that has paradoxically focused mainly on institutions, parties and leaders in a period marked precisely by the active participation of the broadest layers of society, and the workers in particular, in shaping their own collective fate. Basing himself as far as possible on primary sources emanating directly from the workers, the author questions the prevailing view of the workers as essentially unconscious, manipulated actors, anarchistically-inclined prey of unscrupulous demagogues. He concludes that the workers were certainly no less conscious politically than the more educated members of society and that they constituted a vital, creative and dynamic force in the Russian revolutionary process.

David Mandel took his BA at the Hebrew University and Ph.D at Columbia University, where he was appointed Senior Research Fellow in the Russian Institute (1977–8). In the course of his research for this book he spent a year in Leningrad as a Canada–USSR Exchange Scholar (1975). He has taught at the Centre for Russian and East European Studies at the University of Birmingham, the Departments of Political Science at McGill University and l'Université du Québec à Montréal, and the Department of Sociology at l'Université de Montréal. He is the author of several articles on the Russian revolutionary period and labor movement.

THE PETROGRAD WORKERS AND THE FALL OF THE OLD REGIME

From the February Revolution to the July Days, 1917

David Mandel

St. Martin's Press   New York

ISBN 0–312–60393–2

Library of Congress Cataloging in Publication Data

Mandel, David, 1947–
   The Petrograd workers and the fall of the old
regime

   Bibliography p
   Includes index
   1. Labor and laboring classes—Russian
S.F.S.R.   Leningrad—History.   2. Strikes and
lockouts   Russian S.F.S.R.—Leningrad   History
3. Labor and laboring classes—Russian S.F.S.R.—
Leningrad   Political activity—History   4. Lenin-
grad (R.S.F.S.R.)   Politics and government
5. Soviet Union   History—Revolution, 1917–1921.
I. Title.
HD8530.L5M36   1982   322'.2'0947453   81–21237
ISBN 0–312–60393–2   AACR2

For I. K. N. and R. J.

This book was sponsored by the
Russian Institute of Columbia University
in the City of New York

Contents

Page-numbering of the companion volume *The Petrograd Workers and the Soviet Seizure of Power* will follow on consecutively from this book.

List of Tables and Map

Glossary

All dates are given according to the Julian calendar, thirteen days behind the Western Gregorian calendar in the twentieth century.

census society the propertied classes and those members of the intelligentsia that identified with them

chernorabochii literally, black worker; unskilled labourer

conciliator contemptuous term applied to the moderate socialists who argued that an alliance between the workers and peasants and census society was necessary for the survival of the revolution

defencist after February 1917, those socialists who argued that as a result of the revolution the war on Russia's part had ceased to be imperialist and that the people had a duty to support the military efforts of the Provisional Government to defend the revolution

duma elected municipal government

intelligent one earning (or looking forward to earning) a living in an occupation recruited chiefly from among those with a higher or at least secondary education; worker-*intelligent*—a self-taught worker with the educational equivalent of an *intelligent*

internationalist after February 1917, those socialists who argued that the war being waged by the Provisional Government continued to be imperialist and should be opposed; included Bolsheviks, Menshevik–Internationalists and Left SRs

Kadet Constitutional Democrat, member of Russia's liberal party

nizy literally, those on the bottom; the lower classes, the poor

revolutionary democracy (or democracy) the workers, peasants and soldiers and those members of the intelligentsia that identified with them

SR Social Revolutionary, member of Russia's peasant-oriented socialist party, successor to the nineteenth-century populists; in the autumn of 1917 the Left SRs (internationalists) officially formed a separate party

State Duma Russian 'parliament', won as a result of the 1905 revolution; its powers were narrow and the franchise upon which it was elected even more so, especially after the June 1907 *coup d'état*

TsIK All-Russian Central Executive Committee of Soviets of Workers' and Soldiers' Deputies, elected at the First All-Russian Congress of Soviets in May–June 1917

verkhy literally, those on top; the wealthy and privileged

Acknowledgements

In the writing of this book I have many and large debts to acknowledge. My deepest debt is to Leopold Haimson, without whose help this study might never have been realised. His profound grasp of pre-revolutionary Russian society and his intellectual honesty have been an inspiration. Special thanks also to Robert Davies, editor of this series and Director of the Centre for Russian and East European Studies at the University of Birmingham during my truly enjoyable year there in 1978–9, for his valuable critical and editorial comments. Many other colleagues have read versions and parts of the manuscript and offered useful criticisms that influenced its ultimate form. Among these were Seweryn Bialer, Alexander Erlich, Ziva Galilee y Garcia, Ursula Nienhaus, Janet Rabinowitch and Ron Suny.

I am also grateful for the support given me by the Russian Institute of Columbia University, both during my graduate studies and as Senior Research Fellow in 1977–8.

Sincere thanks also to the people who typed various parts of the manuscript and especially to Beverley Colquhoun for a splendid job on the final draft.

Finally, I have a deep personal debt to my family and friends, whose contribution was indirect but whose support and kindness nevertheless played an integral role in the completion of this work.

Montréal   DAVID MANDEL

1 Introduction

No historical event arouses political passions as much as revolution, and no statement about the upheaval of 1917 provokes more con- troversy than the assertion that it was a proletarian revolution, a view which one scholar recently consigned in less than a paragraph to 'the realm of revolutionary mythology'.[1] And yet, a systematic study of working-class attitudes and activity in Petrograd, the heart of the revolution, leads one inexorably to the conclusion that this was indeed a workers' revolution. It was, of course, not only that; so complex and multi-faceted an event cannot be reduced to any simple formula. The Russian Revolution was, among other things, a soldiers' mutiny, a peasant rebellion, a movement of national minorities. Moreover, the autocracy's demise in February was facilitated by the *krizis verkhov*, the disaffection of the upper classes that had ripened towards the end of 1916, embracing even the most conservative elements of society, the landowners organised in the United Nobility, as well as significant strata of the bureaucracy and officer staff, who, if not quite of a revolutionary turn of mind, were still little inclined to join battle to save the discredited regime. Nevertheless, in the struggle for state power that culminated in the Bolshevik-led Soviet seizure of power in Petrograd, it was the working class that led the way, providing the mass movement with direction, organisation and a vastly disproportionate part of the active revolutionary forces.

This book is the first part of a study of a largely uncharted area of the Russian Revolution. Its aim is to offer a coherent account and analysis of the attitudes and behaviour of Petrograd's industrial workers rela- tive to three issues of the revolution that were uppermost in their minds: the war, economic regulation, and the question that eventually subsumed all others — state power.

Until recently Western scholarly work on this period has focused largely on leaders and institutions. Although in the past few years writers have begun to turn their attention to the lower strata of society, studies of the working class that systematically utilise the extensive primary sources now available are still few and far between.[2]

This paucity of monographs on the workers in the Western litera- ture on the revolution invites reflection on some of the assumptions that have predominated in the historiography. To the extent that the urban masses have entered the picture in past studies, they have

appeared principally as an elemental, basically anarchistic force which
the ultimate victors of the battle at the summits of power were able to
harness and manipulate to their ends. Rarely is anything approaching
political consciousness attributed to the workers, and even more rarely
to the great mass of workers that supported the Bolsheviks and soviet
power.

Unfortunately, the view of popular involvement in revolutions as
essentially irrational is still widely held in the social sciences. One
writer has argued that it differs little from the acts of lunatics and
criminals.[3] Historians of the Russian Revolution have similarly explained the workers' radicalism in terms of 'instinctive distrust of
authority in any form', 'apocalyptic hopes',[4] 'visions of a proletarian
paradise',[5] 'blind embracing of maximalist slogans',[6] and the like.
Little or no attempt has been made to investigate the relationship
between the workers' day-to-day experience in the factories and in the
larger society and the goals they pursued. Even less has the assumption
that these goals originated exclusively from outside the working class
been subjected to empirical scrutiny.

A corollary of this is the oft-made claim that it was the most recent
immigrants from the countryside, uprooted, disoriented and un-
schooled in political struggle, who were most susceptible to Bolshevik
propaganda.[7] A more general formulation of this thesis — that socially
unintegrated, 'anomic' individuals, and especially such marginal urban
populations as recent immigrants from the village to the factory, are
the tinder of revolution—has long been part of the sociological
folklore of revolution and has only recently come under fire as a result
of the growing number of studies of popular participation in
revolutions.[8]

Not surprisingly, Soviet students of the revolution have written far
more extensively on the working class and especially since the 1950s
(though much less in the past five years) have produced a number of
impressive monographs based upon a wealth of hitherto unavailable
materials. Yet, they have not been immune from at least one of the
aforementioned assumptions. For all their eulogising of the working
class as the leading force of the revolution, in the last analysis they too
portray the workers basically as objects, if not of their elemental drives
and instincts, then of the leadership provided by the Bolshevik party.
True, the workers follow this leadership as a result of conscious
decisions based upon their increasingly 'correct' understanding of the
objective situation. But this process of radicalisation is generally
conceived in such lineal, unproblematic and inevitable terms that in
the end we are left with very little understanding of its underlying
dynamics. Thus, the overwhelming support of the Petrograd workers
for the moderate socialists and dual power in the early part of the
revolution is dismissed as essentially 'unconscious', the product of the

'petty bourgeois wave' that swept the working class during the war.[9] The possibility that this position may have, in fact, been quite reasonable from the workers' point of view in the post-February period is hardly entertained.

It is these as well as other assumptions examined in this study that have left the immediate experience of the workers, and especially their capacity to interpret and act upon this experience, at the margins of history. It is my hope that this book will contribute towards the correction of this imbalance.

A systematic investigation of the evidence has confirmed me in the view that the workers' participation in the revolution was fundamentally a response to their own experience both in the factory and in the broader societal setting. Even—or rather, especially—the least politically aware and experienced workers, the women and the recent rural immigrants, were not moved by even the most eloquent 'agitation' unless they were able to see a correspondence between the analysis and goals put forward and their own immediate experience.

The growth of support in the working class for the Bolsheviks was, thus, not the result of the party's successful tapping of the workers' irrational impulses but rather an expression of the growing correspondence between the latter's aspirations and the party's programme and strategy. The progressive radicalisation of the Petrograd workers in 1917 was not an elemental drive toward utopia, not a chiliastic movement, but a cautious and often painful development of consciousness. This was an essentially rational process in the basic sense that it involved much realistic mulling over of means and ends.

This is not to argue that the revolution was a coldly calculating affair on the workers' part. Culture, as a sort of lens moulded by historical experience through which the workers interpreted and responded to their immediate experiences, is a non-rational factor that must be an integral part of any analysis of working-class politics. Moreover, the revolution of 1917 did not lack its share of idealism. Affective elements such as class honour, rage, as well as the workers' long-term socialist ideals played no small role. The point is, however, that these factors alone would hardly have proven sufficient to move the rank-and-file worker, struggling at his or her lathe to eke out a living, to support, let alone participate in, so uncertain and perilous a venture as the seizure of state power.

The evolution of working-class attitudes between February and October must be viewed fundamentally in terms of the workers' desire to safeguard the gains of the February Revolution as they conceived it—a democratic republic, an active search for a just peace, and a decent standard of living—in the face of a perceived counterrevolutionary threat from the propertied classes. The demands embodied in the October Insurrection—peace, workers' control and national regulation of the economy, and a firm policy towards the counterrevolution—were first and foremost solutions to concrete problems rooted in the objective conditions of the workers' lives, just as the seizure of power itself was perceived as a defensive response forced upon the workers by the imminent threat of political defeat and economic ruin.

It follows from this that if the evolution of working-class politics in 1917 is to be fully understood it must be viewed within the framework of the shifting relations between classes. This, in fact, is the basis for the periodisation of this study.

The period from the February Revolution to the April crisis marked the so-called 'honeymoon' of the revolution when a certain sense of national unity prevailed, and the workers, though distrustful of the propertied classes, supported the dual power system of soviet control and conditional support for the census government. ('Census society' in contemporary usage referred to the propertied classes and the non-socialist intelligentsia. 'Democracy' or 'revolutionary democracy', on the other hand, referred to the *nizy* (the lower classes—workers, soldiers, peasants and the 'democratic' intelligentsia). In Russia, all of democracy adhered to one or another brand of socialism.)

During the second period, from the April crisis to the July Days, the polarisation that had characterised pre-revolutionary urban society again broke through the veneer of national unity. A majority of Petrograd's workers, suspecting the entrepreneurs of sabotage, alarmed at the growing outspokenness of the census leaders against the soviets, and dissatisfied with the government's foreign policy, began to demand the transfer of power to the soviets—in effect, a dictatorship of 'revolutionary democracy'. But the situation took a bad turn when the moderate socialist leadership of the soviets, as a party to the coalition government, responded with repression to the workers' pressure on it to take power. The soviets, until now vehicles for the realisation of the workers' aspirations, had become obstacles (though the soviets as such, as institutions, were never abandoned). The workers suddenly found themselves isolated by an alliance of the propertied classes and that part of democracy still supporting the Soviet leadership—the intelligentsia, most of the peasantry, and a part of the workers and soldiers, especially outside the capital. It was a political cul-de-sac. To move forward would have meant a split in democracy and civil war.

The July Days and their aftermath, therefore, forced the workers to confront new and frightening issues; if the revolution was not to go down in defeat, could civil war be avoided? And could they go it alone and hope to succeed under such unfavourable odds? The Bolsheviks' winning over of the soviets in the major urban centres during the autumn, representing a certain 'unity from below', reduced the fears of isolation but did not eliminate them. Attachment to the idea of unity within the socialist camp was still strong among broad strata of workers, and the prospect of a split filled them with foreboding. The intelligentsia would certainly be hostile to a soviet régime, and the peasantry was only beginning to become disillusioned in the coalition. The workers hesitated.

But the political and economic situation had become so unbearable that it required only the initiative of the more decisive elements of the working class for the rest to follow and rally to the new soviet government. Many workers still hoped that democratic unity could be restored and civil war avoided, but this hope was abandoned once it became evident that the moderate socialists, arguing that Russia was not ripe for working-class hegemony and the socialist experiments that were bound to follow, would have no part in a soviet dictatorship. Moreover, the entrance of the Left SRs (Social Revolutionaries) into the government, signifying an alliance between the workers and at least part of the peasantry, moderated this sense of isolation. October had finally torn Russian society apart, pitting the *nizy* against the wealthy and educated *verkhi* (upper classes) and setting the stage for a bitter and protracted civil war.

The present volume traces these developments to the July Days, a crucial watershed in the revolution that dramatically revealed the split that had developed within the socialist camp, placing in doubt the essentially peaceful perspectives hitherto dominant among the workers. A second volume to follow will examine the process of reorientation among the workers in the new and perplexing post-July situation, culminating in the October Revolution and the outbreak of full-scale civil war in the spring of 1918.

In my use of sources, in matters pertaining directly to the workers' consciousness and activity, I have relied as far as possible on materials emanating from the workers. I have tried to let the workers speak for themselves in order to allow the reader to enter the atmosphere of the period and the minds of the actors and to make his or her own interpretation of the evidence and draw conclusions. In this way I also hope to lend credence to the contention that the workers were not only no less conscious actors than educated society, but the level of political sophistication among certain elements compared very favourably with that of even the most 'cultured' members of the society, and that the working class as a whole was a crucial creative factor in the development of the revolution. Apart from this methodological concern, these working-class sources, almost all untranslated and not easily accessible to the reader, add life to what otherwise might be a rather dry account of one of the most dramatic episodes of modern history.

The most valuable type of data in this respect are the direct statements of workers 'at the bench' or in their capacity as elected representatives. These can be found in letters to the press, meeting and conference protocols, newspaper reports and memoirs. In the case of elected delegates and published letters, we are often dealing with a more literate stratum of workers. Nevertheless, these people were in close daily contact with the factories and subject to immediate recall by simple majority vote. Even letters were often collectively written and put to the vote of the factory meeting. Election results to factory committees, district and central soviets, dumas (city government), unions and the Constituent Assembly, constitute another important direct source.

One of the more abundant types of data are the resolutions of workers' meetings, the use of which requires special comment. The fact that key parts and even entire resolutions often followed closely upon the wording of central party organs obviously limits their value as original formulations of workers' attitudes. However, a number of circumstances must be kept in mind. First, this was a time of very broad political freedom and, except for a few periods of doldrums, one of great popular interest in the 'burning questions' of the day. Published protocols of factory meetings and archival material show that the typical factory assembly began with a report on a specific issue or on the 'current moment', presented by one or more of the factory's delegates to the Petrograd or district soviet or by special outside speakers. After this, representatives of the various party fractions in the factory were heard. Then followed the debate or *preniya*, often described as 'lengthy and heated', during which workers from the floor could express their views and ask questions. Unfortunately, the secretaries apparently did not feel the need to record these debates, but the very fact that they took place is evidence that the rank-and-file workers had at least a basic sense of the issues. At the conclusion of the meeting, each fraction or bloc would present its resolution. The one receiving a majority of hands was then sent to the press or the Soviet. In this way, even a centrally prepared resolution was at the least an indication of which of the main political positions the majority of workers found most attractive.

Other resolutions, however, were written by local party workers from the factory or district, and though usually based upon central party policy, did reflect more closely local issues, attitudes and moods. Thus, resolutions from specific factories tended to show a strong element of consistency in the nature of their concerns and the degree of militancy. One must also bear in mind that in 1917 the relationship between leadership and rank-and-file was by no means one-sided. Local leaders not only had to take the mass mood into account but they themselves were often infected by it, at times even to the detriment of central party policy. A notable example of this is the behaviour of local

Bolshevik leaders in the July Days and their less than enthusiastic abandonment of the popular slogan 'All power to the soviets', despite official party policy. The Menshevik–Internationalists and Left SRs had similar cause to complain after October when they found the Bolshevik demand for a government responsible exclusively to the soviets tacked onto supposedly internationalist resolutions for an all-socialist coalition.

It is not clear how often resolutions were amended from the floor, but this did occur. In some cases, entire resolutions were offered from the floor and accepted over the opposition of the leadership. The fact that resolutions were usually written in more literary style (the flowery language of many resolutions betrays the style of the self-taught worker-*intelligent* (roughly—intellectual)) should not of itself be taken to mean that they did not express actual attitudes held by workers, if, perhaps, on a less articulate level. Buzinov, a Petrograd worker and SR, described the relationship between the worker agitators and the 'masses' in the following terms:

> The 'self-made' agitator said what was in the head of each person but for which the others, less developed, could not find expression in words. After each of his words, the workers could only exclaim: That's it! That's exactly what I wanted to say.[10]

These resolutions, moreover, were taken quite seriously by contemporaries familar with the labour situation. In October, for example, *Izvestiya*, the organ of the Soviet, and the Left SR *Znamya truda* published an analysis of 169 local resolutions on the issue of state power in an attempt to show the mass attitude.[11] A. L. Popov, a Menshevik–Internationalist, published a collection of documents on the October Revolution in 1918 that consisted almost exclusively of these resolutions. He did not even bother to question their validity as expressions of the workers' positions, even though some of the issues he dealt with were quite subtle.[12]

At least, then, the resolutions can show which political tendency the workers preferred and what issues were in the air. At the most, where this is justified, they can be used as expressions of more specific attitudes and moods.

Another source of information on the workers are political intelligence reports, *doklady s mest*, presented by local delegates at various conferences and party meetings. These were often somewhat coloured by the delegates' personal inclinations, but in the end there was no one to fool but oneself. Press reports, including correspondence sent in by workers from the factories, are another contemporary source.

Leaving the contemporary materials, one comes to the memoirs, the most valuable, of course, being those of workers written as close as possible to the events described. Of the memoirs of non-workers, those of Sukhanov, an editor of the Menshevik–Internationalist *Novaya zhizn'*, are undoubtedly the most enlightening, though his acquaintance with the higher circles of Soviet leadership in 1917 was far deeper than his knowledge of the factory masses.

In the late 1920s under the sponsorship of Gorky, a series of factory histories was commissioned. This was soon terminated under Stalin's rule but was resumed in the late 1950s. These works, which utilise archival and memoir material inaccessible to Western scholars, are of very uneven value but, used in conjunction with more reliable sources, take on a certain significance.

I am well aware of the often limited and partisan nature of my sources, a problem for any social scientist but especially serious for a student of a revolution that tore society asunder. I have made allowance for this, frequently pointing out the particular bias to the reader. I have also not relied on any single type of source in making a major point.

I did not set out to prove a theory and have not selected evidence with that in mind. My purpose was to shed light on the nature of working-class participation in the revolution—to describe and explain how the workers acted and what thoughts lay behind these actions. I have sought to do this on the basis of all the evidence available to me.

It is impossible to write about important historical events, especially one so controversial and deeply political as the Russian Revolution, without having one's own point of view. I have not tried to conceal my sympathy for the workers of Petrograd and their struggles. But this should not be misconstrued as evidence of a *parti pris*. A study that employs the terms 'proletarian' and 'capitalist' is not necessarily less objective than one that uses 'worker' and 'entrepreneur', though it may violate the sometimes superficial canons of scholarly neutrality.

2 Types of Political Culture in the Industrial Working Class of Petrograd

All too often, students of the revolution have approached the workers as a homogeneous mass, only to find themselves confronted with a confused and contradictory picture of working-class politics. Among the workers of Petrograd one can discern three basic types of political culture that coincide roughly with three groups of workers: the majority of the skilled workers and especially those engaged in private industry; the unskilled labourers; and a sub-group of skilled workers drawn largely from among the printers, elements in state factories, and the settled, small property-owning stratum in the outlying suburbs. Since the cultural traits and dispositions brought by each of these groups into 1917 served to filter perceptions and shape responses to events, it follows that an analysis of the different types of political culture is a necessary point of departure for any attempt to understand political consciousness as manifested in the revolution itself.

The Skilled Workers[1]

John Reed referred to the Vyborg District as the 'Faubourg St-Antoine of Petrograd'. Such was its reputation, won during the 1912–14 upsurge in labour militancy, that I. K. Naumov, recalling his arrival from Tula in 1915 as a young worker militant, was moved to write: 'To work in Piter—that is happiness. To work on the Vyborg Side—that is my longstanding dream.'[2]

Statistics on the social and industrial composition of the district offer some insight into the sources of this radicalism. Not only did this predominantly proletarian district have the largest concentration of factory workers (18 per cent of the capital's industrial labour force) but fully 84 per cent of these were employed in the metal industry. In fact, the number of metalworkers alone in the Vyborg District exceeded the total for all industrial workers of any other of Petrograd's districts.[3]

There were basically two types of metal industry: machine construction, involving much skilled and complex work, and the more simple

9

types of production of the metalworking (*metaloobrabatyvayushchie*) factories, such as metallurgy, founding, pipe and wire making, munitions, etc. In the Vyborg District, machine construction accounted for 15 of the 21 large plants. Other districts where the metal industry predominated were typically dominated by one or two giant factories of a mixed type of production. Characterising the vast Putilov Works, the journal of the Metalworkers' Union wrote: 'This factory is a universal one, where metallurgy and machine construction are combined ... It is a plant with a high proportion of unskilled labourers ... Metallurgy in comparison with machine construction has an extraordinary percentage of unskilled labour.'[4]

A 1924 sociological study of Moscow factory workers under the direction of E. Kabo concluded: 'In the worker milieu, skill, literacy and interest in socio-political questions go hand in hand. The greater the skill, the more frequent the attendance of lectures, circles, especially political ones, the greater the number of newspapers read.'[5] The 1918 industrial census, though based on a population smaller than that of 1917, confirms that the highest literacy rates were found in printing and machine construction, the most skilled industries, while conversely, the rate among cotton workers, the least skilled (and predominantly female), was the lowest (see Table 2.1).

TABLE 2.1:   *Literacy of industrial workers in European Russia by type of industry, August 1918*

Industry	Per cent literate workers
Printing	94.7
Machine-construction	83.6
Metalworking	76.5
Clothing	74.9
Chemicals	70.0
Woodworking	69.6
Paper	68.1
Food	66.0
Leather and fur	64.1
Cotton	52.2
All industry	64.0

Source: Based upon A. G. Rashin, *Formirovanie rabochego klassa Rossi* (M., 1958) p. 601.

The cultural differences that set off the skilled workers from the unskilled were striking. On starting work as an adolescent in the forging shop of the Nevskii Ship and Machine-construction Factory, one of the large mixed production plants, A. Buzinov was first struck by the vast cultural abyss between the metalworkers and the workers of the nearby textile mills. But he soon became aware that even within his own factory

> the workers of the engineering shop, the machinists and turners, looked at me from above. I realised the humble position of the hot departments: the founding, rolling and forging shops. Here I saw people of an uncouth and oafish nature, both in their bearing and speech. Through the robust ruddiness one could clearly distinguish in each individual face the coarse features which said that force, not agility of mind, predominates in their work. I saw clearly that beside an experienced founder even a shabby machinist seemed an educated, thinking person. The machinist held his head higher, was more accurate and forceful in his speech. He was able to insert a dozen words, including a stinging bit of irony, where the founder had time for only one, and even that of a rather simple type. With the machinist you automatically felt like talking about something general and not just wages. In short, the worker of the engineering shop was no longer the semi-raw material of the founding and forging shops. Indeed, he seemed himself to have passed through the shaping action of the lathes and tools.[6]

Various contemporary observers noted these differences: a generally higher level of culture, greater facility with words and complex ideas, a keener interest in broader socio-political issues, and a stronger sense of personal dignity.[7]

In part, as Buzinov indicated, these traits were related to the nature of skilled work itself, which was lighter, less mechanical and more thought-demanding. The July 1917 wage agreement in the Petrograd metal industry described the highest skill category as 'independently executing complex and exact work according to drawings and utilising exact measuring instruments'. Workers in category II did work of a 'relatively less exact and complex nature, but requiring a sufficiently lengthy period of training and the ability to work with drawings'. Category III did 'various uncomplicated but responsible work, including exact work of mass production'. Workers in category IV attended simple machines—lathes, presses, ovens, etc. (This would include most work in production of ordnance.) The final category, labourers (*chernorabochie*—literally, blackworkers) involved heavy unskilled work, such as carrying, washing, loading, sorting.[8] A. Shapovalov, a skilled Petersburg metalworker, recalled that 'work on a turning lathe quite often demands high intelligence [*intelligennost*', implying also education, culture], an understanding of technical drawings and knowledge of arithmetic. Some jobs, for example, the turning of cones, also required a certain familiarity with geometry, algebra, and trigonometry.'[9]

The following is a description of the machinist's trade before the introduction of Taylorism, which eliminated much of the mental component of skilled factory labour:

> The machinist of Taylor's day started with the shop drawing and turned, milled, bored, drilled, planed etc. and otherwise machine-and-hand-processed the proper stock to the desired shape as specified in the drawing. The range of decisions to be made in the course of this process ... is enormous ... Taylor himself worked with twelve variables, including hardness of the metal, the material of the cutting tool, thickness of the shaving, shape of the cutting tool, use of a coolant ... etc. Each of these variables is subject to a large number of choices.... But upon these decisions of the machinist depended not just the accuracy of the product, but also the pace of production.[10]

It is true that Russian machine building stood on a generally lower technological level than that of the industrialised West. But on the other hand, the relatively weak and fluctuating nature of the demand for machinery in Russia made the introduction of batch production and a developed division of labour difficult. This in turn placed special demands on the workers to exhibit qualities of resourcefulness and independence. A Soviet student of the pre-revolutionary machine-construction industry found that 'the basic type of machine builder was not the worker-operator but the so-called broad profile worker'.[11]

In sum, skilled metalworking involved a high proportion of non-routine tasks requiring decisions based upon relatively complex calculations involving many variables. Executed according to technical drawings, this work fostered the capacity for independent thought and the ability to move with ease between the abstract and the concrete.

Skilled work required a certain amount of formal education beyond elementary literacy. Shapovalov, for example, decided to attend evening technical school to acquire the knowledge required of a skilled worker.[12] Moreover, since the acquisition of a skill involved several years of apprenticeship, the typical skilled worker, even though often raised in the village, having entered the factory at 14–16 years of age, had already spent a sufficient number of years in the factory to become assimilated into the urban working-class culture.

With skill came a sense of personal dignity, fostered by pride of craft and relative material security. After a few years at the Workshops of the North-West Railroad, the young Shapovalov was advised by an older worker to go to a factory where they build new machines and don't just repair locomotives... Quit the Varshavka, Sashka, you'll learn how to work, you'll gain more experience, become a skilled worker, learn to be bold. You'll stop fearing the foremen, forge freedom for yourself. You'll scorn the danger of finding yourself without work. You'll get a broader outlook of life.[13]

S-skii, a liberal journalist, called the Petersburg workers in general 'the salt of the conscious working people' and proceeded to characterise the skilled metalworkers:

Workers in machine production are always in the forefront of every movement. They are the aristocrats, the progressivists. Turners, founders, blacksmiths, mechanics and machinists—all of these are developed people with a well formed sense of individuality and rather good wages ... At any rate, this group of workers is able to live without especially burning need, given, of course, continuous employment. They are able to rent a flat, a cheap one, but nevertheless a flat, if they are married ... there is a hearth, something of which many worker groups are deprived.

I was never a worker myself, but it seems to me that work in machine-construction factories, despite its burdensome nature, must develop in a man the urge toward individuality. Here there must be room for creativity. The worker must think a great deal, reason in the very process of work. And, therefore, the very essence of his work gives him a push toward self-determination. I personally have had the occasion to talk at my home with many workers for hours on various subjects. In the form of their conversation and even their language, they are almost indistinguishable from our intellectuals. In my opinion, they are more interesting because their judgments are fresher, and their convictions, once taken, are very firm.

The author then describes a change of shift at a machine-construction factory:

A group of workers comes out of the gates. They are wearing work clothes, not exactly in the freshest state, but undoubtedly well-sewn and of durable quality. Their facial expressions are very serious and concentrated. Through the layer of soot, one can see sullen thought at work. They walk unhurriedly and solidly. They talk among themselves—and about matters that generally have nothing in common with the factory they have just left. Over there—one life, the working life. Here—another, the public, with its sharp sociopolitical interests. On the way they buy newspapers, mainly of the

liberal trend. [Under Tsarism, the socialist press was severely perse-
cuted.] On arriving home, the worker will read his newspaper in his
spare time and will, perhaps, disagree with much in it, as liberalism is
for the upper classes (*barskii*), and they, the workers, are essentially
different.[14]

A. Shlyapnikov, a skilled metalworker and prominent Bolshevik
who worked in the factories of the Vyborg District during the war, also
drew a connection between militancy and a better material situation.
Referring to the Vyborg District, he wrote:

In pre-war years, with large war orders, there was a crying need for
working hands; and so employers paid higher wages to attract skilled
workers. This contributed to the concentration of the most advanced
elements in this district. The better working conditions and the
fighting spirit gave the district a certain revolutionary reputation,
and the Vyborzhtsy maintained it with pride.[15]

In fact, metalworking, which predominated in the Vyborg District, was
the highest paid industry, the printers having lost their leading position
during the wartime decline in their industry (see Table 2.2).

TABLE 2.2:   *Average monthly wage of Petrograd
workers by industry, in rubles, 1913 and 1916*

Industry	1913	1916
Metalworking	42.0	51.0
Printing	56.4	38.0
Chemicals	30.0	33.8
Woodworking	41.0	31.3
Leather	36.0	30.7
Minerals	30.7	24.5
Food	28.2	24.5
Textiles	26.0	24.7

Source: P. Leiberov, 'Petrogradskii proletariat v gody
pervoi mirovoi voiny', in *Istoriya rabochikh Leningrada*,
vol. I, p. 470.

In the Russian context, the emergence of these new cultural needs,
the sense of individuality and human dignity and the aspiration towards self-determination, served to intensify the workers' hostility to
the existing order. As these needs grew, so too did the tension between
them and the system that stubbornly prevented their fulfilment. And if
the less developed workers were concerned primarily with economic

issues, their skilled colleagues, as Buzinov noted, wanted to 'talk about something general and not just wages'. For the skilled worker, the struggle had to be conducted on many levels, the economic often taking a secondary place.

In both work and public life, Tsarist society constantly frustrated these new aspirations. The Russian factory régime was a corrupt and degrading despotism, where rights had to be wrested by force, only to be rescinded by management at the first opportunity. From 1905 onward (with a certain pause during the reaction of 1907–11), demands for the recognition of the human dignity of workers, for polite address (especially the second person plural), an end to searches, decent treatment of women, and the like, became dominant issues in the labour movement.[16] Shapovalov recalled how keenly he experienced this clash between his emergent sense of dignity and desire for autonomy, on the one hand, and his subservient, dependent position *vis-à-vis* the boss on the other.

> From my first days in the workshop of Olivier I felt a peculiar duality. I, a revolutionary and Marxist, hating the capitalist system, having set as my goal its total destruction, recognised that capital was pressing me and subordinating me to the will of the boss to such an extent that I was lowering my eyes under his severe gaze, that I was stooping over my machinist's lathe more intensely than I had to when he looked at me. Alas, I had to admit that it was as if two men were living inside of me: one who for the sake of the struggle for a better future for the workers was not afraid of sitting in the Peter-Paul Fortress and in Siberian exile; and another who had not fully liberated himself from the feeling of dependence and even fear. Nevertheless, catching myself on these slavish feelings, I came to hate capitalism and my boss Olivier even more intensely.[17]

The oppression in the factories, however, was but a microcosm of the workers' social and political condition in Tsarist society at large, which was characterised by a despotic paternalism that stifled all attempts at self-expression. Here, too, in the broader social context, the movement did not limit itself to economics, to the struggle for legalisation of trade unions and the like, but fought also for recognition of the workers as full-fledged citizens with their own economic, cultural and political organisations run by and for workers.

The emergence of these needs[18] generated a new type of militant—the 'conscious worker'. 'Behind the Nevskii Gates', wrote Buzinov,

> one now [1906–7] heard the word 'conscious', and the appearance of the conscious worker clearly implied that his opposite was also

present—the unconscious worker. There were few socialist workers [i.e. party members] and they were supported by the conscious workers. The latter were ten times as numerous as the socialists ... Each was, in a way, a 'juridically reasoning individual' (*yuridicheski myslyashchaya lichnost'*) capable of understanding all that surrounded him. They all, to a greater or lesser degree, understood the situation of the workers and their relations with the factory owners. Life itself transformed them into the vanguard of the worker masses. Their native keen wit and worker sensitivity did not fail them when they exposed the hidden ends behind this or that manoeuvre of management. And they were no longer silent. Somehow in their midst, a special type of agitator was created, a man always hammering away at the same point—I would say—of class isolation from the exploiters. In the persons of these agitators life had hammered a wedge between workers and owners that no party agitator, not so closely tied to the masses as they, could have done ... This self-made agitator spoke of that which each worker had in his head but, being less developed, was unable to verbalise. After each of his words, the workers would exclaim: 'That's it! That's just what I wanted to say!' He would seize upon a subject that could not claim a very wide scope, but rather one of the simplest kind ... It would have to do with a screw and its thread. But the confrontation of a whole series of such details, among which a worker passes his whole life, gave this speech a special persuasiveness. For each worker, be he as benighted as the dark night, it became clear that under his very nose amazing things were going on, and this in itself posed the question: 'And after that, what else is going on that he, like a mole, does not see?'[19]

Buzinov emphasises here what 'class consciousness' has traditionally signified: a grasp of the workers' oppressed economic and political situation in society. But in the Russian labour movement, the term 'conscious worker' was actually a much broader concept embracing an entire code of conduct that included such varied aspects of social life as relations with women, attitudes towards the use of alcohol, theft, relations with management, etc. The 'conscious worker' was not only a fighter for the economic and political rights of the working class: he was also an *intelligentnyi* person in the broad Russian sense of the term. A. Babytsyn, a skilled locksmith at the New Parviainen Machine-construction Factory in the Vyborg District, recalled how some of the workers on pay day would go directly to the taverns to drink or play billiards amidst the whine of the gramophones.

But the conscious part of the workers spent their leisure in a different manner: many went to the People's House, attended performances at the 'Komediya' theatre, visited museums. But they did not spend their wages only on distractions. One day, Nikolai Mukhin, a worker in our shop, approached me and with the caution characteristic of the underground activist asked if I could aid arrested workers who were suffering for the interests of the working class.[20]

Another worker expounding on the nature of interpersonal relations among workers, wrote: 'Only a conscious working person can truly respect a human individual, women, cherish a tender child's soul. We will not learn from anyone but ourselves. We, the conscious working people, have no right to be like the bourgeois.'[21] In the autumn of 1917 the committee of the Izhorskii Factory passed a rule that anyone involved in theft of factory property be fired. The union would be notified of the grounds for dismissal: 'for theft, which disgraces the conscious proletariat'.[22]

Buzinov noted that the 'conscious workers' 'were no longer silent', that this consciousness had an active bent. And yet, these 'self-made agitators' were not party people; they were acting solely upon an inner compulsion to raise their fellow workers to their own level. In the worker, wrote a contemporary observer of the labour scene, L. M. Kleinbort:

> the spiritual process is an active one. Once the voice of the individual has begun to speak in the worker, he can neither sit under a bush ... nor limit himself to words ... The strength of this process is in its dynamism: the upper strata of the proletariat raise up the backward strata to their own level.[23]

This active orientation was crucial to the ability of a comparatively small stratum of workers to exert its influence over the entire class and also helps to explain the relatively swift assimilation of large numbers of peasant newcomers into the labour movement.

It is interesting that even the Ministry of Trade and Industry, headed by one of Russia's biggest bankers and staffed largely by former Tsarist officials, referred to the skilled workers as the more 'conscious' element. In a March 1917 survey of Petrograd's factories it reported that

> In a whole series of cases the [factory] committees are able to introduce a certain order and discipline into the worker masses, and it is generally observed that the influence of the committees and their significance are greater the more conscious the workers. Therefore, their authority is rather significant, for example, in the metalworking factories. And the opposite is true: very insignificant where the majority of workers are relatively uncultured.[24]

Thus, metalworking, consciousness,[25] culture, discipline and organisation are linked in this report. Indeed, although the Vyborg District metalworkers were the most active and radical element of the working class, they were the farthest from being the anarchistic masses that later Western historiography has often made them out to be. In fact, they especially prided themselves on their discipline and organisational abilities, as the following report on the 18 June 1917 demonstration makes clear: 'The Vyborzhtsy arrived in strict formation on the Plains of Mars. "What district is this?", shouted a voice from the crowd. "Why, can't you see? Exemplary order! That means it's Vyborg," proudly replied the leader of the column.'[26] Malakhovskii, commander of the Vyborg District Red Guards, wrote of the local workers:

> And the people we had there in the Vyborg District were the pick of the crop—each one a fine lad. Whomever you poked, he would not make you blush. And, in truth, we never had reason to ... Such gratifying soil as the workers of the Vyborg District allowed us to organise the Red Guards such that all to the last man were utilised... While the Red Guards of the other districts also numbered in the thousands, they showed themselves to be much weaker in action. On the day of the uprising, they came from various districts and even from Kronstadt to learn from us how to organise the Red Guards.[27]

One of the most important characteristics of the political culture of the skilled metalworkers was what Buzinov termed 'class isolation from the exploiters'. The essence of the 'conscious worker's' agitation was 'to hammer a wedge between workers and owners'. In strikingly parallel fashion, S-skii observed that the workers would disagree with much that they found in the liberal press because 'liberalism is for the upper classes, and they, the workers, are essentially different'.

This aspiration towards 'class isolation' from census society was more than the desire for self-determination. It stemmed also from a deeply held sense of the irreconcilability of the interests of worker and the propertied classes, a position that expressed itself in the desire to keep all workers' organisations under the sole control of workers and, where this was not feasible, to gain at least an equal footing with representatives of census society. Thus, a police survey of the labour movement during November 1915 in Petrograd observed that the most discussed issue of the period had been consumer cooperatives and that at meetings on this, worker orators 'expressed the desire to do without any material aid from the industrialists, who were gladly offering material support in the founding of co-operatives'. Similar attitudes were expressed in the factories in regard to the cooperative opened by the Petrograd Society of Factory and Mill Owners (PSFMO). At Erikson, for example, the majority pointed out that the Society is totally dependent upon the factory owners, and since co-operation is one of the forms of the general workers' movement, it is necessary to think along lines of our own worker societies, independent of the owners.

The report also noted that interest in insurance and sickness funds was growing:

> However, one observes of late in the worker population the tendency towards isolation of their activities from any sort of pressure from the authorities or the entrepreneurs. Here, too, one feels the shift towards pure autonomy ... This tendency ... can be observed at all workers' meetings without exception.[28]

And the same attitude prevailed in the sphere of worker–management relations within the factories, where all forms of toadying or even socialising (often referred to as 'fraternisation') were frowned upon. The ideal was a clean separation.

On the political level, this irreconcilability manifested itself above all in the almost universal rejection of liberalism. The Constitutional Democrats (Kadets), the liberal party, proved incapable of winning even the smallest working-class following. Indeed, the stratum of workers in question tended to reject the liberal bourgeoisie even as potential political allies. This was one of the major reasons the Mensheviks enjoyed relatively little support among them, especially in periods of labour offensive. Buzinov recalled that even after the revolutionary mood of 1905 had subsided and the sobered workers grew more reform-minded, at their meetings, 'from each word spoken ... a sharp line separating the workers from the ruling class emerged. One could sense the spiritual growth of the workers during the past two years.'[29] Even Buzinov, though an SR, as a 'conscious worker', took the sentiment for 'class isolation' as a sign of spiritual growth.

The other side of this irreconcilability was the very keen sense of class honour that played such an important role in the workers' tenacity in struggle, turning strikes for economic and legal demands into questions of honour to be won regardless of the price.[30] It was this sense of class honour that moved the 48-year-old Putilov worker, Skorinko, to lash out at his son for 'allowing himself' to be beaten by officers for speaking in defence of the Bolsheviks:

> And you stood for it, you wretch?! You should have given him one in the mug. With an inkwell, a revolver, a chair. A worker should not endure a blow from a bourgeois. You hit me?—There, take one back? Ekh, you *zasranets* [shithead]![31]

It was class honour that inspired such statements in 1917 as 'Better to fall a pile of bones than to live like slaves' or 'We will still fight, and if we perish, it will be in an honest battle and we will not retreat from the struggle'.[32]

While a full analysis of the sources of this irreconcilable outlook is not possible here, some elements readily present themselves. First, Russia on the eve of the revolution still bore many traits of a society based upon juridically defined estates. Elections to the State Duma, for example, were held by curia defined by a mixture of estate and property (class) qualifications. This in itself naturally fostered attitudes of separateness among classes. Secondly, the reality of the Russian social situation was such that the interests of the propertied classes, as they conceived them, were, in fact, quite opposed to the aspirations of the workers. Even the 'Workers' Group' of the War-Industry Committee, one of the more conservative elements in Russian Social Democracy during the war, whose chief goal was to effect a political alliance between the workers and bourgeoisie, could not ignore this. In a letter to the workers of Petrograd in December 1916, it stated:

> The propertied classes have always feared the people, but now, having lost faith in their own forces, they turn to the popular movement and especially to an active demonstration by the working class.
>
> Of course, they would like this intervention to take place on their own terms, for their own interests—to get the most for themselves and give as little democracy as possible to the workers. But the working class is conscious enough not to let this happen. The bourgeoisie wants political reform, a liberal regime; we will secure our goal—the maximum democratisation of the country. The bourgeoisie wants a government responsible to the Duma [elected by a very unequal suffrage weighted toward the propertied classes]; we—a provisional government resting not on the Duma but on the organised people. The bourgeoisie will try to maintain the current forms of cruel exploitation; the working class will demand a series of social reforms that will facilitate their struggle against exploitation and the exploiters. The bourgeoisie wants to give freedom to its annexationist appetites; the proletariat and democracy will protest decisively against all military coercion and will strive for a peace acceptable to the workers of all countries.[33]

There was also a third, more psychological element. Shapovalov, for example, recalled how deeply disturbed and galled he was as a conscious revolutionary worker to observe in himself feelings of dependence and timidity towards his boss. And precisely because of these feelings, he came to hate the entire system even more intensely.

But the same sentiments also gave rise to fear among the 'conscious workers' that if they lowered their defences and failed to maintain total separation, they might ultimately yield to these impulses and be dominated, in a sense swallowed up, by the owners. Thus, the anger and the fear, originating from a common source, fed the same intense striving for 'class separateness'.

The other side of 'class separateness' was the equally strong desire for class unity among workers. These workers typically referred to themselves as a 'worker family' or 'one whole harmonious proletarian family',[34] and felt that they should not fight among themselves, that there should be agreement on strategy and tactics since, after all, they shared common interests and a common enemy. More than once they showed their impatience with what they termed factionalism and misplaced pride in the party leadership. As the Menshevik, Lev Lande, wrote:

> The wish for unity had run strong in the labour movement through-out the February period, and it did not die easily even after October. At bottom, it sprang from the belief that the working class had to remain united if it were to fulfil its historical role. Therefore, though it increasingly clashed with reality, all parts of Russian social democracy in 1917 paid some lip service to the masses' yearning for a single, united labour party.[35]

Lande is clear that the yearning for unity came 'from below' and that the leadership was forced to take it into account. But at the same time, this position was always a principled one: the workers would not compromise basic programmatic goals even for the sake of this unity. Nevertheless, the desire for unity played an important role throughout the labour movement, causing the workers to hesitate before actions that might divide their ranks.

Of course, in the absence of other political and economic resources except their numbers, a premium was naturally placed upon solidarity. But unity also filled a deeply psychological need: just as the avoidance of close contact with census society was a means of dealing with servile tendencies in face of authority, so too the support of the 'collective' aided in overcoming these inclinations. Shlyapnikov noted a duality in the metalworkers of the Vyborg District that is strikingly reminiscent of the conflict that Shapovalov experienced. According to Shlyap-nikov, during the war, wage differentials were often quite large within the same shop and even among workers performing the same tasks:

> It ... occurred quite often because our metalworkers were accus-tomed to collective struggle, while demands for simple wages and much else in factory life called for a certain amount of personal

restraint, persistence and the ability to stand up for oneself, each person alone, sometimes without the common support.[36]

A. Buiko, a Petrograd worker raised in the village, recalled the tremendous feeling of strength he drew from the sense of belonging to the collective:

> In the first years before I outgrew my still peasant attitudes, I felt myself alone and constantly experienced fear before other people. But once I grew close to my comrades, I began to feel unshakeable ground beneath my feet. Confidence and assurance appeared: 'I am not alone—there are many of us. We are all as one!' The consciousness of this imparted so much energy that it lasted for the entire ensuing struggle.[37]

In the factories the social pressure towards unanimity was very great and this expressed itself in 1917 in a tendency to pass resolutions unanimously, or with abstentions only. Similarly, an important tool for enforcing labour discipline was to have the recalcitrant worker answer publicly before the general assembly.[38]

One final trait that should be mentioned was the fundamental internationalism of this stratum of workers, both in relation to ethnic groups within Russia and towards the war and the struggles of the oppressed peoples abroad. Though the Petrograd working class was overwhelmingly Russian, there were significant minority groups.[39] Yet, if ethnic antagonism existed, it played no visible role in the labour movement. One of the most famous strikes of 1912–14, the 102-day strike at the Lessner Machine-construction Factory, was sparked by the suicide of a Jewish worker driven to despair by the taunts of a foreman. In 1917 itself, candidates with such obviously Jewish names as Izrailevich or Kogan were prominent among elected delegates in mass working-class organisations.[40]

The workers' internationalism on the war issue was forcefully demonstrated in 1917. 'Down with the war' was a key slogan of the February Revolution. Even the initial patriotic wave that swept up broad strata of workers throughout Russia found only a weak and relatively short-lived echo in Petrograd, and, according to the police, little remained of it by the autumn of 1915.[41] N. I. Potresov, a right-wing Menshevik and a defencist (even prior to the February Revolution) bitterly lamented in 1915 the fact that the 'German invasion' had 'aroused even the most stagnant elements of bourgeois society', while it 'awakened nothing in the proletarian masses', no response worthy of the 'most revolutionary class of today's society'.[42] In the summer of 1917, the Putilov workers donated 5000 rubles for a banner with the inscription: 'We swear to achieve the brotherhood of all peoples. Long live the Russian Revolution as the prologue to the Social Revolution in Europe.' This was presented to the Pavlov Regiment in an elaborate ceremony on the Plains of Mars. It hardly seems likely that the workers would spend their money on slogans they disapproved of. Similarly, it is unlikely that the workers would pass resolutions condemning Kerenskii's closing of the Finnish Parliament for its vote for internal autonomy had they, like the Kadets, nurtured 'greater Russia' sentiments. One should also bear in mind that the Petrograd workers did not have far to look to see the international character of capital. The textile industry was largely British owned, and the metalworking factories bore such world-famous names as Siemens, Erikson and Nobel. In addition, much of the administrative and technical personnel was of foreign origin.

The Unskilled Workers

The unskilled workers were the least active element of Petrograd's working class. In labour circles they were often referred to as the *malosoznatel'nye massy* (literally—masses with low consciousness) and sometimes merely *boloto* (the swamp).

By far the largest single group in this category were the women. V. Perazich, a Petrograd union activist, wrote of the textile workers: 'Our masses in general at that time [early 1917] were still totally benighted ... Only very few had managed to become conscious proletarians.' He explained this by the composition of the work force: during the war the mills had lost their activist skilled male cadres to the front and the war-related industries. 'It reached a point where women appeared even on the mules where they had never worked before, and among the women at this time there were still too few conscious workers.'[43]

Women were almost invariably employed at menial unskilled and semi-skilled work. In textiles, food-processing, chemicals and shoemaking, women were typically to be found in the largely unskilled production jobs, while the men did the skilled work in maintenance, setting up the machines and supervising the women.[44] Even in the more skilled industries, such as metalworking and printing, women almost always did unskilled tasks.[45]

If skilled labour fostered analytical thought and other intellectual qualities, unskilled work deadened the mind. 'The weaver and spinner', wrote S-skii,

> are of a totally different type [than the skilled metalworkers]. They are the slaves of the machine. The machine has devoured them with all their essence. It is stubbornly mechanical work ... Here the people are numbers. Here, on the faces is written that which is most

terrible in a work atmosphere: the hopelessness of labour. People grow dull, go to seed ... [There is a total] absence of demand for individual creativity.[46]

Women's jobs in metalworking were essentially the same. A woman who assembled hand-grenades in an exclusively female shop of the Optical Factory left this account:

I am sitting on a stool, bending my head over a protective glass. On the other side of the table lies a sheet of cardboard with tiny slits. From a tiny box lined with khaki I take 40 capsules instead of the regulation 20 and insert them into the slits. I dip the brush into a bottle and cover the detonator with glue. With the point of a wooden stick, I put on it a tiny golf leaf circle and press it down with a small hammer. My hand repeats these movements learned by rote, and my body is locked in motionlessness.

At that moment, the foreman Yanikeev appeared behind my back. 'You're breaking the rules, sweetie! Haven't I explained it to you? Or aren't you Russian? ... I've had it fooling around with you rule breakers. Collect your pay in two weeks.'

We tried to prove to him that there was no defective output nor had there been. We could not deny the fact of breaking the rules ... Masha and I were saved from dismissal by the revolutionary events of February 1917.[47]

In this uncomplicated work of less than five operations, there was no room for independent thought. Initiative, in fact, was discouraged even, as in this case, when it raised productivity.

Women were the lowest paid workers: the average wage in textile was less than half of that for metalworking in 1916 (see Table 2.2). And women were doubly exploited. Not only did their wages fail to secure anything close to a decent standard of life, but they were totally under the thumb of unscrupulous administrators and foremen who often showed no qualms about exploiting their weaknesses both economically and sexually.[48] The 'decent public' looked upon them as little better than prostitutes.

Literacy among women workers was low, though the gap between male and female literacy narrowed considerably in the lower age groups (see Table 2.3). Indeed, except for the few skilled male workers, it was typically from among the youth of the textile mills that militants were recruited.[49]

But perhaps even more than the mechanical nature of their work and the low level of literacy, it was the women's entire mode of life that militated against their being drawn into public life. The woman worker typically began to earn a wage at the age of 9–11 or even earlier,

TABLE 2.3:   *Literacy of women textile workers, metalworkers, and all industrial workers, by age, August 1918*

Age	Per cent of literate workers		
	Women textile workers	Metalworkers	All industrial workers
to 14	70.0	93.6	80.6
15–19	62.8	92.1	77.1
20–24	51.7	88.6	68.2
25–29	38.6	87.2	66.2
30–34	28.6	86.7	64.2
35–39	19.9	81.1	59.2
40–44	15.1	79.7	58.2
45–49	10.7	72.6	51.9
50 +	7.9[a]	62.8	42.3
All	37.5	82.6	64.0

[a] 50–54 only.
Source: Based upon Rashin, *Formirovanie rabochego klassa Rossi*, p. 602.

serving unlimited hours as a nanny, at work in a peasant's garden or
tending the local noble's cattle. Later, she would leave the village to
work in the city as a seamstress, mill hand or salesgirl. Mill work and
childbirth, concluded Kabo, 'lead to the early destruction of the
organism, leaving no energy or time for acquiring elementary literacy.
As a result, almost all of the textile workers, who average 33 years of
age [in this sample of Moscow workers] are physically exhausted and
intellectually semi-literate or completely illiterate.'[50]

The woman worker's life was a closed one, an almost unbroken
passage between home and mill that kept her isolated from the larger
society, outside of the dynamic influence of the labour movement. Her
intellectual horizons went scarcely beyond family and shop. 'Working
beside a man at the factory', wrote the Bolshevik women's paper
Rabotnitsa,

at the mills for 11–12 hours, and receiving for her work a significantly lower wage, miserable pennies, is not the woman, whose organism
is weaker, also burdened with necessary and heavy housework? Is it
easy for her after the endless grinding work at the mill, when the man
can relax, partake in public life, read and converse with comrades
about what he has read, instead of all this, forgetting herself, to give
each free minute to the care of the children? They have to do the
washing, and mend the linen, and feed them. And with what will you
feed them when goods grow continually dearer and the earnings are

so small? . . . In this sort of calculation, in these cares and worries about the household, passes all the free time of the woman worker with a family, and she hardly has any time for rest, for her personal life. Exhausted, sick from unhealthy, endless mill work, knowing no peace at home, from morning to night, day in and day out, month after month, the worker mother drudges and knows only need, only worry and grief. Her life passes in gloom, without light. She ages quickly: she is also broken, has suffered her fill in the very years when a person should enjoy the full blossoming of her forces. And she dies having known no happiness in life; she perishes like a broken young tree.[51]

A tendency towards passivity, the absence of initiative and persever-ance in struggle, a general indifference to public life, along with a weakly developed sense of class solidarity and low political literacy—these were some of the characteristics of the political culture of the unskilled women worker. 'How many times', asked another article,

have we heard that a strike in this or that enterprise failed . . . because 'among the workers there were many women'; that several factories did not support their comrades at work 'because' among the workers employed there are many women; that a strike ended prematurely and was consequently lost 'because' among the workers are many women? . . . Why, women are the least conscious group . . . They sign up less in the unions than men, they go less frequently to clubs and lectures.[52]

'We have never adhered to the collective actions of the proletariat', wrote a woman from the Kenig Thread Mill (2500 women and 80 men).

And if women workers in some departments do declare a strike, the workers in the other shops do not come to the aid of the first. This, Kenigtsy, is what our isolation and lack of organisation have led to: they exploit our benightedness. And so it will be until we stop regarding our boss as a benefactor and ourselves as slaves . . . The majority of the women workers, including our mill, drag behind at the tail end of the labour movement. There is not the intensity, the energy required in the struggle against capital.[53]

Kabo found that among her 30 women respondents, the overwhelm-ing majority showed a complete ignorance in all questions of 'political and artistic life'. Only nine had read newspapers before the revolution. 'The great majority of women', she concluded, 'do not interest themselves in matters of politics and culture, have no reading habits and cannot remember what they read or when.'[54]

One of the reasons for their reluctance to participate in public life was fear. 'They hold more firmly to the present', wrote *Rabotnitsa*, 'fear risk more acutely, for themselves, for their children. And it is harder to arouse them to strike, to convince them of the need to carry it to the conclusion.'[55] In part, this stemmed from their sense of family responsibility and the insecurity of their material situation. But it was also a question of upbringing and social background. Even young women often feared activism. For example, when elections to the directorate of the health insurance fund were held at the Laferme Tobacco Factory in 1914,

> The older women said: What do we need a fund for? They'll dock us and we'll get no aid. Anyway, we're too old to give birth. But even among the young workers many were frightened by the elections. Some even cried when they were elected: And what if we get into trouble because of this? What if they arrest us? [These were legal organisations.] One young worker even said: Thank God! when she learned that she was too young.[56]

Women often exerted a restraining influence on the activist tendencies of their husbands. One woman, recalling her relationship with her late husband, noted:

> In those days I would often get angry at my husband when he went off to some meeting or as he rather often sat reading a newspaper. 'Is that any business of ours to read newspapers? It is fine for gentlemen to indulge in that, but what can we get out of reading it?'[57]

Although the discussion to this point has been limited to women workers, it must be emphasised that it was not sex but the level of skill and the social characteristics associated with it in Russia that were the primary determinants of political culture. Thus, women engaged in the needle trades, the only skilled industry with a significant proportion of women[58] and which typically required two to three years of trade school or apprenticeship, were quite unlike their unskilled sisters. The three seamstresses interviewed in Kabo's study were all literate, two with two years of formal schooling and one with six. The overall literacy rate for women in the needle trades was 68.2 per cent as compared with 37.9 per cent in cotton.[59] Of the remaining 27 women in Kabo's study, only three had any formal schooling. All three seamstresses were urban bred, daughters of workers. In contrast, seven of the eight textile workers interviewed were raised in the village in peasant families. Kabo's interviewers described these as 'downtrod-

den', 'uncultured', 'underdeveloped', 'uninterested in public life';
while the seamstresses were perceived as 'energetic', 'intelligent',
'capable', and two of them were actively involved in public affairs.[60]

Indeed, the relatively few skilled women workers bore a far greater
resemblance to their skilled male counterparts than to the unskilled
women. And the converse is also true: the unskilled men, the *chernorabochie*, were very similar to the unskilled women in both social
background and political culture. And like the women, they were
referred to by Mensheviks and Bolsheviks alike as 'undeveloped',
'backward', 'of low consciousness'.[61] Referring to the 1912–14 upsurge, Kleinbort wrote that 'it was indeed the arrival of the *chernorabochii*, coarse, uncultured, illiterate ... that complicated more
than ever the struggle of the working class for its human dignity'.[62]
Also like the women, they were engaged in exhausting, repetitive
work, received a bare subsistence wage at best (though more than the
women),[63] and tended to stand aside from the labour movement.

Unskilled labour in general, and especially during the war, was
drawn heavily from the countryside. T. Shatilova, a Bolshevik who was
active in efforts to organise the chemical industry in Petrograd before
the revolution, observed that 'in the chemical plants the majority of
workers directly involved in production were *chernorabochie* ... with
weak ties to the city and weakly imbued with proletarian attitudes'.[64]
S-skii also wrote of a 'huge mass of unskilled *chernorabochie* the
majority of which were *prishlye*'[65] (literally—arrivals; the term could
refer to any immigrants but was most often used for peasants), and the
Menshevik–Internationalist Bazarov described them as 'casual elements, *prishlye* turned into workers during the war'.[66]

The chief objective difference between male and female unskilled
labour was that women, regardless of the length of their industrial
employment, tended to remain at unskilled work; the unskilled men,
however, gradually moved into semi-skilled or skilled work as they
acquired experience. For men, unskilled work and recent arrival from
the village tended to go hand in hand; not so for the women.

From the point of view of political culture also there was a difference
in the histories of men and women unskilled workers. The longer the
men remained in the urban factory setting, the more they gradually
shed their peasant ways of life and thinking, the more they became
'proletarianised'. On the other hand, as Kabo concluded, 'the milieu
from which a woman came and the nature of her activity left a more
significant imprint on her [than on the man]'. And the reasons are
clear: 'Here, all the basic characteristics inherited from the recent past
which we have described are tied in the tight knot of a closed family life
and have maintained intact the wretched culture of the urban and rural
poor. Life has somehow passed these people by, giving them small and
infrequent joys and leaving as their lot an abundance of deprivation
and trouble.'[67]

Since the recent arrivals tended to see their stay in the factory as temporary, or at least had not yet developed a sense of identification with the urban working class, their commitment to the collective goals of the labour movement was at best weak, their chief interests being land and personal economic betterment. A journalist in the Menshevik–Internationalist paper *Novaya zhizn'*, comparing the Putilov workers to those of the Trekhgornaya Textile Mill in Moscow, wrote that 'in the first, there is a clear understanding of class interest; in the second, the fundamental issue is land'.[68]

Strike statistics show that unskilled workers responded more readily to short-term economic goals than to the longer-term, especially political, aims of the labour movement. In the first half of 1914, a period of particularly intense labour militancy and class conflict, the textile workers not only took a less active part in the strike movement as a whole (despite their numerical preponderance in Russia) when compared to the metalworkers, but they were still heavily involved in economic actions at a time when the metalworkers were almost entirely absorbed in the political movement (see Table 2.4).

TABLE 2.4: *Participants in economic and political strikes in 1914 in European Russia in metalworking and textiles*

	Economic strikes	Political strikes
Metalworking	87773	661426
Textiles	115532	160336

Source: M. Balabanov, *Rabochee dvizhenie v Rossii v pod"ema 1912–14* (M., 1927) p. 62.

But apart from the issues of interest and class identity there were also more purely cultural traits influencing the unskilled workers' mode of participation in the labour movement, traits in many ways reminiscent of the mentality of the Russian peasantry. One of the most crucial characteristics that distinguished the skilled urbanised workers from their rustic unskilled colleagues was the ability to generalise in social life, to orient themselves in the more abstract, remote public issues that had no concrete referent in the workers' immediate personal life. This quality is akin to what C. Wright Mills termed the 'sociological imagination', the capacity 'to grasp history and biography and the relations between the two in society'.[69] The extent to which this ability developed depended on many factors, including the level of literacy and education, the nature of work and the like. But many students of peasant culture have noted the peasants' inability to see past the confines of the farm or village, an inability conditioned by the limited nature of the relations between peasants and the world outside.[70] A Petrograd Soviet agitator working among the peasants of the Yamburg Uezd in the summer of 1917 reported back that all the social questions were raised at the meetings he had managed to organise, but 'matters of state-wide significance were very little examined due to the peasants' lack of preparation, their failure to grasp their importance'.[71]

If the peasants lived in a largely natural world where the primary relationship was between family and nature, the world of the urban factory workers was predominantly a social one in which the satisfaction of all vital needs underlined their dependence upon the rest of society: the employers for livelihood, landlords for shelter, peasantry for food, fellow workers in production and struggle, etc. The different social situations of the workers and peasants were reflected in their reading habits, as summarised by Kleinbort:

> The peasant 'who loves to read' ... conducts his economy 'more rationally' ... 'is more open to innovation' ... What is most valuable in a book is that which is 'useful', which can be used here and now in the economy, at the village assembly, in relations outside the village. If beside this practicality the village discovers some understanding of the book in the sense of general development, it is a very rare book indeed that devours the reader, swallows him up to such an extent that he forgets his manure, his cattle, the fuss around his home and person ... He is passive, analyses little, looks for sermons, lectures.
> ... [But] least of all do we find calm in the worker reader. Reading a book, he reacts strongly to this or that part of it, even more strongly than one might have expected. Accordingly, the book for him is not a sermon or a lecture. Living at the factory, he sees and experiences much. Therefore, the book is the same as life for him. That this is so is shown by the indifference to utilitarian knowledge and the increase in reading of social books – the opposite of what is undoubtedly taking place in the village.[72]

Not that the workers were impractical dreamers. For they read newspapers the most, and next to belles-lettres, preferred books on the 'workers' question, in the same way that peasant readers demand books "on land"'.[73] However, technical literature that would have aided them to raise their skill levels interested them little. As one worker stated: 'When you put in 12 or 15 hours in a row, it makes you sick to even remember your trade, let alone read about it.'[74]

The unskilled workers, like the peasants, also displayed a rather narrow and concrete circle of interests. If Buzinov recalled that with the machinist one felt like talking about something general, not just wages, and S-skii observed that the skilled metalworkers, upon leaving the factory, discussed broad socio-political issues, the woman worker who read newspapers preferred to read 'only about our factory ... accidents and trials ... or something my husband points out'.[75] The unskilled workers, thus, related to public life, and to politics specifically, through their concrete everyday needs and experiences and one should be careful about attributing their tendency to concentrate on economic issues solely to lack of interest in specifically working-class goals, especially since in 1917 peasants and workers shared many of the same political interests, standing together in opposition to census society which favoured continuation of an annexationist war, opposed state regulation of the economy and was less than enthusiastic about transferring land to the peasants.

Similarly, the inertia of the unskilled workers, their low level of participation in the labour movement in general, also had parallels in the peasants' oft-noted fatalism and passivity, which some have connected with the uncertainties that pervaded peasants' agricultural pursuits subject to the whims of nature.[76] However, 'passivity' is not quite an accurate characterisation of the Russian peasantry, which showed itself capable of periodic outbursts of extremely militant collective action that tended, however, to peter out quickly in the absence of concrete results, only to be followed once more by long periods of relative quiescence. Moreover, these outbursts were not generated spontaneously from within peasant society, but almost always occurred in response to changes outside the village system that somehow challenged the legitimacy of the established order.[77] Lacking any systematic conception of the working and dynamics of society, they exploited opportunities sent them in much the same way as they made use of favourable climactic conditions. Once, however, the opportunity appeared to have passed, there was no turning to organisational work, no concern for consolidating forces, but rather a retreat to old patterns and preoccupation with local issues and solutions.

The unskilled workers showed a strikingly similar pattern of participation in the labour movement. Buzinov recalled how the 'lower stratum of the working class' fell into a state of lethargy as the revolutionary wave of 1905–6 receded. 'A kind of indifference to everything existing and to the future took hold of it.'[78] B. Ivanov, a Moscow baker, wrote of the 'mass workers' who were 'tied to the land' and 'undeveloped' (*malosoznatel 'nye*): 'In moments when his spontaneous energy drives him to battle ... he goes forward with hot decisiveness. But if some obstacle arises in his path, his strength is immediately smashed at the first decisive rebuff of capital.'[79] In 1907 the bakers had conducted two successful strikes and the 'mass workers' were demanding a third, against the opposition of the 'conscious bakers', the 'proletarianised' elements free from ties to the village. The latter preferred to postpone the strike in order first to gather forces and resolve organisational problems that required attention. But the 'mass worker ... took circumstances very little into consideration. His field of vision was limited to the union and he did not consider the state of the entire movement in the country as a whole.' When the strike failed, the union lost credit in the eyes of these workers, but the other group, which had received the least, stuck with it.[80] Similarly, during the reaction of 1907–11, it was the skilled metalworkers who constituted the great majority of the union membership in Petrograd. In 1907 and 1908, of 8459 members, only 16 per cent were unskilled. Of the workers who joined in 1909 and 1911, only 10 and 5 per cent respectively were unskilled.[81]

Yet another characteristic of the unskilled workers which had a counterpart in the peasantry was their heavy dependence upon outside leadership. As the Petrograd Soviet agitator cited above noted, 'The peasants still do not understand what happened and believe someone will issue them an order "from above" to which they will submit. And when the matter is explained to them, they reply: "He is an anarchist." '[82] While Buzinov wrote of self-made agitators appearing from the midst of the metalworker masses, Perazich explained the 'backwardness' of the textile workers by the departure of skilled male leadership during the war. Yet, despite constant repressions that purged thousands of militants during the war, the Petrograd metalworkers were able continually to put forward new leaders and to intensify their economic and political activism.

But not all elements of the peasant's political culture retained by the unskilled workers were inimical to the political consciousness of the skilled workers. For example, the desire to maintain closed ranks was at least as strong among the peasants, whose *skhody* (assemblies) were famous for unanimous decisions. And as for 'class separateness', it was a rare peasant, indeed, who would allow his- or herself to be represented by a member of the nobility.

However, these traits could not contribute to the radicalisation of the recently arrived peasant until the initial uprootedness and sense of alienation from the working class were overcome. To cite Buiko again: 'In the first years before I outgrew my peasant attitudes, I felt myself alone and continually experienced fear before other people.' It is true, on the other hand, that in periods of dynamism in the labour movement, this initial transition could be quite swift.

Nor can one say that the skilled workers had 'outgrown' all the deeper peasant attitudes. For unconscious traces remained that could take root and develop under the right conditions. One cannot help but feel that the impatience and often outright scorn that skilled workers showed for the 'village' were to some degree a reaction to remnants of peasant traits they were still fighting in themselves. This was certainly true of the peasants' tendency to kowtow before authorities, a tendency in himself which infuriated Shapovalov, for one.

F. N. Samoilov, a dedicated Bolshevik activist and deputy to the Third Duma from the workers' curia in Ivanovo–Voznesensk, recalled how he was forced to move to an almost rural suburb of the town when his wife fell ill in 1909. Although he had been born in the village, as a skilled textile worker he had behind him 17 years of uninterrupted factory work and no economic ties to the land. Nevertheless, the surrounding woods and fields had a definite effect on him.

> Behind the cottage was a large level piece of land overgrown with thick grass that seemed like a convenient place to work. When I looked at it, my hands begged for work. At first, I restrained myself but soon I could no longer hold back. The peasant in me finally awoke and the blood of my ancestors, father, grandfathers and great-grandfathers began to boil wildly in my veins. The land attracted me irresistibly to itself ... In the course of many days, I spent all my free hours from work at the mill on the plot ... I experienced the inexpressible pleasure of the muzhik-ploughman who ploughs his strip with the greatest love and care.[83]

This idyll was cut short by Samoilov's brief arrest in connection with his past activity in the now defunct textile workers' union. When he returned he found the crop destroyed by stray cattle and promised himself 'never again to yield to petty property-owning peasant moods'. But he did yield again when he moved to a new working-class district on the edge of town where he was again eventually arrested. Of course, this was a period of dark reaction when labour activism was difficult and unfruitful, and after this second lapse Samoilov never did give in to 'peasant moods'. Nevertheless, he considered himself a 'conscious worker', and his tone, while somewhat amused, is also clearly apologetic.

The 'Worker Aristocracy'[84]

If, despite the above qualifications, the two types of workers described can be viewed as opposite poles on a series of continua of related social and cultural characteristics, the 'aristocracy' was a group quite apart, sharing many traits with the other skilled workers, but differing fundamentally in other crucial ways. For these were also skilled workers (though only a small stratum of this category) and to a significant degree 'conscious proletarians'—politically literate, 'cultured', active, with a developed sense of class consciousness.[85] However, they did not share the skilled metalworkers' irreconcilability towards census society.

In this category, which drew its members from among the printers,[86] skilled workers in state factories, and the settled, small property-owning stratum of workers, the printers formed the largest and most important sub-group. Their union had traditionally been Menshevik and remained so, except for a brief period following the October Revolution, into 1920.[87] As skilled workers, the printers were urbanised and almost 100 per cent literate; their work required the exercise of considerable intellectual skills, and their wages were on a par with metalworking. It was not a privileged material situation[88] but rather the specific nature of the printing industry, its structure and traditions, that not only muted the antagonism towards census society that characterised the skilled metalworkers but actually gave rise to a certain positive sense of kinship with the intelligentsia and through it with liberal society as a whole. The printers had a real sense of belonging to what the Mensheviks termed 'the vital forces of society'.

And there was, in fact, an intellectual aspect to the work of the typesetter, who in this period, when manuscripts were often untyped, required at least a basic understanding of the text to work with sufficient speed and accuracy. In addition, continuous exposure to materials at best of a liberal orientation, and at worst reactionary, could not but leave traces in the workers' minds.[89] There was also more direct contact with educated society. According to one early history of the Petersburg union, 'type-setters, especially those working on periodical publications, were in direct contact with journalists who, while visiting the composing room, never refused a request by a printer for clarification . . .'[90]

The printers also tended to set themselves somewhat above the mass of workers. Before 1905 they referred to themselves not as 'workers' (*rabochie*), but by the more genteel 'toilers' (*truzheniki*), or 'free artists of the graphic arts', 'literary smithies' and even 'commanders of the leaden army', and their printing plants were 'temples of art'.[91] As the printers were drawn more into the general movement, these attitudes were attenuated but they never fully disappeared.

There is also evidence that printers were recruited from the higher social strata to a greater extent than other workers. The above cited history of the printers' union claimed that while metalworkers almost invariably came from working-class or peasant families, typesetters in Petrograd 'came from all strata, including often very intellectual type-setters from strata that were foreign to the working class, scions of the bourgeoisie'.[92] This is supported by Kabo's study in which of the nineteen printers, six were from 'employee' (*sluzhashchie*, denoting white-collar, non-manual salaried occupations, including administrative and technical positions) families, six from working-class families and another six from the peasantry. In contrast, only two of the seventeen metalworkers were of 'employee' origin, with six of working-class background and eight peasant. This can perhaps be taken as an indication of the higher status attributed in society to the printing trade—it was not so much a 'step-down' for an administrative employee, for example, to set his son up as a printer's apprentice.

In contrast to metalworking, textiles, chemicals, etc., printing still retained many features of a craft industry. To a large extent, this was a question of the relatively small size of printing establishments where the average work force was only 121, as compared to the city-wide industrial average of 409.[93] As in all small plants, relations between owners and administration, on the one hand, and workers, on the other, tended to be of a more personal and paternalistic nature.[94] The direct and informal character of these relations worked against attitudes of 'class isolation' and irreconcilability. Moreover, the small size of the work force and the economic instability that characterised small enterprises placed the workers in a weaker position *vis-à-vis* the owners and made control by the latter, who knew the workers individually, often by name, relatively easy. In March 1917, the Factory Inspectorate reported:

> It is very important to note that work in the small and medium sized enterprises of Petrograd is proceeding in a relatively normal manner. Work is being done in shifts longer than eight hours, and although the workers demand higher wages, these claims are very moderate. The reason for this lies in the fact that the workers are less organised and also in the *closeness of the owners to the workers, thanks to which they have great influence over the workers.*[95]

The workers of small enterprises also lacked the sense of power that their colleagues in the large factories derived from membership in large collectives.

In addition, among the small owners in the printing industry one could find former workers who still had acquaintances at the presses, and, according to Tikhanov, a Petrograd printer, informing and toadying were still quite prevalent during the war:

> An extremely popular expression of the slavish sentiments toward the 'father-benefactors' were the anniversary and name-day celebrations, for which the workers would give money and then celebrate together with the boss ... Of course, the administration valued this and encouraged it with sops.[96]

Another element in the structure of the printing industry that weakened class identity and solidarity was the institution of the *kompaniya*, an exclusive cartel-like association of skilled printers who took on quantities of work at higher rates in return for swift execution. The *kompanii* were self-regulating, with an elected 'elder', who enforced conditions and discipline established by the *kompaniya*. Although outsiders were rarely admitted, they were taken on at lower wages when the *kompaniya* had more work than it could handle by itself.[97] In this way, some of the printers themselves became employers.

Many of these characteristics of the printing trade fostered a sense of superiority towards the less 'cultured' elements of the working class, something that was evident in the printers' early reluctance to be called workers. The 'conscious' metalworkers, as noted, also shared a certain scorn for the 'village', but this was to a large degree sublimated and even overcome in efforts to raise up the unskilled masses to their level, to unify the working class around their own standards and goals. Given their insistence on 'class isolation' from census society and their fears of being dominated and coopted if they cooperated with it, this was the only path open for the struggle to improve their collective lot. The printers, on the other hand, were much less in a position to follow this, since not only did they have no fear of cooperation with liberal society, but they believed it an indispensable condition of success. Moreover, the unskilled masses, once aroused to political life, tended most often towards the skilled metalworkers' position of irreconcilability.

One of the political expressions of the printers' identification with the 'vital forces of society' was their defencism during the war, much stronger here than in other industries. Basing himself on personal recollections and the contemporary press, Tikhanov noted that 'the poison of patriotism was especially potent among the printers, who were in direct contact with it through the press and books'. The Printers' Union paper came out against Karl Liebknecht, the only Social Democratic deputy in the German Reichstag to vote against war credits, and published Plekhanov's letter to the Duma deputy Buryanov advising him to vote for war credits.[98] Kudelli similarly wrote that 'the broad masses of Petrograd, . . . although affected by the chauvinist frenzy, were not so for long. The greatest tribute to chauvinism was paid by the printers, the workers of the Arsenal Factory, the railroad depot of the Putilov Works and certain others.'[99] Tikhanov also recalled printers being involved in such 'bourgeois' organisations as liberal philanthropies and the city duma in efforts to ameliorate the workers' economic situation—clear violations of the norms of 'class isolation'.[100]

The printers, thus, found the Menshevik concept of 'vital forces', i.e. a coalition of the workers, intelligentsia and liberal census elements as the instrument of revolutionary change, quite compatible with their own outlook on society. They felt more comfortable with such an alliance than with the Bolsheviks' 'democratic dictatorship of workers and peasants', in which, as they saw it, the *stikhiya*, the elemental, anarchistic masses of peasants and 'unconscious' workers, would set the tone. At the same time, the Mensheviks, as a *bona fide* 'workers' party' (in contrast to the peasant emphasis of SR populism) with a more intellectual accent and composition than the Bolsheviks, appealed to their self-image as 'worker-*intelligenty*'.

The other elements of the 'worker aristocracy' were characterised by a similar absence of irreconcilability and an affinity to liberal society. In the state factories, as in the printing enterprises, this was fostered by the more paternalistic nature of worker–management relations. But unlike the printers, at least a part of these skilled state workers did enjoy a privileged material position that bound them more closely to the existing order and the upper strata of society. A. Anotonov, a worker of the state-owned Obukhovskii Steel Mill, wrote of a stratum of 'highly skilled workers, whom the administration tried to neutralise by giving them apartments in small houses with truck gardens and other small sops'.[101] At the state Factory of Military-Medical Preparations, there was also a 'handful of highly skilled workers who lived in state apartments and received relatively high wages and medals'. Many of these had refused to strike in 1905–6.[102] According to Tikhanov the system of sops

> in the state enterprises reached the point of awarding medals and even gold ones and hereditary titles. For example, after Easter the workers return to work. Suddenly, in full uniform, with crosses and stars, the director appears. He walks up to the nearest worker, greets him with a handshake, pronounces 'Christ has arisen!', and kisses him three times. So he does with all the others.[103]

Such scenes of 'fraternisation' were almost unthinkable in private metalworking factories after the revolution of 1905 and especially after 1912. One should also bear in mind that workers in state factories were a part of the state bureaucracy and that long-time skilled workers could not but be affected by the bureaucratic ethos of state service that pervaded the administration and which also worked against any clean separation of workers from management.

There is also evidence that in at least some state enterprises wages and conditions were better on the average than in private industry. This was the case, for example, at Obukhovskii where positions were especially coveted and could be obtained only upon recommendation from old-timers. Shotman, who had worked at this factory, cites this as one of the reasons it was so difficult to conduct revolutionary agitation there.[104] At the Government Paper Printing Plant the work day had been only eight hours even before the 1905 revolution, and the workers had their own elected elders.[105]

In an article on the state Patronnyi (Cartridge) Factory, a defencist stronghold in the red Vyborg District, *Izvestiya* offered three reasons for its 'backwardness'. First, it was a state enterprise and had been subject to the 'barracks regime' that had prevailed in state plants before the February Revolution, making revolutionary agitation and collective actions very difficult. As a result, the workers were not 'propagandised' and had little tradition of participation in the labour movement. Secondly, the labour force was 55 per cent female, a fact that was apparently intended to speak for itself. In general, state metalworking factories, even more than private industry, were heavily involved in unskilled ordnance production, employing great numbers of unskilled workers. Finally, this was an 'unusual case' in that the skilled workers were defencists—unusual because in the private factories the skilled workers were typically the most radical element, the natural leaders that pulled the unskilled masses after them.[106] By contrast, in the state plants any spontaneous radical tendencies among the unskilled masses had first to overcome the moderating influence of the local leadership cadres. For this reason, even the women of the textile mills were 'Bolshevised' on the whole weeks and even months before most of the state factories, since they did not have to overcome the influence of local defencist skilled workers who enjoyed special prestige as workers of the same factory. (Although the foremen in the textile mills were also defencist, even Kadet sympathisers, they were not trusted by the workers, who saw them as representatives of the management.)

One outstanding exception to the conservatism of the state enterprises was the Sestroretsk Arms Factory, located in a resort town outside the capital, just three miles from the Finnish border. The work force here, producing rifles for the army, was skilled—it was not, as in most other state metalworking factories, the case of a small stratum of privileged skilled workers in an unskilled mass. This factory also had more than its share of revolutionary agitators, as it served as a haven for Petersburg activists who were finding the capital a bit too hot. It also was used as a way-station for smuggling illegal literature and even arms into Russia.[107]

Owning property, especially land, even on a small scale, had a definite, conservative influence on the politics of workers. Nowhere was this more evident that in the semi-rural suburban Nevskii District of Petrograd, which remained an SR stronghold for most of 1917 only to become the centre of anti-soviet worker sentiment in 1918. Shotman recalled that

> The main mass of workers consisted of a settled element that had worked at the factory continuously for several years. There were, for example, some who had worked 20 or even 30 years consecutively ... Many workers had their own small houses; there were even those

who had several houses which they rented out. Naturally, among this category of worker it was useless to conduct any sort of agitation for the overthrow of the existing order ... Only the youth, and even so, not the sons of the old-timers, but the outsiders, were more or less receptive to agitation ...[108]

In times of crisis, such semi-rural factory settings were often the scene of conflict between the long-time local residents and the workers who had come from the outside, since 'the local worker, owning his home, cow, truck, garden and pasture-land, in critical moments for the factory has the possibility of working for lower wages than the worker from outside whose entire well-being depends upon the factory wage. The worker from among the local residents, owning private property, is also a sort of patriot of his factory and very sensitive to its fate.'[109]

The ownership and cultivation of a plot of land drew workers away from participation in public life. As Samoilov noted:

The greatest part of my time away from the factory [was spent] working in the garden ... This new situation ... began to affect me in a very soporific manner, strongly distracting me from questions of politics ... The whole arrangement created the illusion of peace and calm and a certain sense of contentment with one's lot.[110]

Not surprisingly, this type of worker found the SRs' populism, with its emphasis on 'the people' and on land, more to his liking than working-class social democracy.

As Shotman hinted, there was a certain generational element involved here. Kleinbort described the 'old-timers' (*starichki*) as 'workers who had served 12–15 years in one place. They are aloof, closed groups that have their privileges. Of course, they fear politics, any issues or aspirations. They live in the past; dream of their little home. They say: We lived better before.'[111] This was not, however, a characterisation of all older workers, though age and family responsibilities did foster a more cautious approach to life. It was rather the specific stratum of settled workers, who by virtue of long, continuous and faithful service in one factory had received certain privileges, amassed a little property and developed a sense of loyalty to the administration. The younger, militant elements, of course, looked on this with scorn and disgust. 'Try, try old-timers', wrote a worker of the Russko-Baltiiskii Wagon Factory. 'Soon, for your 25 years of service you will receive a watch and 25 rubles. But remember that if you get sick, they will kick you out like a worthless, squeezed-out lemon, like an old rag.'[112]

The Generational Factor

This typology is not a rigid set of categories into which all manifesta-tions of working-class consciousness neatly fall. Rather it represents basic tendencies within the working class, tendencies which were attenuated, strengthened or otherwise modified, depending on a host of more specific, local factors. Some of these will be treated in the following chapter, while others will be dealt with as they appear in the course of the study. But one that requires further development at the outset because of the exceptional role it played is that of age.

While there appears little basis for the assertion that generational conflict was a major factor underlying political differences in the working class, there can be no doubt that the younger workers, regardless of the industry in question or the level of skill, were among the most militant and radical elements while the older workers tended to be more cautious, reluctant to take risks. The reputation of the younger workers was such that a conference of the Ministry of Internal Affairs and representatives of the Petrograd Council of Metal Entrep-reneurs decided in 1910 that workers under 21 could not take part in the general assemblies of the union. Bulkin, who was the union's secretary explained: 'The aim was to remove from union affairs the most fervent and active elements.'[113] The important role of the factory youth in February and October 1917 is also well documented.[114] 'As always', recalled one worker of the October period, 'the youth was in the front, cheerful, content.'[115] In the less skilled industries, such as textiles and chemicals, and also in the state factories, it was the youth that formed the militant nucleus and who were most attracted to the Bolsheviks.[116]

The youthfulness of the Bolshevik Petrograd organisation (with 28 000 workers in October 1917—two thirds of the city's membership[117]) is striking. In L. V. Golovanova's incomplete, but representative, listing of Bolshevik district committee members in the first half of 1917, over one-third were under 27 years of age, 60 per cent were under 32 and only 18 per cent were over 37: 74.1 per cent of these were workers.[118] Since these were quite responsible, mostly elected positions, one can assume that the average age in the organisa-tion as a whole was even lower. A. F. Smorodkina, a worker at the Optical Factory, recalled that

at that time there was still no Komsomol and not even a hint of the youth organisations that appeared later, such as 'Labour and Light'. Youths who had barely turned twenty were, at times, hardened fighters for the revolution. They joined the party at 17–18 or even 16 years, conducted illegal underground activity, often sat out time in jail and exile. They had experience in political work among the masses.[119]

Naumov, a worker at the New Parviainen Machine-construction Factory was only 22 in 1917, yet had already been to jail and was a member of the Bolshevik Petersburg Committee, the Vyborg District Committee (both even before the February Revolution), a delegate to all three city party conferences in 1917, a factory delegate to the Petrograd Soviet and a member of the Central Soviet of Factory Committees.

The high level of literacy among young workers, a product of the development of the Russian elementary school system towards the end of the nineteenth century, was clearly a crucial factor in this activism. For the young generation of Petrograd workers was almost completely literate (see Table 2.5).

TABLE 2.5: *Literacy of Petrograd metal-workers, by age and sex, early 1918*

| Age | Per cent of literate workers | | |
	Male	Female	All
up to 20	98	81	94
21–30	95	70	89
31–40	90	47	85
41–50	84	48	82
50 +	51	21	74
All	92	70	88

Note: This table is based on a sample of 10196 workers.
Source: *Metallist*, no. 6 (18 June 1918) p. 10.

The youth were avid readers, and what they read shaped much of their outlook on life.[120] Kleinbort found that over one half of the members of workers' educational societies before the war were under 23. 'You see old-timers only in exceptional cases.'[121] Similarly, membership in workers' clubs was overwhelmingly under 25 years of age.[122]

The younger workers, of course, were less likely to be married and burdened with family responsibilities. And it was almost axiomatic in the Russian labour movement that married life discouraged activism.[123]

Over the ages, youth has been characterised by enthusiasm, rebelliousness and militancy; and the Russian working-class youth was not an exception. However, the direction these qualities took was by no means 'innate' or 'instinctual' but was determined by the youth's socio-economic situation. Not only among the workers, but in all classes and strata the youth were at the forefront. A report from Revel in October 1917 stated that the movement to establish soviets of landless peasants was sluggish 'because the youth, which is the most active element, has been called away into the army'.[124] In the peasant movement of 1906–7, it was also the younger generation that led the way.[125] The same was true of census society, where the youth of the Junker schools of Petrograd was really the only element prepared actively to take up arms against the soviets in October 1917.

To a large extent, the rise of the younger workers like Naumov to positions of responsibility was facilitated by the departure of older activists from the movement. Of course, many members of the old guard remained. Shlyapnikov and Gvozdev were only the most prominent of them. But even among those who stayed, a substantial part preferred more moderate positions which did not correspond to the militant mood of the youth. The older activists were a different type of worker-*intelligent* than the generation that reached maturity after the revolution of 1905–7. The former, despite serious tensions, had developed under the guidance of the intelligentsia and in an atmosphere of sympathy (even if paternalistic), not only on the part of the intelligentsia, but of all liberal society. These workers learned from the intelligentsia, modelled themselves after it. After the 1905 revolution, however, society grew increasingly polarised along class lines, and the intelligentsia began to lose its enthusiasm for the workers. It 'ran headlong', wrote Kleinbort, 'and the working class found itself left to its own resources'.[126] This 'flight of the intelligentsia', as the workers saw it, produced a deep sense of betrayal.[127]

Thus, the new generation matured in conditions of relative isolation from society. Unlike their 'fathers', they could not feel that they were part of an all-national liberation movement. It was these conditions that fostered the 'conscious' metalworkers' irreconcilability towards liberal society. Only the printers, partly because they enjoyed a special relationship with the intelligentsia by virtue of the nature of their profession, retained something of the self-image of the old worker-*intelligent* as a part of the 'vital forces' of society.

Whether it was fatigue that came with age and the burdens of family life, the experiences of the abortive revolution of 1905 and the deep reaction that followed it, or apprehension at a movement developing more and more in isolation from the rest of society, the older workers, though not inactive, tended to take a back seat after 1907. Shlyapnikov, recalling an encounter with old comrades who had left the movement and were 'weighed down by life', wrote of the 'transfer of the red banner from the older to the more energetic generation of workers'.[128] In 1912, the Siemens and Shukkert Electrotechnical Factory opened a new branch in the Moscow District of Petrograd. 'It is interesting', wrote Bulkin

> that the so-called 'old' factory ... where long-time settled, and highly skilled workers, predominated, followed the lead of and was continually pushed forward by, the new factory ... where there were predominantly non-local, less skilled and younger workers. At the 'new factory', the workers were both more mobile and more active.[129]

The Siemens Factory was but a microcosm of the shift in the centres of workers activism in Petrograd after 1905–7 from the old factory districts such as Nevskii and Petergof to the relatively newer machine-construction factories of the Vyborg District.

Clearly, the Petrograd working class was not all sewn of the same cloth. Though sharing a common socio-economic situation as factory wage-labourers, they were divided culturally in significant ways, the result of the differing natures of their work and social backgrounds. And yet, unity, that longed-for and elusive prize, was achieved at the crucial junctures of 1917—in February and October. To explain how this came about requires a detailed study of the interaction between these cultural elements and the objective conditions and events of 1917. This is the task of the following chapters.

3 The Social Composition of the Industrial Working Class of Petrograd and its Districts

On 1 January 1917, 392 000 industrial workers were employed in Petrograd,[1] which had a population of 2 412 700.[2] (The category 'industrial worker' includes non-managerial personnel employed in factories, mines and quarries (excluding transport, construction, etc.) with over 10 workers or not less than 10 h.p. mechanical power. Estimates of the total vary slightly. Another figure often cited is 384 000. Since the difference is not very significant, depending on the source, both figures will be used here.) In addition, some 24 000 worked outside the capital in factories that were economically and politically connected to the capital.[3] These 416 000 workers represented 12 per cent of Russia's three and one-half million industrial workers in a total population of 134 million.[4]

Over 60 per cent of Petrograd's workers were employed in metalworking (see Table 3.1) a fact that left its imprint on the entire course of the labour movement not only in Petrograd but Russia as a whole. By contrast, in the Central Industrial Region (Moscow and five surrounding provinces), metalworkers made up only 18.6 per cent (192 000 of 1 030 000) of the work force. Here textiles dominated—cotton alone employed 42.7 per cent of all workers.[5]

Industrial concentration, too, was higher than in the rest of Russia—as much as 40 per cent above the average.[6] This congregation of large masses of workers under one roof—38 plants of over 2000 each accounted for over two-thirds of the total work force[7]—strongly facilitated political education and communication, imparting great strength to collective actions.

Wages in Petrograd were also the highest in Russia, though significantly offset by the higher cost of living.[8]

One-third of Petrograd's workers were employed in state factories, a reflection of the historic dependence of Russia's metalworking industry on the state (and on foreign capital). In all, there were 134 414 workers in 31 state plants, with another 6768 in two large railroad workshops.[9]

TABLE 3.1: *Distribution and average concentration of Petrograd workers by industry, 1 January 1917*

Industry	Number of factories	Number of workers	Per cent of all workers	Average number per factory
Metalworking	379	237369	60.4	626.3
Textiles	100	44115	11.2	441.2
Chemicals	58	40087	10.2	691.2
Paper, printing	218	26481	6.7	121.5
Food processing	70	15773	4.0	225.3
Woodworking	81	6754	1.7	83.4
Leather, shoes	50	12627	3.2	252.5
Mineral processing	32	3900	1.0	121.8
Others	23	5722	1.5	248.8
	1011	392828	99.9	388.5

Source: *Materialy po statistike truda*, vyp. I, p. 10.

In the course of the war, Petrograd's industry underwent tremend-ous expansion, especially in the war-related branches of metalwork-ing, chemicals and to some degree, the clothing industry (see Table 3.2). Most striking was the growth in metalworking, which alone accounted for 83 per cent of the new jobs. The relative weight of

TABLE 3.2: *Changes in number of workers employed in Petrograd by industry, 1 January 1914–1 January 1917*

	Number of workers					
	1914		1917		Change 1914–17	
Industry	in 1000s	%	in 1000s	%	in 1000s	%
Metalworking	100.6	41.5	235.9	61.3	+135.3	+134.5
Chemicals	21.6	8.9	42.9	11.2	+21.3	+98.6
Textiles	40.1	16.5	36.2	9.4	−3.9	−9.7
Food processing	22.7	9.4	15.5	4.0	−6.8	−30.5
Printing	23.1	9.5	19.4	5.0	−3.7	−16.0
Clothing	10.2	4.2	14.7	3.8	+4.5	+44.1
Woodworking	5.0	2.1	5.2	1.4	+0.2	+4.0
Paper	4.4	1.8	3.6	0.9	−0.8	−18.2
Other	14.9	6.1	8.6	2.2		
All	242.6	100.0	384.6	99.2[a]	+142.0	+58.5

[a] Less than 100 per cent due to rounding.

Source: Rashin, *Formirovanie rabochego klassa Rossi*, p. 83.

metalworking in the labour force grew from 42 per cent in 1915 to over 60 per cent in 1917.

In this wartime expansion, there was a disproportionate growth in the number of women workers (see Table 3.3). Although in absolute terms the increase was about the same for both sexes, the relative increase in the female labour force exceeded that for men by over 50 per cent, bringing the adult female component up to 33.2 per cent from 25.7 per cent in 1914. In metalworking, woodworking and printing, the most skilled industries, despite very significant growth in the number of women workers, men continued to predominate. But in textiles and food-processing, which were mainly unskilled and where women had long since become prominent, they now formed a majority. Both of these industries underwent a decline in the absolute number of male workers, due not only to an overall drop in the work force but also to the widespread movement of men of draft age into defence-related industry in search of military deferments. In leather and shoes and chemicals, the sexes had become more or less evenly balanced, with the former experiencing the largest decline in relative size of the male work force. (Shoe-making still employed a significant proportion of skilled workers, while leather-processing, involving heavy physical work, could not easily be done by women.)

TABLE 3.3:   *Changes in number of industrial workers in Petrograd, by age and sex, 1914–17*

| | Number of workers | | | | | |
| | Adult men | | Adult women | | Under 16 years | |
Year	1000s	Per cent of work force	1000s	Per cent of work force	1000s	Per cent of work force
1914	158.4	65.2	61.6	25.4	22.9	9.4
1917	231.2	58.5	129.8	32.8	33.8	8.6
% Increase		46.0		110.7		47.6

Source: Based on Stepanov, *Rabochie Petrograda*, pp. 34 and 36.

There were four principal sources of recruitment into the labour force during the war:

1. peasants, mainly women, juveniles and men above draft age;
2 wives and children of workers, craftsmen, workers from small workshops and other non-industrial working-class occupations;
3. evacuees from factories in Poland and the Baltic provinces; and
4. urban petty bourgeois and bourgeois elements seeking to avoid the draft.

Unfortunately, data on the relative size of these categories are scant and allow only for rough estimates.

The head of the Labour Section of the People's Commissariat of Labour, A. Anikst, reported in 1920 that there had been at least 170 000 'wartime workers' in the factories of Petrograd in 1917, with 150 000 in metalworking and 20 000 in chemicals.[10] A. Antonov, a Petrograd metalworker prominent in industrial management during the civil war, cited similar figures.[11] Two Soviet historians, I. P. Leiberov and O. I. Shkaratan, using archival materials, have calculated that about 70 per cent (116 000) of the male workers of Petrograd were of draft age in 1914. Of these, no more than 15 000–20 000 were actually drafted, the others receiving deferments for war-related work, health or other reasons. Thus, they estimate that 200 000–220 000 or 52–57 per cent of the industrial workers of January 1917 had been in the factories at the start of the war,[12] approximately the same figure given by Anikst and Antonov (about 55 per cent).

Among the newcomers, peasants were by far the most numerous category. *Novaya zhizn'*, citing the Commissariat of Labour, reported that about 150 000 workers constituted 'an element in one way or another tied to the village and interested in the factories only in connection with military deferment'.[13] Evidence from individual factories confirms this. At the Sestroretsk Arms Factory, of the 3286 workers that arrived between January 1914 and July 1917, the majority were peasants; among the new male workers alone, 1875 came from the village.[14] A. Smirnov, a worker of the Skorokhod Shoe Factory, wrote that the new workers who came in 1915–16 were 'predominantly women who had come from the village'.[15] The Petrograd Pipe (Trubochnyi) Factory witnessed such an influx of this element, that, according to one of its workers, it became known as a 'peasant factory'.[16] Even at the Phoenix Machine-construction Factory, with a more skilled work force, 20 per cent of the male newcomers were peasants.[17]

Nevertheless, the economic ties to the land among Petrograd's industrial workers were significantly weaker than in the rest of Russia. According to the August 1918 industrial census, 19.5 per cent of those employed in Petrograd when the data were collected had owned land before the October Revolution, and 7.9 per cent had worked it through members of their family. In all of European Russia these figures were 30.0 per cent and 20.9 per cent respectively; in Moscow—39.8 per cent and 22.8 per cent; and in Ivanovo–Voznesensk, the 'Russian Manchester'—35.7 per cent and 22.6 per cent.[18]

Data on the other categories of newcomers are even more limited and less reliable. One estimate of the number of industrial evacuees, based upon figures for a 10-day peak period, puts them at 15 000–20 000.[19] The rest consisted of non-industrial elements from the urban poor and the middle and upper strata of society. At Phoenix about 23 per cent of the newcomers were artisans.[20] In January 1917 33 800 juveniles (under 16 years) were working in Petrograd's factories. There were also significant numbers of janitors, doormen, cabbies, etc., as well as wives of industrial workers. As for the wealthy elements that took on factory work (some arriving at the plant in cabs), a special commission at the Putilov Works reported in the autumn of 1917 that 7 per cent of the (approximately 36 000) workers here were elements 'foreign' to the working class.[21] Other factories, however, appear to have purged these people soon after the February Revolution.

In sum, despite very significant changes in the social composition of the Petrograd working class, it managed to retain a strong urbanised core that had experienced one of the most intense periods of labour activism in Russian history, the upsurge of 1912–14. Thus, revolutionary Petrograd, as an industrial centre, retained those characteristics that had traditionally set it apart from all others in Russia and placed it at the forefront of the labour movement: predominance of metalworking with a large machine-construction component and the most concentrated, urbanised, skilled and best paid work force.

The Geographical Factor—Social Composition of the Districts of Petrograd

It is not always possible to account for the attitudes and moods that predominated in a given factory solely on the basis of the socioeconomic background of its workers or past and present conditions at the plant. Social geography, the sociological nature of the physical environment, also often played a role in shaping attitudes and influencing actions. This, and the fact that much data on working-class consciousness focus on the district level, call for a brief survey of the social make-up of Petrograd's districts.

The geographical factor asserted itself in various ways. For example, the location of most printing shops not in the predominantly industrial and working-class peripheries but in the centre, populated by the more affluent and educated elements, undoubtedly reinforced the ties felt by the printers towards 'society' as well as their perceptions of the power of the propertied classes compared to the workers. By contrast, working in the militant atmosphere of the Vyborg District with its large cadre of skilled metalworkers, its homogeneous proletarian population and revolutionary reputation, the wartime newcomers were more quickly assimilated into the prevailing spirit of working-class radicalism here than elsewhere.

In general, the geographical proximity of a militant skilled work force to one inclined towards passivity by the nature of its social background often had crucial consequences for the latter. The Treugol'nik Rubber Factory in the Narva District, for example, with an overwhelmingly female and unskilled work force, had never struck during its entire pre-1917 history except when 'taken out' by the more active workers from the relatively nearby Putilov Works or some other factory. This was the case even during the mass poisoning at Treugol'nik in 1913.[22] This widespread tactic of 'taking out' (*snyatie*) involved the arrival of a group of already striking workers at a factory, who through shouts and the occasional throwing of stones, breaking down locked gates, and, if it came to that, physical threats, persuaded the timid or reluctant workers to join. Sometimes this was even prearranged, so that the workers could later claim they had struck under threat of violence. The workers of the quiescent Kersten Knitwear Mill, also overwhelmingly female and peasant, were given the name *kolbasniki* (from *kolbasa*—sausage) because of the boss's custom of treating them occasionally to sausage and tea while he kept them over time. Because the few Bolsheviks here were in any event poor orators, reinforcements would be called in for meetings from the neighbouring Vulkan Machine-construction Factory.[23]

In districts where one or two giant factories (over 5000) dominated numerically, they would also often exert a very strong influence on moods and attitudes in the smaller plants, which tended to look to them for guidance. The Putilov Works, to cite the most striking example, enjoyed prestige far beyond the Petergof District and even the capital. Its participation in any collective action, by virtue of its numbers alone, made success so much more certain. In the early February Days, for example, a meeting of the workers of the main workshops of the N.W. Railroad decided to send a delegation to the Putilov workers to see what they were doing before taking action themselves.[24] In the Vyborg District, the workers of the James Beck Textile Mill traditionally sought aid and advice on economic and political matters from the nearby New Lessner Machine-construction Factory.[25]

Distance from the centre also played a certain role in isolating workers from the heated atmosphere and burning issues and made access to left socialist agitators difficult. This was especially important in factories with a relatively unskilled work force which could not supply its own internationalist leadership. In such cases, the local 'intelligentsia'—the clerical and technical personnel, foremen, etc., who were almost invariably defencists—had little trouble, especially in the early period of the revolution, in holding sway over the workers. This was the situation, for example, in the Porokhovskii District with its two large state-owned chemical factories. The delegate from this district to the Bolshevik Petersburg Committee reported in October:

'Till the Kornilov Days, there was a predominance of Mensheviks and SRs. Now the mood is ours ... Distance from the centre hurts our cause.'[26] Similarly, the Left SR *Znamya truda* wrote

> The district, thanks to the absence of paths of communication, is in especially unfavourable conditions. It is only with difficulty that we are able to tear lecturers away [from the centre] ... Despite the lack of homogeneity (there are many peasants taken on because of the war) interest in the political life of the country continues to grow ... We especially feel the absence of intellectual forces [favourable to us]. But thanks to this, one notes an extremely gratifying fact: the appearance of agitators and propagandists from among the workers themselves. There is a collegium of orators—17 workers. In the near future the district will be able to conduct party work by its own forces alone.[27]

This was written in August. The Vyborg District, by contrast, had been supplying not only itself, but other districts of the city and even nearby provincial towns, with agitators and organisers from the start of the revolution.

Finally, one should be aware that these districts were not merely administrative units but also, and this is especially true for the working-class districts, social entities. One need only recall the pride taken by Vyborg District workers in their revolutionary reputation. In Buzinov's memoirs, too, one senses the 'Nevskii District patriotism', to the point, in fact, where he almost sees the district as the centre around which the 1905 revolution turned. In 1917, workers took part in demonstrations not only as members of their factory but marched in their district columns. This identity was reinforced by the existence of district soviets and dumas. The districts in 1917 did in fact show characteristic patterns in their political positions and actions.

One can see from the map (p. 51) and Table 3.4 that industry generally ran along the outskirts of the city, while the centre, consisting of the First and Second City Districts, northern Moscow District, east Vasilevskii ostrov and south Petrograd District, had few, if any, large factories.

The Vyborg District[28]

The role of the size (absolute and relative) of the industrial working-class population and the predominance of metalworking, especially machine construction, in accounting for this district's militancy and radicalism has already been noted. Another closely related characteristic of the Vyborg District was the social homogeneity of its population (see Table 3.5). The Menshevik–Internationalist paper

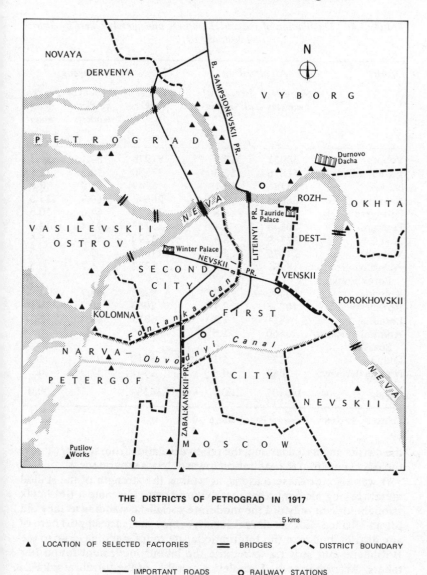

THE DISTRICTS OF PETROGRAD IN 1917

0   5 kms

▲ LOCATION OF SELECTED FACTORIES   ══ BRIDGES   ⌁⌁ DISTRICT BOUNDARY

──── IMPORTANT ROADS   ○ RAILWAY STATIONS

Iskra referred to Vyborg as 'our exclusively proletarian district',[29] and in this respect it surpassed all others. The sheer size of the working-class population and the strength of the local cadres of proletarian militants and leaders[30] imbued the workers here with a sense of their independent strength, while the 'exclusively proletarian' character of

TABLE 3.4:   *Distribution of industrial workers and metalworkers by district,*
1 January 1917

District	All industries		Metalworking		
	Number of workers	Per cent of all workers	Number of workers	Per cent of district's workers	Per cent of all metal workers
Vyborg	68932	17.9	57978	84.1	24.5
Vasilevskii ostrov	51876	13.5	37530	72.3	15.9
Narva	38784	10.1	6549	16.9	2.8
Nevskii	38208	9.9	26641	69.7	11.3
Petrograd	37840	9.8	24444	64.6	10.3
Petergof	36148	9.4	33753	93.4	14.3
First City	32769	8.5	13299	40.6	5.6
Moscow	21079	5.5	11012	52.3	4.7
Polyustrovo-Porokhovskii	18931	4.9	1262	6.7	0.5
Kolomna	10480	2.7	9237	88.1	3.9
Rozhdestvenskii	10233	2.7	2063	20.2	0.9
Lesnoi	6811	1.8	6015	88.3	2.5
Admiralty, Kazan', Spasskii	5660	1.5	1865	32.9	0.8
Okhta	4273	1.1	3110	72.8	1.3
Novaya derevnya	3083	0.8	1631	52.9	0.7
Total	385107	100.1	236389		100.0

Source: Stepanov, *Rabochie Petrograda*, p. 30.

the district and its leadership, the relative isolation from society (across the river) nurtured the aspiration towards 'class separateness'.

It was also for these reasons, as well as the strength of the skilled metalworking element, that the Vyborg District became a Bolshevik stronghold. Not only did the moderate socialists, standing as they did for an alliance with the liberal society, enjoy the least support here of any district, but even the Internationalist groups standing close to the Bolsheviks but striving to reunite the labour movement found few takers. According to L. Leont'ev, a member of the 'Mezhraionka', a group of Internationalist Social Democrats formed during the war to work for unity, it had considerable appeal among Petrograd workers, both Menshevik and Bolshevik. 'Only on the Vyborg side did it develop weakly.'[31] It will become clear later that on one level, at least, the socialist unity slogan was an appeal for the restoration of the alliance between the workers and radical intelligentsia that had largely broken down after 1905–7. It is not surprising, therefore, that the

TABLE 3.5:   *Industrial workers employed in districts as percentage of total district population*

District	Number of workers	District population	Workers employed as percentage of district population
Vyborg	68932	150465	45.8
Petergof[a]	36148	91000	39.7
Nevskii	38208	190000	20.1
Vasilevskii ostrov	51876	268000	19.4
Narva[a]	38784	208900	18.6
Kolomna	10480	96000	10.9
Moscow	21079	194000	10.8
Petrograd	37840	360000	10.5
First City	32769	414600	7.9
Okhta	4273	60789	7.0
Rozhdestvenskii	10233	166000	6.2
Admiralty, Kazan', Spasskii	5660	311590	1.8

[a] Separate figures for Narva and Petergof were not available and were calculated on the basis of the 1915 *uchet* in *Statisticheskii spravochnik po Petrogradu* (1921) Table 1.

Source: Based on *Vedomosti obshchestvennogo gradonachal'stva Petrograda*, 17 April 1917, cited in Golovanova, 'Raionnye komitety RSDRP (b)', pp. 41–57; and Stepanov, *Rabochie Petrograda*, p. 30.

Note: This is not the actual concentration of workers since not all lived in the same district in which they worked, although the poor state of municipal transport allows one to assume that this was generally the case. These figures also do not include family members not employed in industry. They are, therefore, only relative indicators of social homogeneity.

Vyborg workers in October were the most active participants in insurrection and gave the initially all-Bolshevik government the most unqualified support, showing little apparent concern over the near total isolation of the working class not only from census society but from the great majority of the socialist intelligentsia as well.

Certain physical traits of the district also contributed to its characteristic organisation, activism and swift response to the issues of the day. Almost all the factories were relatively large (well over 500 workers) and located along the banks of the Neva or Bol'shaya Nevka Rivers or along the parallel and nearby Bol'shoi Sampsion'evskii Prospekt, the district's main thoroughfare, making for easy communications. Secondly, as the map shows, although entirely separated from the 'bourgeois' centre of the city by the river, the district's factories were actually very close to the centre where the official heart of Russia beat. This proximity made the district readily accessible to all the latest news and rumours, while making the centre especially vulnerable to the direct response of the workers. In all other districts the factories were on the outer peripheries, generally as far as possible from the centre.

Petergof and Narva Districts

The Petergof District stood next only to Vyborg in working-class concentration. It consisted of two sub-districts, one populated mainly by the workers of the Putilov, Til'mans and Langezipen Factories; the other with many small commercial enterprises and a population of small shopkeepers and white-collar employees. As noted, the Putilov Works had a dominant influence here as well as in the Narva District. (In popular usage and party circles, 'Narva District' also included Petergof, and these adjacent districts were usually treated as one.)

Except for a relatively brief period in June and early July 1917, the district did not play a leading role in the political movement. This, in fact, had been the case since the start of the war, something that can be largely explained by the mass influx of peasant and urban non-working-class elements as the factories expanded into ordnance production. The Bolsheviks did not win firm control of the district soviet until after the July Days, though on economic matters they enjoyed considerable support from the very start of the revolution.[32]

The Narva District, to the northeast of Petergof, was much less proletarian in composition and considerably less active. Of its three sub-districts, only one was industrial. The only large metalworking enterprises were the workshops of the Baltic and N.W. Railroads. Narva had the smallest proportion of metalworkers of any industrial or semi-industrial district. The two largest factories were the Treugol'nik Rubber Factory with 15 000 workers (about two-thirds female), about 40 per cent of the district's industrial work force, and the Government Paper Printing Plant (about 8000 workers), one of the most conservative factories in the city. The remainder of the workers were in factories making heavy use of unskilled female labour.

Vasilevskii ostrov

This island in the estuary of the Neva River was the second largest industrial district, though its population was quite variegated. The industrial areas were situated in the port area to the south and on Golodai Island in the north, away from the 'Point', which formed an integral part of the city centre, directly across the bridge from the Winter Palace, the Admiralty, Army Headquarters and other key sites. Here, at the very tip of the island, was the Petrograd Stock

Exchange. On the eastern part, along Bol'shoi and Srednyi Prospekts and the intersecting 'lines', lived members of the nobility, merchants and high state officials, whose stately homes built in the 'empire style' can be seen to this day. This was also the capital's centre of higher education, with the Russian Academy of Sciences, the university Institute of Mining, Academy of Arts, Bestuzhev Women's Higher Courses, as well as several *gimnazii*, a *realschule*, two commercial schools and a municipal high school.[33]

The district had 16 large factories, with the Petrograd Pipe Factory employing one-third of the entire work force. Like the other large metalworking plant, the Baltic Shipbuilding Factory (8000 workers), it engaged large masses of unskilled workers for the production of shells and other ordnance. Besides several smaller electrotechnical factories, the remainder of the district's industry was varied, with five textile mills, several leather factories, and a few tobacco-processing plants.

Next to the Vyborg District, Vasilevskii ostrov became one of the strongest centres of support for the Bolsheviks, who, in bloc with the Internationalists, won control of the Soviet as early as mid-May.[34] In part, this was a function of the size of the industrial population, making for a stronger sense of class identity, and also of the significant number of skilled workers here when compared with most of the other districts.

Another important element in the political situation of this district was the presence of a large body of students, the radical elements of which supplied many of the agitators and organisers that the workers themselves were not always able to put forward. According to Golovanova's data, 30.6 per cent of the members of the Bolshevik district committee between February and July 1917 were intellectuals, while 57.6 per cent were workers. This was the highest proportion of intellectuals (and the lowest proportion of workers) of any of the major industrial districts (see Table 3.6).

Another consequence of the presence of radical intellectuals was the relatively strong support the Internationalist groups enjoyed. Leont'ev, cited above, recalled that 'our strongest district was Vasilevskii ostrov', and in 1917 itself this was one of the few districts where the Menshevik–Internationalists were a significant (albeit secondary) force among the workers. (In September, the Menshevik–Internationalist organisation here entered the Bolshevik party, almost en masse.) The issue of the worker–socialist intelligentsia alliance was so prominent here at least in part because of the tradition of contact with and, to a degree, dependence upon, the district's radical students and intellectuals.

Petrograd District

The population of this district, which consisted of seven islands sand-

TABLE 3.6   *Social background of identified Bolshevik district committee members. March–June 1917*

District	Per cent workers	Per cent intellectuals	Per cent others	Total identified members
Vyborg	89.5	8.8	1.7	57
Narva-Petergof	85.7	10.7	3.6	28
Nevskii	83.4	16.6	0	12
Petrograd	82.1	10.7	7.2	28
Second City	76.7	13.3	10.0	30
Porokhovskii, Liteinyi, Okhta and Railroad	64.3	28.6	7.1	14
Moscow	63.6	18.2	18.2	11
Vasilevskii ostrov	57.6	30.6	11.8	26
First City	50.0	50.0	0	16
Rozhdestvenskii	35.7	28.6	35.7	14
All districts	74.1	18.2	7.7	236

Source: Golovanova, 'Raionnye komitety RSDRP (b)', appendix, Table 7, p. 13

wiched between the Vyborg District, the centre and Vasilevskii ostrov, resembled the latter in its social heterogeneity, though the working-class element was considerably smaller. (In popular usage Novaya derevnya was sometimes included in this district.) The southwest and central sections were quite well-to-do, while the workers, as usual, inhabited the outlying west and northeast shores. Here were several large factories (averaging 1500 workers[35]), with machine construction represented by the Langezipen, Vulkan, Shchetinin and Lebedev Factories, as well as a tram depot. But such highly skilled factories far from predominated. There were at least three textile mills, Kersten, James Beck and Leont'iev Bros, the state-owned Factory of Military Medical Preparations (about 3000 workers, two-thirds women[36]), and some of the city's largest printing houses, including the State Printing Plant, Pechatnyi Dvor and the Otto Kirkhner Printing House and Bindery.

As one might expect, the Petrograd District, as a whole, was less radical than the three above: the Bolsheviks won control of the Soviet here only at the start of August, and even so, the Mensheviks and SRs formed a strong opposition right into October, when they were finally dislodged. The political temper of the district was thus uneven, a reflection of the industrial mix of the district, in which highly skilled machine-construction enterprises existed alongside such conservative bastions as the State Factory of Military Medical Preparations and the large printing houses.

Moscow District (Moskovskaya zastava)

The majority of the eleven large factories here were located at the south central end of Petrograd, where Zabalkanskii Prospekt became the Moscow Highway. The industrial population was about evenly distributed between metalworking and the other branches of industry. Leather was heavily represented by the Skorokhod (6500—the largest in Russia) and the Nevskii Shoe Factories (1600), together employing close to one-third of the district's industrial work force.[37] Among the electrotechnical plants were Dinamo (2300, of which 1000 were women[38]) and Siemens-Shukkert. There were also two wagon-building plants—Rechkin and Artur-Koppel', a tram depot and the Municipal 1886 Power Station. Beyond these to the south were about a dozen small factories and hundreds of workshops employing few or no hired workers.[39]

Workers formed a relatively small part of the district's population, which consisted of a large well-to-do element (to the north) and a larger white-collar and petty bourgeois (shopkeepers, artisans, etc.) stratum. This was one of Petrograd's four SR centres (the others being Nevskii, Okhta and Porokhovskii), and as late as September 1917, the SRs held eight of the twenty seats in the Soviet. The relatively small size of the skilled work force does not seem to have been a major factor in this, since it was precisely the metalworking factories that gave the SRs the strongest support (though it is true that these plants were greatly inflated by unskilled workers during the war). In part, SR sympathies seem to have been related to the semi-rural character of the factory setting and to the effects of small property ownership on the settled skilled elements. This explanation tends to be supported by the fact that the other three SR centres were also in semi-rural outlying areas in the south and east of the city. (Actually these were not even incorporated into the city until June 1917.)

Nevskii (-Obukhovskii) District

Located in the southeast corner of the capital at a considerable distance from the centre (to reach it one took the train running between Tsarskoe Selo and Nikolaevskii Station), the Nevskii District consisted of two sub-districts, each dominated by a giant mixed metalworking plant—the Nevskii Shipbuilding and Machine-construction Factory and the state Obukhovskii Steel Mill (13 000). The two other large metalworking enterprises were the Aleksandrovs-kii Locomotive Factory and the repair shops of the Nikolaevskii

Railroad. The latter three were state-owned. In addition were four large textile mills, two paper mills, a soap factory, a wax factory, the State China Factory and a number of smaller plants also relying heavily on semi-skilled or unskilled labour.

The Nevskii District stands out as the most moderate of all the industrial and semi-industrial districts of the capital and the firmest support of the SR defencists. Some of the reasons for this conservatism, which is striking given the relatively large and concentrated worker population and the predominance of metalworking, have already been touched upon. Of the four largest factories, three were state-owned. The largest, Nevskii and Obukhovskii, were situated well outside the city in the midst of villages. In fact, the address of the Nevskii Factory was selo Smolenskoe. Its work force was to a large extent recruited from the neighbouring villages of Rogatkovo, Lesnozavodskaya and Murzinskaya.[40] Local workers of the Obukhovskii Factory who owned plots and kept cattle were called 'Rybatskie korovniki' (cowherds from the village of Rybatskoe).[41] Although a centre of activism before and during 1905–7, the district had faded into the background during the 1912–14 upsurge, when the labour movement picked up once more but in isolation from 'society'. Only in the spring of 1918, in the opposition movement to the soviets, did the district again become politically active, demanding a more broadly-based government and the convocation of the (all-national) Constituent Assembly.

Kolomna (Sub-)District

Officially a sub-district of the Second City District, Kolomna had its own soviet in 1917 and was treated as a separate district in party circles. This was the only industrial area in the Second City District, location of three large shipbuilding factories—Franko-Russkii (6500 workers), Admiralty and New Admiralty (both state-owned, together with 2500 workers). Franko-Russkii, being private, was the more radical and it dominated the district politically. By mid-May the Soviet, from the start under strong Bolshevik influence, fully supported the demand for soviet power.

Second City District

Consisting of the Admiralty, Kazan and Spasskii (and, officially, Kolomna) sub-districts, this was the very heart of the city, the 'bourgeois' centre, without any large-scale industry. Commercial enterprises, army barracks and state institutions dominated the scene. Here were many of the state ministries, the theatres, museums, palaces, libraries, bank headquarters. This was the 'hostile territory' through which worker demonstrators had to pass on their way down Nevskii Prospekt.

First City District

In the centre of this district was the Nikolaevskii Railroad Station, connecting the capital to the rest of Russia. It was here that Nevskii Prospekt began its route through the city. Occupying about one-quarter of the city's land area (as of February 1917), it consisted of three sections: Liteinyi, with the luxurious homes of the nobility and big bourgeoisie; the Moscow section, with a large number of printing houses; and the Aleksandr-Nevskii section, where workers of the Nikolaevskii Railroad Workshops and the nearby textile mills, Novaya Bumagopryadil'nya, Kozhevnikovskaya and Aleksandr-Nevskaya, and a few other factories lived. The Liteinyi District had two large state-owned ordnance factories—Orudiinyi and a branch of Patronnyi (about 6000 workers together), but the main source of employment in the district was the multitude of commercial enterprises. Accordingly, the basic population consisted of white-collar workers, professionals and property-owning elements.

Rozhdestvenskii District

Large-scale industry in this district, site of the Tauride Palace and Smol'nyi Institute, was limited to two large textile mills—Nevskaya Bumagopryadil'naya and Nevskaya Nitochnaya (together about 4000) and a tram depot. There were also several small electrical and metal factories, the largest being Ouf, Shpigel' and Opticheskii. The district also had many military units. As one local Bolshevik put it: it was a district of 'petty bourgeois and semi-intelligentsia' with few workers.[42] Golovanova's data show that only about one-third of the district committee members were workers, the lowest proportion for any district.[43] The make-up of the non-census part of the population accounts for the strength of the Menshevik–Defencists in the Soviet until well past July when it began to shift in an internationalist direction.

Okhta and Porokhovskii Districts

These adjoining, isolated and semi-rural districts, situated in the east end of the city across the Neva, were the other two centres of SR support in 1917. In Okhta, where there was almost no industry, the great majority of workers were employed in semi-artisanal

workshops.[44] The Porokhovskii District, on the other hand, was dominated by two state-owned chemical plants (together about 18 000)
employing a very large peasant element.

This completes the outline of the major social and economic influences
on working-class consciousness in Petrograd. The picture obtained is,
admittedly, not a simple one, but as the following pages are intended to
show, it does provide a framework for a coherent analysis of working-
class attitudes and behaviour as manifested in the revolution of 1917.

4 The Honeymoon Period— From the February to the April Days

From the standpoint of the evolution of working-class politics in 1917, the dominant issues of this period revolved around the question of the workers' relationship to census society. The February Revolution left the workers ambivalent on this score. The historical experience of the labour movement had bequeathed a legacy of deep and pervasive distrust of the bourgeoisie, which had generally been hostile to working-class aspirations. But this distrust was now counter-balanced by two new factors: the workers' unwillingness to assume responsibility for running the state and economy, and the ultimate, if belated, rallying of census society to the cause of the revolution.

This ambivalence found its political expression in the system of dual power: formally, state power resided in an all-census government standing on a platform agreed upon with the Soviet; but the Soviet reserved for itself the right to 'control' this government and ultimately to intervene directly when it saw fit. And as far as the workers were concerned, the Soviet was the sole source of legitimate authority in Russia, the Provisional Government merely an executor of its will.

In the economic sphere, the workers were at once more and less radical. While they refused to yield on the social aspects of the revolution, as they conceived it, regardless of the threat this may have posed to their political alliance with census society, they nevertheless showed no intention of challenging the economic dominance of the capitalists. One must add, however, that even in the early weeks of the revolution, one could discern a certain wariness among the workers regarding the intentions of the owners and management and the first hints that the workers would not stop even before direct intervention into administration if they felt the interests of production and the revolution called for it.

In this way, a hesitant alliance was established between the working class and census society, each eyeing the other with unconcealed suspicion.

Background to February—The Labour Movement During the War

The February Revolution in Petrograd occurred against the immediate background of growing economic dislocation, military reverses and the deepening alienation of all classes from the Tsarist régime.

At the root of the economic problems lay the war and the backwardness of the Russian economy, which was simply unequal to the task of meeting the needs of the front and the rear. Moreover, the Tsarist state proved incapable of organising the economic base that did exist. The military reverses were in large part a result of these factors. While census society was turning away from the régime for its inability successfully to prosecute the war and hold the increasingly militant workers in check (without, however, daring actually to break with it), the workers' anti-government mood was fired by the deterioration of their economic conditions caused by a war which, by the winter of 1916, the majority had come to view as imperialist, as well as by the severely repressive political régime.

In the winter of 1916–17 the workers experienced the effects of the war and economic crisis in the form of production stoppages due to shortages of fuel and raw materials, declining living standards resulting from the galloping inflation and the outlawing of strikes, scarcity of consumer goods and the appearance of long queues before bakeries and food stores. Work conditions had also deteriorated, overtime was unlimited, laws protecting female and child labour abrogated. The management, now virtually free of all restraints and enjoying the active support of the state, met workers' demands with the very real threats of the front, jail or exile. The labour press, trade unions and most other forms of workers' organisation had been shut soon after the outbreak of war, the Bolshevik State Duma delegates exiled to Siberia for anti-war agitation. So efficient was police repression that the average career of the underground activist was reduced to only three months.[1]

In the eyes of many observers, the eve of the war in Petrograd had had the markings of a revolutionary situation reminiscent of 1905.[2] The strike of 6–12 July 1914, the culmination of a movement begun in 1911–12, started as a protest against a police attack on the Putilov workers and soon escalated into a general political strike, replete with barricades and pitched battles.

The mobilisation and intensified repression put an abrupt end to this movement. The anniversary of Bloody Sunday, 9 January and May Day 1915 were not marked by strikes or street demonstrations as in previous years. But the spring and summer of 1915 saw a resurgence of strike activity, though it was now predominantly economic in nature except for a strike of 30 000 workers protesting against the bloody repression of a textile strike in Ivanovo-Voznesensk in the summer of that year.

But if in the first year of the war less than one-third of the 180 864 worker-days lost were due to political strikes, in the second year a full one-half of the 596 039 worker-days lost were due to political actions.[3] On 9 January 1916, 100 000 workers put down their tools. In February, the Putilov workers began an economic strike which soon put forward the political demands of the Social-Democratic minimum programme, and over 100 000 workers struck in solidarity.[4]

The movement in the autumn of 1916 continued to grow, its political character becoming more and more pronounced, culminating in a protest strike of 120 000 workers against the court martial of Baltic sailors accused of membership in an underground Bolshevik organisation. Confronted with a lockout, the workers responded with yet another strike. The largest strike of the war to date occurred on 9 January 1917, with estimates running between 200 000 and 300 000. No one at this point foresaw a revolution only six weeks away, but the potential of this mighty upsurge of militancy was not lost upon the workers' leaders. The Executive Committee of the Bolshevik Petersburg Committee (PC) reported: 'The success of the demonstration of January 9 very much raised the spirits of the masses. In the factories the mood is very buoyant and politically conscious; this opens wide revolutionary possibilities.'[5] In the six months from September 1916 to the start of the revolution a little over one million worker-days were lost in Petrograd, three-quarters of these in political strikes.

The February Revolution—The Birth of Dual Power[6]

The general strike that resulted in the overthrow of Tsarism grew out of two separate actions. On 17 February one of the shops of the Putilov Works struck for higher wages and the reinstatement of several dismissed activists. Other shops soon joined, and when on 22 February the administration declared a lockout, the whole 36 000 work force struck. A strike committee was formed, and delegations dispatched to other factories to drum up support. One of these prophetically informed Kerenskii, then a Trudovik (right-wing populist) duma delegate, that this could be the beginning of a major political offensive.[7] But no one guessed just how close the dénouement was.

International Women's Day fell on 23 February, and the mood among the women workers was very militant against the background of high prices, the queues and especially the recent disappearance of bread from a number of bakeries. The day began with meetings featuring anti-war speeches, but no other actions were planned. Among the Bolsheviks, who tended to be the most militant, the strategy was to conserve energy for a decisive general strike on May Day.[8] Nevertheless, in the Vyborg District the women workers of several textile mills quit work and, gathering outside the nearby metalworking factories, easily persuaded the men to join them. I. Gordienko, a worker at the Nobel Machine-construction Factory, recalled the following scene:

> On the morning of February 23 one could hear women's voices in the lane which the windows of our department overlooked: 'Down with the war! Down with high prices! Down with hunger! Bread for the workers!' Myself and several comrades were at the windows in a flash ... The gates of No. 1 Bol'shaya Sampsion'evskaya Manufaktura were wide open. Masses of women workers filled the lane, and their mood was militant. Those who caught sight of us began to wave their arms, shouting: 'Come out! Quit work!' Snowballs flew through the window. We decided to join the demonstration ... A brief meeting took place outside the main office near the gates, and we poured out into the street ... The comrades in front were seized by the arm amidst shouts of 'Hurray!', and we set off with them down Bol'shoi Sampsion'evskii Prospekt.[9]

That day, the demonstrators concentrated their efforts on 'taking out' (*snyatie*) the other factories. Singing revolutionary songs, the crowd would stop in front of a factory and exhort those inside to join. If no response followed, some would steal inside to agitate, and, that failing, to threaten. At Metallicheskii, the administration took the precaution of locking the gates, but the crowd broke them down. Along the way, the workers disabled trams and attacked isolated policemen. Several bakeries and food shops were sacked. The geographical goal of the movement from the very outset was Nevskii Prospekt, the city's main thoroughfare. But the police were still able to keep most demonstrators from crossing the river. According to the Okhranka (secret political police), 87 534 workers from 50 factories struck that day.[10] Although anti-war and anti-government slogans could be heard from the start, the most popular on that day by far was 'Bread!'.

On the morning of 24 February, the workers appeared at their factories as usual but after brief meetings again took to the streets. Events followed the pattern of the previous day, and clashes with the police became more and more frequent. Bread was still the most widespread slogan, but anti-war and anti-government cries were gaining in prominence. The strikers now numbered about 200 000[11] and came from all districts of the city. Now students began to appear in significant numbers. The demonstrators were also more successful in getting across to the centre. Among certain army and Cossack units there were signs of favourable disposition towards the demonstrators.

The next day the City Governor's office reported 240 000 striking workers (Leiberov's estimate: 305 000). For all practical purposes the strike had become general. Non-working-class elements—artisans, white-collar employees, members of the intelligentsia—joined in larger numbers, creating an atmosphere of general sympathy that further raised spirits. The police were now definitely on the run, moving only in groups on the street. Anti-war and anti-government slogans predominated alongside calls for a democratic republic and the other traditional Social-Democratic demands: the eight-hour work day and the convening of the Constituent Assembly. Nevskii Prospekt belonged to the demonstrators.

It was at this point that the people began to sense that the movement would end in victory, that what was happening was a revolution. A police informer reported on that day:

> Since the military units did not hinder the crowd and in individual cases even took measures to paralyse the initiative of the police, the masses have acquired a sense of certainty that they will go un-punished, and now after two days of unhindered marching about the streets, when revolutionary circles have put forward the slogans 'down with the war' and 'down with the government', the people have become convinced that the revolution has begun, that success is with the masses, that the government is powerless to suppress the movement since the military units are not on its side, that victory is close since the military units will soon cross over to the revolutionary forces.[12]

On Sunday, 26 February, the number of strikers remained about the same as the previous day. The police began to retaliate by firing into the crowds, especially on Nevskii Prospekt, but the crowds scattered only to reassemble as soon as the shooting died down. The sacking and firing of police stations began. Isolated cases of mutiny among the garrison occurred.

27 February marked the victory of the revolution. Virtually the entire Petrograd working class was out. From the morning, crowds approached the barracks in efforts to persuade the soldiers to join them. By afternoon, the mutiny was a mass phenomenon. The remainder of the day was spent in firing police stations and liberating political prisoners.

Meanwhile, at the Tauride Palace, seat of the State Duma, the two remaining Social-Democratic (Menshevik) deputies, Chkheidze and Skobelev, along with the recently freed Menshevik-Defencist leaders of the 'Workers' Groups' of the Military-Industrial Committee and a number of independent Social-Democratic intellectuals (Sukhanov and Sokolov), seized the initiative in organising a Soviet of Workers' Deputies to take charge of the movement. Declaring themselves a Provisional Executive Committee (EC), they set up military and food commissions and invited the factories to send delegates to the Soviet that evening.

In another section of the palace, the State Duma, having recently been dissolved by the Tsar, met in 'private session' (still reluctant openly to defy the will of the autocrat) and formed a Provisional Committee of Members of the State Duma for the Restoration of Order and for Contacts with Persons and Institutions.

On the night of 28 February–1 March, these two bodies, the one speaking in the name of revolutionary democracy, the other for census Russia, reached an agreement on the formation of a government constructed exclusively from among the census delegates of the Duma. The Duma Committee, for its part, accepted the Soviet's programme, including full political freedoms, political amnesty, and immediate measures for the convocation of a Constituent Assembly. On 2 March, the soviet plenum approved this arrangement overwhelmingly, though emphatically qualifying its support of the Provisional Government upon the latter's conscientious execution of the Soviet's programme. The plenum also decided to establish an 'observation committee' to monitor the activities of the government. The dual power system was born.

The Workers' Attitudes on State Power and their Relationship to Census Society

The idea of a soviet of workers' deputies, part of the legacy of the 1905 Revolution, was close to the hearts of the workers, and the question of its election was raised in some factories as early as 25 February, even before the initiative of the Provisional Executive Committee (EC) of the Soviet.[13] At the same time, however, there can be little doubt that the overwhelming majority of the workers were not prepared for the Soviet itself to take power and that the dual power arrangement hit upon by the EC corresponded to their own understanding of the tasks at hand.

At the 2 March plenum, the formula of conditional support, '*postol'ku-poskol'ku*' (inasmuch), was passed by 400 votes to 19. But the establishment of an 'observation committee', which had not been among the EC's recommendations, indicated the existence of a somewhat greater distrust of the census government among the rank-and-file delegates than among the leadership.

Some Bolsheviks and the Menshevik–Internationalist Bazarov spoke against the position of the EC majority. The protocols note that 'in the debate a current emerged that rejected any possibility of contact with the Duma Committee and demanded the creation of a Provisional Revolutionary Government by the Soviet of Workers' and Soldiers'

Deputies' (W and SD).[14] But as Shlyapnikov, a member of the Russian Bureau of the Central Committee (CC) and the Soviet's EC, admitted, even many of 'our own people' voted with the majority.[15] And the Bolshevik Petersburg Committee in its majority also rejected the slogan of a Provisional Revolutionary Government to be created by the Soviet in favour of a lukewarm formula of conditional support for the government: 'We *will not oppose* the Provisional Government [PG] inasmuch ...'.[16]

In the factories, the attitude to the Soviet's position was also overwhelmingly favourable, with many of the resolutions passed at meetings closely echoing the Soviet. An 8 March meeting of the workers of the Izhorskii Factory, a mixed production metalworking plant in Kolpino, near Petrograd, resolved: 'All measures of the PG that destroy the remnants of the autocracy and strengthen the freedom of the people must be fully supported on the part of democracy. All measures that lead to conciliation with the old régime and that are directed against the people must meet a most decisive protest and counteraction.' The resolution went on to state the necessity of defending by all means the SD minimum programme, the 'Three Whales'—the democratic republic, the eight-hour day and the confiscation of lands and their transfer to the peasantry—and it called upon the Soviet to appeal to the working classes of the world and conclude a democratic peace.[17] Nevertheless, despite the profession of support for the government, the very mention of the possibility that the government might turn against the people betrays a basic distrust. The resolution is at once an expression of support and a threat.

Yet even this formulation appears relatively positive when compared to many other resolutions. A meeting of leatherworkers in early March expressed support for the Soviet's tactics on power (significantly omitting any direct expression of support for the government itself) but added that 'even now, when all classes are caught up in the powerful revolution created by the workers and soldiers, we must not completely trust the bourgeoisie. We must establish unremitting control of the Soviet of W and SD over it.'[18] Even more explicit is the resolution of the general assembly of the Petrograd Cable Factory on 3 March. Having heard a report of the factory's Soviet delegate, it resolved (by about 1000 to 3) that

> We consider the most essential issue of the current moment to be the establishment of strict control over the ministers who were appointed by the State Duma and who do not enjoy popular confidence. This control must be constituted by representatives of the Soviet W and SD.[19]

Similarly, on 3 March, about 2000 woodworkers meeting in the

Chinzelli Circus declared that they 'trust only the Soviet W and SD'. Calling on the latter to exert vigilant control over every step of the PG, the resolution instructed the Soviet 'to immediately inform the workers and soldiers and the whole population of this [any retreat by the PG from its promises] and to call them out into battle against it'.[20]

The workers' resolutions of March all point to a conclusion that was obvious even to the leaders of census society: the PG itself had little legitimacy in the eyes of the workers, and the support that they did give it was a function of the legitimacy and 'control' of the Soviet. In fact, the Duma Committee had attempted to persuade Skobelev, Chkheidze and Kerenskii, members of the Soviet EC to enter the government. Failing this, Milyukov insisted that the Soviet at least express publicly its support.[21] It was the Soviet, not the government, that issued the call to end the general strike. All this was a conscious admission of the government's lack of authority among the masses. Nor was this the case in Petrograd alone. An analysis of workers' resolutions from the provinces found all addressed either to the Soviet or to Kerenskii;[22] none to the PG.[23]

In their actions too, the workers showed that for them the Soviet was the real source of authority. Thus, several state factories turned to the Soviet, not the government, to sanction changes they had made in the administration.[24] Others asked the Soviet to enact various reforms. When on 4 March the general assembly of the Patronnyi Factory decided that alcoholic beverages should go the same way as the old régime, it resolved to 'enter into contact with the Soviet to work out a decree on its prohibition'.[25] Many factories specifically petitioned the Soviet for a law on the eight-hour day[26] and almost all turned to the Soviet to issue an appeal to the peoples of the warring countries.[27] When suspicions or open conflicts arose in relations with management, it was again the Soviet that was summoned to investigate.[28]

The only wage- or salary-earning groups to express direct support for the government were white-collar employees and railroad workers. The latter, especially outside the big cities, constituted a huge semi-proletarian mass with strong peasant ties and were under the influence of the Kadets and right-wing socialists from among the higher administrative personnel.[29] The white-collar employees (*sluzhashchie*) of the Russian Company of United Machine-construction Factories pledged 'full support to the PG and the Soviet in their responsible work to create a new organisation of society and to summon the Constituent Assembly'.[30] Similarly, the workers and employees of 26 railway lines resolved jointly to 'support the Soviet and the PG'.[31] According to Tanyaev's history of the railroad workers in 1917, they indeed viewed the PG as a popular democratic government. 'No other part of the working class placed so much hope in it.'[32]

On the other hand, despite the misgivings and qualifications, there were few industrial workers in Petrograd who did not accept dual power as a viable arrangement. The only exceptions were in the Vyborg District. A large meeting on 1 March at the Sampson'evskii Brotherhood was extremely hostile to the State Duma and its Provisional Committee and voted by a large majority to subordinate the Committee to a Provisional Revolutionary Government.[33] Another meeting at the Brotherhood hall on 3 March called on the Soviet 'to remove the PG of liberal bourgeoisie and to declare itself the Provisional Revolutionary Government'.[34] According to the Bolshevik worker Sudakov, meetings here were famous for their anti-Duma and anti-PG tone.[35] The Vyborg Menshevik organisation indirectly confirmed the existence of such a mood in the district, at least among some of the workers, reporting that 'with the exception of the attitude to the PG, all questions—land and the future political system—are being decided clearly and categorically'.[36] And the Menshevik paper wrote: 'The calls to overthrow and even to arrest the PG that we heard from irresponsible street orators in the first days of the revolution evoked applause but they led to no practical results.'[37]

Within the Petrograd Bolshevik organisation itself, apparently only the Vyborg District (500–600 overwhelmingly working-class members in March 1917) held to this left position. In fact, the PC was forced specifically to forbid the distribution of the Vyborg organisation's leaflet containing the 1 March resolution of its general assembly demanding the resignation of all members of the Duma, that 'pillar of the Tsarist regime' and the formation of a Provisional Revolutionary Government.[38] Shlyapnikov comments that the Vyborg Bolsheviks, 'somewhat apt to force events', were for immediate, even armed, struggle by all means against the PG.[39]

It is possible that support for soviet power at this early date was somewhat more widespread than these few items of evidence indicate, since before the formation of the PG and its endorsement by the Soviet on 2 March, some factories seem merely to have taken for granted that the Soviet itself would become the government. The Soviet delegate elected at the Shchetinin Aircraft Factory in Novaya derevnya, next to the Vyborg District, presented the following mandate: 'The general assembly of workers ... has elected Grachev to the Provisional Revolutionary Government—the Soviet of Workers' Deputies ...'[40] Similarly, the Schlusselburg Powder Factory on 1 March mandated its Soviet delegates 'to enter into relations with the Provisional Revolutionary Government to receive information and directives'.[41]

Moreover, immediately upon Lenin's return in early April (before the April crisis, the first open clash between the workers and the government), several Vyborg metalworking factories passed anti-government resolutions. One can thus surmise that Lenin's support for soviet power and the eventual victory of this slogan within the party facilitated the open expression of views that were already held by some workers but which had been suppressed in face of the apparently unanimous support for dual power and the failure of the local Bolshevik cadres, bound by party discipline, to put forth an alternative.

On 4 April (actually before Lenin's arrival), the general assembly of the Nobel Machine-construction Factory resolved:

1) that the liberation of the working class is the affair of the workers themselves 2) that the way of the proletariat to its final goal— socialism—lies not on the path of compromises, agreements and reforms, but only through merciless struggle—revolution 3) that the bourgeoisie has taken into account the danger that threatens it from the proletariat and from time to time arranges a blood-letting of the working class: in 1905 we had January 9; 1912—Lena; after Lena—Kostroma (June 1915) and Ivanovo-Voznesensk (August 1915) 4) that the working class cannot trust any government comprised of bourgeois elements and supported by the bourgeoisie 5) that our PG, composed almost totally of bourgeois elements cannot be a popular government to which we can entrust our fate and our great victories.[42]

This extreme statement of irreconcilability towards the bourgeoisie based, significantly, upon an historical argument and not upon the current situation, in the prevailing atmosphere of support for dual power, stopped short of concrete proposals for action. But a meeting of 5000 workers and soldiers went a little further, unanimously demanding legislation on the confiscation of land in favour of the people, the eight-hour work day, a war tax on the capitalists, arming of the workers, a declaration by the PG, with the agreement of the Allies, rejecting all annexations and retributions and calling for immediate peace talks, and finally, the publication of all secret treaties.

These five main demands of the people, of course, will not please the bourgeois–aristocratic government, by which we mean the PG. Putting forth these demands we will let all those parts of the people that are waivering and trusting the PG know the impermissibility of the existence of such a government.

In the case of the inevitable refusal by the PG to directly and unconditionally satisfy these basic demands of the people, the Soviet W and SD must declare itself the unique supreme power and publish in its name these and other laws needed by the people.

Such a second stage of the revolution by its example (and not by declaration) will have an effect on the toilers of the other countries and, in particular, Germany. The German people, seeing against them a workers' government, will more boldly turn against their own oppressors, against Wilhelm and the bourgeoisie. That is when the truly defensive war will begin ... Until then the war will be one of plunder.[43]

In addition, two other Vyborg factories, the Old Parviainen Foundry and Mechanical Factory and Russian Renault (13 and 15 April respectively) called directly for soviet power.[44] But in all these cases, again, the rejection of census society rested not so much upon anything that had already occurred, but rather upon an implicit analysis of the class nature of the bourgeoisie, itself based upon historical experience. To the majority of workers, and particularly those recently arrived from the village, who shared neither this experience nor the analysis, such conclusions seemed totally unwarranted, indeed dangerous. They needed contemporary and concrete proof, the kind the above quoted resolution wanted to provide.

Even aside from the mass of resolutions in favour of the Soviet's position, the overwhelmingly 'revolutionary defencist' attitude among the workers towards the war points indisputably to their support for dual power. Rejecting what they saw as the imperialist aims of all the belligerent governments, the workers declared, nevertheless, that 'we will not under any circumstances allow Wilhelm and his underlings to fill the place left by Nikolai the Last. We want peace without annexations and retributions, peace which the toiling masses of the warring countries will sign. The Soviet of Workers' and Soldiers' Deputies and the Provisional Government must facilitate such an agreement.'[45] Since the imperialist inclinations of the Russian bourgeoisie and its unflinching support for the war under the old régime were well known to the workers, their support for a war of defence conducted by a census government could only mean either they believed the bourgeoisie had undergone a change of mood or, much more likely, that the Soviet, through its 'control', could ensure the adherence of the government to a democratic and active peace policy. Even factories that subsequently proved among the most radical, such as the Franko-russkii Shipbuilding Factory, apparently shared this belief, calling on the people to exert

> energetic influence on the PG in the aim of forcing it to make a categorical declaration on the war in the sense that Russia in this war no longer pursues annexationist goals. On the other hand, we consider it extremely necessary that the PG immediately press the states allied with Russia to make similar declarations.[46]

On the war issue, the Bolsheviks did put forward an alternative position, but one that made little sense to the workers and even aroused considerable hostility. The party retained the pre-

revolutionary slogan 'down with the war', arguing that the 'bourgeois
government' was imperialist, but nevertheless continued conditionally
to support the 'bourgeois government'. As a result, many workers saw
'down with the war' as a threat to the revolution itself. And the
Bolsheviks had trouble explaining their contradictory position. At the
First Bolshevik Petrograd City Conference in early April, the worker
Naumov complained:

> The masses do not understand our calls to end the war. Something
> here is missing. Those who ask: Does it mean sticking the bayonets
> into the ground?—are right. That is what the masses say. We have to
> clarify it for the masses and ourselves. One feels that something is
> lacking.[47]

Given the Bolsheviks' premisses, the more consistent stand would
have been to call for the replacement of the census government with
one formed by the Soviet, one that would and could conduct a
revolutionary defensive war as well as an active democratic peace
policy. It is not surprising, then, that the only place where there was
any support for the Bolshevik position on the war was the Vyborg
District.[48] For it was only here that there was any readiness to oust the
census government. (After the return of Stalin and Kamenev in
mid-March, the editorial policy of *Pravda* did, in fact, take a sharply
defencist turn and changed again only after Lenin's arrival.)

But if the great majority of workers supported the Soviet leadership
on dual power, their positions were still not identical, and it was,
significantly, over the war issue that this discrepancy first revealed
itself. While the workers took for granted that the government,
voluntarily or under pressure, had adopted the Soviet's peace policy,
the architects of dual power were far from certain about this. And yet,
they went ahead and agreed to support the government. Thus, Rafes, a
Bundist, reports that Sukhanov, who had a major hand in the negotiations, argued that 'there can be no talk of the participation of democracy in the PG, since this would mean participation in the war being
conducted by them'.[49] Sukhanov himself wrote that in the negotiations
both sides avoided the question of the war, knowing that it would lead
to a collision.[50] This discrepancy may also explain why the Soviet
plenum did not object to Kerenskii's entering the government, while
the Soviet EC had opposed it.

These differences first surfaced around the 'Liberty Loan', launched
by the government in early April. The Soviet EC endorsed the loan by
21 votes to 14 on 7 April, but the plenum decided to wait until the
government had shown concrete initiative towards securing a democratic peace. However, on 22 April, the plenum gave in, endorsing the
loan against the opposition of only 117 Bolsheviks and

Internationalists.[51] But in the factories, almost everywhere, opinion was strongly hostile both to the loan and the EC's endorsement of it. The most common reaction to the appeal to support the loan were resolutions demanding a special tax on capital and war profits and a government initiative to press the Allies to renounce all annexationist aims. On 10 April, the engineering department of the Russko-Baltiiskii Wagon-construction Factory resolved (by over 400 to 7):

> Recognising that the 'Liberty Loan' has as its aim the continuation of this fratricidal war which is of benefit only to the imperialist bourgeoisie, we do not consider it possible for the socialist pro-letariat to take part in this loan. At the same time we recognise that the matter of supplying the army with all it needs requires financial means and we point out to the Soviet that this money should be taken from the pockets of the bourgeoisie that has instigated and continued this slaughter making millions in profits from this bloody frenzy.
>
> We energetically protest against the conduct of the 21 members of the EC of the Soviet of W and SD who accepted the 'Liberty Loan' and we consider such an attitude to the cause of the proletariat a betrayal of the International.[52]

Indeed, the Soviet's support for the loan served as the first occasion for the recall of delegates. At the Novaya Bumagopryadil'nya Mill, both delegates, Menshevik sympathisers, were censured and recalled for agitating in favour of the loan.[53] At the Skorokhod Shoe Factory, the four SR delegates ignored the factory general assembly's rejection of the loan and went ahead to vote for it at the district soviet. These, too, were recalled, and Bolsheviks elected in their place. One of the four, however, offered a public recantation and was left at his post.[54]

But as strong as the reaction on the 'Liberty Loan' issue was, it did not produce any perceptible shift in the workers' attitudes towards dual power (or, for that matter, towards the moderate socialist leadership of the Soviet, whose stock may have fallen somewhat but, nevertheless, remained high). Once again, only from the Vyborg District came urgings for the Soviet to take power.

Dual Power in the Light of pre-February Attitudes

The 'Liberty Loan' episode, however, underlines a problem implicit in the entire preceding analysis: given that the workers' support for the government was so guarded, their distrust of the aims of census society so profound, and their readiness to make concessions for the sake of this alliance so small, why, in fact, did they lend their support to dual power rather than opt directly for a government of revolutionary democracy through the soviets? But before attempting to answer this, we must ask if the workers' position in March 1917 represented a break with, or a continuation of, their pre-revolutionary positions.

From the start of the revolution on 23 February until 2 March there is little evidence for the existence of any concrete ideas among the workers on the nature of a transitional government. The revolution's slogans were the Social Democratic 'Three Whales', but these said nothing about an interim government. Nor did the socialist parties offer much guidance. According to Sukhanov, the leaders did not even raise the issue. When the Soviet met for the first time on 27 February, this seemingly most urgent question was not even discussed.[55] A police report of a meeting of 26 Bolsheviks and Menshevik–Internationalists on 26 February on Vasilevskii ostrov contains a resolution which limits itself exclusively to questions of tactics for street fighting.[56] At this point, all attention was focused on one goal—the overthrow of the autocracy. Only on 27 February did the Bolshevik Central Committee issue its call to set up a provisional revolutionary government with its organising centre at the Finland Station in the Vyborg District. But by this time, the Soviet had already been formed.

But if the workers failed to express any clear ideas on the provisional organisation of state power, it is still possible to examine their attitudes toward the State Duma and census society for the period immediately preceding the insurrection.

These attitudes found their clearest expression in the debate over participation in the War-Industry Committees and the workers' response to the tactics of the 'Workers' Group'. The War-Industry Committees were established in the summer of 1915 by the Congress of Representatives of Trade and Industry to facilitate the organisation of Russian military industry. In the autumn of that year, the leadership of the Central War-Industry Committee, which included such prominent capitalists as A. I. Guchkov (future Minister of War in the first Provisional Government) and A. I. Konovalov (future Minister of Trade and Industry), obtained permission to organise two-stage elections to 'Workers' Groups' that would be attached to the committees. This electoral campaign was the first legal opportunity since the outbreak of war for public discussion by workers of the government's domestic and foreign policy.

Three main currents emerged. The Bolsheviks and Left SRs decided against entering the committees since that would mean participation in the war effort. However, they would participate in the first stage of the elections and exploit the legal opportunity for anti-war and revolutionary agitation. Menshevik–Internationalists, such as Chkheidze, while opposed to the war, supported participation in the committees, but solely with the aim of organising anti-government forces and fighting to ameliorate the conditions of the working class.[57] Finally, Menshevik–Defencists, such as Gvozdev, admitting that the war aims of the government were imperialistic, nevertheless stood for defence of the country against the Germans, at the same time as they advocated the overthrow of Tsarism as the principal means of this defence.

The meeting of electors took place on 27 September and gave the Bolsheviks a majority of 90 to 81. However, Gvozdev disputed the validity of these elections on the grounds that a Bolshevik worker had substituted himself for an elector from the Putilov Works who had declined to participate.[58] A second meeting of electors was held on 29 November, during which the Bolsheviks and Left SRs walked out. Those remaining voted unanimously (with eight abstentions) for participation.

On the surface, it might appear that the issue was the attitude to the war. But in fact, both the Bolsheviks and the Menshevik–Internationalists opposed participation in the war effort, even under the guise of defence; yet the latter rejected the Bolsheviks' boycottist position. Even the Defencists equivocated in their position on the war. As Maevskii, a Menshevik–Defencist member of the 'Workers' Group' wrote: 'Defence of the country was understood by the Workers' Group, despite what the anti-defencists said, not as the establishment of civil peace or reconciliation with the old régime, but first and foremost as an irreconcilable struggle against the Tsar and autocracy.'[59] Only towards the end of 1916 did the defencism of Gvozdev's group emerge clearly, causing Chkheidze and other Menshevik–Internationalists finally to disown the Workers' Group.

What was really at issue—and what had always been the fundamental bone of contention within Russian Social Democracy—was the question of revolutionary strategy and, specifically, the relationship between the working class and census society in the revolutionary struggle. The war, which was wholeheartedly backed by the bourgeoisie, was only one aspect of the more general issue debated at the electors' assemblies. Speaking at the first assembly in November 1915, Emel'yanov, a Menshevik–Defencist worker from the Trubochnyi Factory, argued:

This war, as any other, is conducted only in the interests of the bourgeoisie, not the workers. Such is our principled view of the war. And still our opponents call us nationalists ... And yet, following the Zimmerwald Conference, we merely repeat: 'peace without annexations and retributions'. We strive for this peace in union with all of revolutionary democracy. How can we achieve such a peace? Our opponents do not go together with other classes. They are thinking of a revolutionary overturn which they will achieve solely by their own forces, while the achievement of this goal and of peace is possible only through the mobilisation of all the vital social forces of the country around our slogans ... The only salvation of the country lies not in technical defence, not in participation in committees and commissions on defence, but in the radical change of all our lives in the interests of democracy ... If you adopt this point of view, then the mobilisation of all vital forces of the country standing for the democratisation of public life is necessary for the democratisation of the public order. We disagree with our opponents in our evaluation of the active forces: they trust solely in their own forces in the revolution; we strive to rally all those strata of Russian society that are able to strive for the democratisation of the public order and that want to fight ... The political struggle isn't a call to strike, not a meeting in front of the factory, not a loud resolution or outcry, but a long preparation for struggle ... Our enemies say that we betray the interests of the revolution and they say so chiefly because of our evaluation of the bourgeoisie. Our bourgeoisie cannot reconcile itself to the rule of autocracy and itself strives towards power, but in a cowardly and slavish manner. We shall criticise and push it towards a decisive battle with the obsolete régime. In the final battle [i.e. for socialism] we must depend on our own forces, but in the struggle for political freedom we must go in contact with the bourgeoisie.

Emel'yanov added that questions of labour policy could also be raised in the committees, noting that the laws protecting female and child labour had been abrogated and that low-paid Chinese and Persian workers were being imported. Participation in the committees would open legal possibilities for organising the working class. He concluded: 'Our aim is victory over the internal enemy, a rebuff of the German army and peace without annexations or retributions.'[60]

Dunaev, a Bolshevik worker, replied:

The Military-Industry Committees are an institution of the liberal bourgeoisie—say our opponents. We can march arm in arm with them. It follows that Guchkov [Chairman of the Central W-I Committee] will go hand in hand with us against the contemporary Stolypins. This same Guchkov, who together with the deceased Stolypin, hanged our comrades? Chinese, Persians and Koreans are being brought in. To listen to Gvozdev and Emel'yanov, it would seem that the government is bringing them in, and the industrialists have nothing to do with it. But comrades, tell me, who is it that needs these coolies and Persians? ... The coolies are being imported by the liberal industrialists, the same industrialists with whom you are about to enter into an alliance against the yellow peril. Female and child labour is being used widely now. Who sought the abrogation of the miserable rights of the women and children? The aristocracy? ...

No, this was sought by the Guchkovs, Konovalovs and Ryabushins-
kiis. The factory owners pressed the buttons, and the rights of the
workers were abrogated. This is whom you call revolutionary elements and invite to go arm in arm with you. All the attempts of the
workers to improve their situation have ended in their being sent to
the front at the direction of the factory owners. Where are our
comrades from Lessner, Phoenix and the other factories? They were
sent by messieurs the liberal factory owners to the front and the jails.
This is honoured company! And with its help they want to create the
organisation of the working class. Our opponents say that we
depend only on our own forces, and you, messieurs liquidators,
desire to conduct the struggle in union with all revolutionary forces.
Fine. Where, then, do you seek your allies? Did you go to the
peasantry? No, you need something different. You go to the
Military-Industry Committee and act in the backyard of a bourgeois
organisation. [Noise, protests.] This is where you seek allies for
yourselves, in the bosses' organisation, who before the war organised lockouts and are now stuffing their pockets on war orders.
[Noise, agitation.] You used the occasion with Kudryashev and
decided to arrange new elections. To whom did you appeal? To the
worker masses? Did you go to the factories and mills and conduct
agitation among the workers? No, you went to Guchkov and some-
where behind the scenes, hidden from the workers, conducted some
sort of shady negotiations. In union with Guchkov you want to
undermine the will of the entire Petrograd proletariat ... [At this
point Dunaev was cut off by the chair.][61]

These two speeches offer a graphic illustration of the basic issue
separating Bolsheviks and the Mensheviks: the relationship of the
working class to the bourgeoisie. The Bolsheviks and their supporters
were irreconcilable on this score, basing themselves on the long history
of intimate cooperation between capital and the Tsarist state against
labour, on the conclusion that the bourgeoisie needed the Tsarist state
against a working class that it feared to face alone. The Mensheviks, on
the other hand, held that at least a part of the bourgeoisie was liberally
minded and that under working-class pressure these 'vital forces' of
census society could be—indeed had to be—forced to break with the
régime. As a corollary, they tried to draw a clear line between the
economic struggle, directed against capital, and the political struggle
against the Tsar.[62]

Maevskii nicely summed up the differences underlying the debates
on participation in the War-Industry Committees:

The Workers' Group saw the coming revolution not only as
bourgeois but also correctly evaluated the role that could be played

by such misshapen representation as that of Fourth Duma. Fighting the Bolsheviks and the semi-Bolsheviks, the Workers' Group had often to stress that, whatever the Duma was now, in a revolutionary upsurge it could be transformed into a base for the future revolution. It was necessary to fight boycottism and indifference to the Duma, i.e. to fight against Bolshevik agitation ... The supporters of the Workers' Group argued before the workers the need, in the name of the revolution, to coordinate their efforts with those of certain circles of the progressive bourgeoisie and to use the Duma as an all-Russian centre, which, in its clashes with the government, could focus the attention of the entire nation. In their criticism of the Workers' Group, already then, we saw the Bolshevik and semi-Bolshevik argument that contrasted the internationalism of the proletariat to the task of national defence, the proletariat to all other classes as a single solidly reactionary bourgeois mass.[63]

Of course, there was also an intermediate position, such as that of the worker Kuz'min, who stated that, while he put no hope in 'Guch-kov and Co.', the legal opening should be exploited to aid and organise the workers. At Kuz'min's plant, the Trubochnyi Factory, under the guise of giving reports, they had been able to hold meetings and conduct agitation.[64] Thus, the final vote in itself did not necessarily imply acceptance of the defencist position. Even so, the vote both times was very close, allowing one to conclude that a good half of the workers of Petrograd opposed even the intermediary position of the Menshevik–Internationalists of 'non-organic' participation. These workers rejected any semblance of political cooperation with the bourgeoisie or the war effort. In view of the extremely limited opportunities for organisation and the deteriorating economic situation of the workers, the support for this position should not be taken lightly.

But what best showed the workers' actual attitude was their failure to support tactics of the Workers' Groups. Maevskii admits that attempts to encourage the workers to exert pressure on the Duma by sending delegations to its chairman or to those of the different factions met

in broad worker circles with chronic Bolshevik-boycottist outlooks covered over with verbal radicalism ... The only form of movement which, with the aid of the Bolsheviks and semi-Bolsheviks, certain circles of the Petrograd working class had mastered was 'strikism', which in the opinion of the Workers' Group and its supporters, in conditions of war, was the least active and effective of forms. The representatives of the Workers' Group spared no effort to make the masses, infected by Bolshevik maximalism, understand the simple revolutionary truth—that not every measure, even if externally super-radical, is really revolutionary in content.[65]

Despite the continuous growth and politicisation of the strike movement during the war, until 1917 no working-class action had anything to do with the State Duma. Sukhanov confirms that the '[Workers'] Group enjoyed no popularity among the worker masses. The overwhelming majority of the conscious proletariat of the capital and also in the provinces took a strongly anti-defencist position and were sharply hostile towards the cooperation with the plutocracy by a small group of Social Democrats headed by Gvozdev.'[66]

When at the October 1916 session of the State Duma a number of census delegates made some strongly oppositional noises—it was here that Milyukov gave his famous 'stupidity or treason' speech[67]—the Workers' Group decided that they 'could not wait until the working class realised the revolutionary significance of organised intervention into the clash of bourgeois society with the autocracy' and so decided to call a strike for 14 February, the opening of the Duma session. The striking workers were to go to the Tauride Palace.[68] The Bolsheviks and Menshevik–Internationalists, for their part, supported the call to strike but agitated against going to the Duma.[69]

According to the police, 90 000 workers struck on the fourteenth but only two small groups, numbering in the low hundreds, were reported in the area of the Tauride Palace and they were quickly dispersed.[70] Maevskii claims that the movement was forestalled by extreme police measures.[71] But this argument is weak, since even on the first day of the revolution the police were not able to keep determined demonstrators from the city centre.

In fact, the workers began to show interest in the Duma only after the victory of the revolution, on the afternoon of 27 February, when the soldiers mutinied en masse. For the first four and a half days, when the movement had been predominantly working class, the Duma had been ignored. The common goal of the demonstrators had been Nevskii Prospekt, with gathering points at Kazan' Cathedral, Znamenskaya Square, and the corner of Liteinyi and Nevskii.

Why Dual Power in February?

However, it was not the case, as Trotsky and Sukhanov both imply, that only or mainly soldiers went to the Tauride on 27 February.[72] The Soviet historian, Burdzhalov, correctly observes that there were many workers, including Bolshevik workers, among these crowds.[73] Several of these worker Bolsheviks, on being freed from jail, stopped only long enough to remove their chains and arm themselves before setting off directly at the head of a Cossack regiment for the Tauride Palace.[74]

Clearly, something had changed with the victory of the revolution, and Maevskii appears justified in his claim that the strategy of the Workers' Group, 'after certain errors', was finally adopted by the working class in the February Revolution.[75] Certainly, the Bolsheviks were genuinely surprised suddenly to find themselves in a minority in the Soviet, since they had had the strongest underground organisation.[76] At the time, they tended to explain this in terms of technical and organisational factors: the Bolsheviks, being largely an underground organisation, were little known to the wider circles of workers; the Mensheviks and SRs were better speakers; the Bolsheviks were engaged in street fighting when the elections took place, while the Mensheviks and SRs were in the factories, etc. But to Shlyapnikov, at least, these arguments seemed one-sided. The revolution had indeed created a new situation. 'What had begun as a proletarian movement [had] taken on an all-national character. One had to evaluate slogans and agitational tasks accordingly.'[77] Here Shlyapnikov hints at the crucial shift produced by the revolution in the workers' consciousness: on the one hand, the form the revolution had taken did indeed create an appearance of national unity; on the other hand, the victory itself gave rise to an intense longing for national unity that predisposed the workers to accept this appearance as reality. Something, indeed, had changed. 'The events of February', observed the Left SR paper, 'made people forget what only a few days earlier had been their irreconcilable differences with the landowners and capitalists. It seemed like all were united.'[78]

Much at the time supported this feeling of national unity. After all, had not the Duma finally adhered to the revolution, making its victory so much easier, since the Duma alone could command the allegiance of the state and military bureaucracies and of census society generally? And had not the Duma Committee accepted the Soviet's programme? Was not the capital's entire population sporting red ribbons?[79]

On the highest levels, too, the political leaders of census Russia were preaching the gospel of national unity and reconciliation. The Central Committee of the Kadet party proclaimed on 3 March:

> The old régime has disappeared. The State Duma, having forgotten party differences, united in the name of the salvation of the Fatherland and took upon itself the creation of a new government ... Let all differences of party, class, estate and nationality be forgotten in this country ... Let the hope burn strong in all hearts that this time we will be able to avoid ruinous disunity [an allusion to 1905–6].[80]

Thus could the February Revolution appear as a vindication of the Workers' Group, and this, no doubt, was not lost upon the workers. All the same, in view of the unhappy history of working-class–bourgeois relations, one can at least understand Shlyapnikov's surprise at 'how easily the worker masses were taken in by the trap of national unity and the unity of revolutionary democracy, in which the capitalists were included'.[81]

Part of the answer lay in the reigning atmosphere after the victory—a strange mélange of euphoria, disbelief and anxiety, all of which nudged the workers towards the alliance with census society.

It would be difficult to exaggerate the elation that seized the workers, once conscious of victory. Participants often described the mood in dream-like terms, a state of intoxication, as being swept up by an irresistible force. N. Tolmachev, a Bolshevik worker at the Nobel Machine-construction Factory, wrote to his family in the first week of the revolution:

I congratulate you on the joyous holiday of Russian liberation, my dear ones. In these days of general amnesty, please amnesty me for my criminal silence. Caught up in the revolutionary movement, I thought of nothing and no one, forgot everything and everyone ... On February 22 on my way to work, I found myself in a demonstration of 20 000 persons and I wasn't able to regain my senses till the last few days. I was everywhere of course: at the first demonstrations and during the shooting, and when the troops rose, then together with the soldiers in the arsenals of Peter-Paul, stole revolvers, rifles, rode in a car to arrest police, was at meetings, assemblies, spoke myself. In such days one cannot stand aside. And only in the last few days have I sobered up. Having fallen into the whirlpool of events, you become a chip of wood, carried along and spun around.[82]

A woman at the Treugol'nik Rubber Factory recalled the exhilaration, the sense of coming of age:

I can't express my joy ... I considered myself lost forever at the boss's. And suddenly I was resurrected, I grew up. That night I put on Russian boots and my husband's cap, a worker's overcoat, said farewell to my children and left. I didn't appear at home for four days, till March 2. My family thought I had been killed.[83]

The left Bolsheviks and Left SRs, who were convinced that the struggle had really only just begun, could only sit by and let matters take their course. 'The people are expressing a state of intoxication with the great act that has been accomplished', wrote Kollontai to Lenin and Krupskaya. 'Amidst the feverish commotion, amidst the desire to create, to build something new, different from what went before, the note of the already achieved victory rings too loudly, as if everything has already been done, completed.'[84] Mstislavskii, a Left SR leader, described his feelings at the 2 March Soviet plenum that overwhelmingly ratified the dual power arrangement:

The most sensitive [of the Bolshevik delegates] refrained from speaking. For was this the place, at the matins, to preach one's

disbelief? Not to convince but only to darken human joy, joy that for
many was the first ... I envied these people who believed so
sincerely that it was all over, that the revolution was completed—the
last bullets will be fired, and a whole new way of life will begin to
flow in a broad powerful current, and we will gather in the fruits of
the February exploit ... But I could not help feeling that it was not
so, that ahead lay a difficult path ... one through which it would not
be so easy to cut with a single blow, as the first knot had been cut in
the February Insurrection.[85]

However, as important as the appearance of national unity and the
joy of victory were, the Petrograd workers did not simply decide to
bury the hatchet but retained very strong reservations and suspicions
concerning their new-found allies and demanded guarantees in the
form of Soviet 'control' over the government. There was yet another
factor in the immediate post-February situation that argued strongly
for the alliance and without which dual power would hardly have won
the overwhelming support it did. This was the fear of counterrevolution and the related fear of civil war. Although the Soviet may have
been in control of Petrograd, in those early days no one had any idea
what the rest of the country, and in particular the army at the front,
were up to. Rumours were afoot of loyal troops headed for the capital.
And troops had indeed been summoned but were won over to the
revolution before reaching their destination.[86] Rafes recalled the
Petrograd of this period:

> There was no certainty in the durability [of the victory] in any district
> of the capital ... The mood of the outsider elements, the public, was
> the same—at every shot, they ran for the gates. There were no trams
> in those days. We had to walk for miles but we felt no fatigue. All
> were feeling such a mood of exhilaration that the distance did not
> tire them.[87]

In some factories, workers only with great reluctance acceded to
their election to the Soviet. At the James Beck Textile Mill on 28
February, the general assembly elected a spinner, I. A. Tikhonov,
known to the workers for his political activism dating back to the 1905
revolution. But Tikhonov, tears in his eyes, pleaded to be let off the
hook—he was married, had been exiled in 1906 to his native Tver
Gubernia, if the old régime were to return, he argued, he would have a
rough time of it. At last he yielded, but the story was repeated in
electing his deputy.[88] At the Thornton Mills, the workers finally
decided to elect the factory committee en masse, 'since they are, by the
way, all single'.[89]

One of the first acts of the workers upon returning to the factories
was to destroy the administration's 'black book' of 'undesirables',

workers blacklisted by the Society of Factory and Mill Owners. At Thornton, all the personnel cards were burnt, despite the director's assurances that they had no political significance. The workers, noting English writing next to the names, decided to burn the cards for good measure.[90]

Given this state of uncertainty, it was important to the workers to retain census society on the side of the revolution, or at least not actively opposed to it. It was one thing to overthrow the government in the capital, but quite another to obtain the allegiance of peasants and soldiers throughout the country and to set the state and economic machines working efficiently. The workers did not feel prepared to attempt this on their own. They needed the authority that the Duma presumably enjoyed outside the capital and especially within educated society.

S. Skalov, a Bolshevik worker, explained why he had led a group of insurgents to the Duma on 27 February rather than go to the Finland Station to set up a provisional revolutionary government:

> I felt that I acted correctly when I didn't go to the Finland Station to group our forces there separately. When we went to the Tauride Palace, on the corner of Shpalernaya and Liteinyi Prospekt we saw a note, I can't remember from what organisation it came, inviting all workers to gather at the Finland Station. By such self-isolation we would immediately have opposed our own very weak organisational forces to those of the State Duma and by this would have untied its hands, giving it full freedom of action and independence, with all the consequences ... We could not go against the Duma on 27 February 1917, nor was there any reason to. We were too weak organisationally, our leading comrades were in jails, exile and emigration. Therefore, it was necessary to go to the Duma, to pull it into the revolutionary current ... It was necessary to create revolutionary chaos, to terrorise all initiative of the Duma directed against revolutionary action; and this was possible only by being inside the Duma, filling up, so to speak, all its cracks with revolutionary reality.[91]

Similarly, speakers at the First Bolshevik City Conference in April sought to explain how census society found itself in power as a result of the revolution:

> When the Soviet of deputies was formed—then state power was proposed, but the workers did not consider it possible to take power into their hands ... Did the Soviet of Workers' Deputies act correctly in refusing power? I consider that it did. To take power into our hands would have been an unsuccessful policy, since Petrograd is not all of Russia. There, in Russia, is a different correlation of forces.

With its relative weight, the proletariat in Russia could not take power—that would have caused civil war.

Another delegate confirmed this:

When the proletariat still feared to take power into its hands, at that time the bourgeoisie made its way to the Duma and began to issue proclamations and meet deputies. Our best workers, fearing counterrevolution, facilitated the accidental composition of the Soviet of W and SD.[92]

The Mensheviks put forth a similar argument in support of dual power, warning that a breach in the united all-national ranks of the revolution through an attempt to wrest power from the PG would only play into the hands of those forces of the past yet to be completely destroyed. The Soviet, it was argued, 'cannot enjoy authority in broad strata of the bourgeoisie. Yet, at the given stage of our economic development, the leading role in economic life cannot but belong to the bourgeoisie . . . If the Soviet W and SD took power, it would be an illusory government, one that would lead to the outbreak of civil war.'[93]

This spectre of civil war, raised at the very start of the revolution, became an inseparable feature of the political landscape of 1917, even as the term itself gradually took on new content. Fear of civil war, and its counterpart, the desire for broad revolutionary unity, continued to haunt the political consciousness of the working class well past the October Revolution.

Finally, one should bear in mind that the government was, after all, only provisional, and scarcely anyone could have suspected that the convocation of a Constituent Assembly would be ten months off. Moreover, in Petrograd, at least, the Soviet controlled all the armed force, and this bolstered the belief that it could effectively 'control' the census government for the interim.

As for the minority of workers centred in the Vyborg District, they submitted to the overwhelming will of the worker and soldier masses once it clearly emerged in the first week of March. For here, too, there was a great concern for unity—not national unity, which these workers considered a sham, but the unity of revolutionary democracy, of workers and soldiers (peasants in military greatcoats) that had made victory possible.[94] But these workers needed little prompting to rally behind Lenin, who declared upon his return in early April that it was better to remain in a minority. 'For one Liebknecht is worth 110 defencists of the type of Steklov and Chkheidze.'[95] This was a constant feature of working-class consciousness in 1917: in the end, the longing for unity always yielded to questions of principle. At any rate, it was only a matter of a few months before this minority of irreconcilables grew into a majority of the Petrograd working class.

5 The February Revolution in the Factories

Although the workers lacked a clear conception of the political arrangements immediately to follow upon a successful insurrection, they had very definite ideas about the social and economic benefits the revolution should bring. In their conception of the revolution, the political task of establishing democratic freedoms was integrally bound up with specific socio-economic reforms. 'Will political freedom [alone] aid [the workers to live] in human fashion?' asked a worker delegate at the 5 March session of the Petrograd Soviet. '[It is necessary] to secure the minimum conditions of existence, the eight-hour day, a minimum wage. With the old conditions still in existence, freedoms are useless.'[1]

The social content of the workers' conception of the revolution included three basic elements: the eight-hour day, a significant improvement in wages and conditions, and the 'democratisation of factory life'. In their minds, these were part and parcel of the democratic revolution; they were not seen as a challenge to the capitalist system or to the fundamental rights of private property.

The entrepreneurs, however, did not share this view. To them, 'social' meant 'socialism'. Harking back to 1905, they were inclined to see the worker as a basically anarchist element who would move on to socialist experiments at the first opportunity. The French ambassador, Paléologue, recalled a conversation in June 1915 with the prominent banker and industrialist A. I. Putilov, in which the latter described the coming revolution as 'horrifying anarchy, endless anarchy, anarchy for 10 years'.[2] This fear of the unleashed masses had been, in fact, a major reason for the bourgeoisie's weak and indecisive opposition to the autocracy. In a speech before a March conference of the Council of Private Railroads, Nekrasov, Minister of Communications and a well-known 'leftist' in liberal circles, tried to assuage these apprehensions.

There is no need to be frightened by the fact that social elements are now beginning to appear. One should, rather, strive to channel these social elements in the correct direction ... The essential thing is the rational combination of the social moment and the political, and by no means to deny the social moment, to fear it ... What we must achieve is not social revolution but the avoidance of social revolution through social reform.[3]

This, indeed, was the initial strategy of the Petrograd industrialists: to make concessions with a view to calming the workers and gaining time until the revolutionary enthusiasm abated. But it is obvious from the very purpose of Nekrasov's talk that the owners and the workers were from the outset far apart on the 'social' issue.

In a sense, the position of the Soviet EC majority paralleled that of the entrepreneurs in its desire to keep separate the economic and political aspects of the revolution and to postpone the struggle for socio-economic reforms until the revolution was politically consolidated. The Menshevik *Rabochaya gazeta* stated this explicitly:

> Our revolution is a political one. We destroy the bastions of political authority, but the bases of capitalism remain in place. A battle on two fronts—against the Tsar and against capital—is beyond the forces of the proletariat. We will not pick up the glove that the capitalists are throwing down before us. The economic struggle will begin when and how we find it necessary.[4]

The Eight-hour Day

The eight-hour day, one of the Social-Democratic 'Three Whales', was a demand that was very dear to the workers. Economic on the face of it, workers and capitalists alike considered it equally political. On 19 March, the workers of the Moscow Military-Industry Factory declared: 'We consider the establishment of the eight-hour day not only an economic victory but we see it as a fact of enormous political significance in the struggle for the liberation of the working class.'[5] 'We have secured the eight-hour day and other freedoms', asserted the Conference of Factories of the Artillery Authority.[6]

The question of ending the general strike was first raised at the 5 March session of the Soviet. The chairman, Chkheidze, stated in his report that although Tsarism was not yet totally destroyed, it had been beaten sufficiently for work to begin, with the understanding that if the need arose all would leave the factories again. He recognised that the workers could not continue under the old conditions and promised that the Soviet would begin working out new ones as soon as production resumed. This report provoked 'passionate debate',[7] during which five workers and five soldiers took the floor. The workers insisted that the strike continue until the eight-hour day and better work conditions were won, one of them complaining that 'many have forgotten about many promises—they do not speak of the longstanding slogan of the proletariat, the eight-hour day'. In the name of the world proletariat, he called upon the assembly to take the decision to introduce this reform.[8] The soldiers, however, demanded an immediate end to the strike.

The vote was 1170 to 30 to return to work. In part, the size of the majority reflected the resolution's promise immediately to work out economic demands to be presented to the owners. But in part it also reflected the workers' concern for the unity of revolutionary democracy, their fear of losing the support of the soldiers, who were understandably worried about war production.

It soon became clear, however, that the Soviet's resolution was out of step with the dominant mood in the factories. A Soviet agitator explained: 'When I told them of this decision, in my heart I felt that we could not do this: the workers cannot win freedom and not use it to ease the burdens of their labour, to fight capital.'[9] A number of factories simply refused to submit and protested what they felt to be the undemocratic nature of the decision. The organisational committee of the Moscow District Soviet resolved (27 to 10 with 2 abstentions):

> Taking into account the decision of the Soviet of W and SD on the immediate return to work, a decision taken without preliminary discussion in the localities by the workers and soldiers themselves, we find that this resolution is incorrect and therefore we have decided to postpone the resumption of work for two days and immediately to raise the question for re-examination by the Soviet. In addition, the Moscow District Committee finds it necessary to begin immediately the reorganisation of the Soviet W and SD.[10]

At the Military-Medical Preparations Factory the workers called the decision 'premature and autocratic' and decided to continue the strike.[11] When a Menshevik–Defencist maintenance mechanic at one textile mill called for a ten and a half hour day in solidarity with the Allies, asking the workers to consider what their English comrades would think, one of the women replied: 'We have sacrificed so much. Do we really have to wait for instructions from abroad?' The meeting resolved to end the strike only after securing the eight-hour day.[12] Of the 111 factories reporting to the Petrograd Society of Factory and Mill Owners, only 28 had resumed work by 7 March, the date set by the Soviet.[13]

It is worth noting that it was by no means the more politically radical factories that evinced the greatest opposition to the Soviet's decision. In fact, the Bolshevik PC reported on 7 March that 18 factories in the Vyborg District, a majority, were working.[14] The Lessner Factories voted by 7000 to 6 to return to work even though the Soviet's decision was considered premature.

> But in the aims of the coordination and unity of all of the revolutionary forces of the country, we obey the decision of the Soviet W and SD and declare that on the first call of the representatives of the

workers and soldiers we will leave work for further struggle on the basis of the fundamental slogans of the proletariat and peasantry—eight-hour day, republic and confiscation of all land for the benefit of the peasantry.[14]

One can clearly see at work here the strong sense of discipline of the skilled workers. It is also reasonable to assume that the skilled elements of the working class were more conscious of the need for unity against the threat of counterrevolution than the less skilled, less urbanised workers, whose militancy on economic issues in 1917 stood in contrast to their general political inertness.[16]

In fact, most factories eventually heeded the Soviet's call but only after introducing the eight-hour day on their own initiative, in 're-volutionary fashion' (*yavochnim poryadkom*), by simply quitting after eight hours or demanding time-and-a-half for 'extra'. On 8 March, the Petrograd District Soviet concluded after hearing reports from the factories:

1. that the decision of the Soviet W and SD on the return to work met with strong resistance on the part of the proletariat of the Petrograd side and that this decision was carried out in very unharmonious fashion
2. the resumption of work in the majority of cases was and is being accompanied by the introduction of the eight-hour day and a number of other improvements of labour.[17]

Few factories actually agreed to forgo the eight-hour day. The state-owned Promet Pipe Factory resolved that 'the eight-hour day can be introduced only gradually, in any case, not immediately'.[18] At the Nevskii Machine-construction and Shipbuilding Factory in the Nevskii District the workers voted not to introduce the reform 'because of the circumstances of the present time'.[19] Both factories were moderate socialist strongholds in 1917.

The matter was finally resolved on 10 March when the Soviet and the Petrograd Society of Factory and Mill Owners reached an agreement which included the eight-hour day. That the owners saw this as only a temporary concession, hoping to recoup their losses at a later date, was made clear at the 16 March meeting of representatives of Petrograd-based firms with the Minister of Trade and Industry, A. I. Konovalov. The meeting, in fact, never got around to its stated agenda because of the amount of discussion the reform generated. B. A. Efron, Chairman of the Society, stated flatly: 'The agreement reached in Petrograd is a real concession for the regulation of work life in the capital, and the workers themselves [!] consider that in the present circumstances it is only temporary.' He spoke against the possibility of limiting the work day to eight hours, arguing that the owners simply could not afford to pay time-and-a-half. The conferees, with the concurrence of Konovalov, resolved that 'Now is not the time to introduce the eight-hour day. One must approach this question very carefully.'[20]

The position of the moderate Soviet majority found its expression in a *Rabochaya gazeta* editorial of 10 March cautioning the workers against those calling for the eight-hour day. It reminded them of 1905 when the same demand helped to drive the bourgeoisie away from the revolution, resulting in a lockout that proved disastrous to the movement. The editorial proposed first to consolidate the workers' political position and only then to proceed with the economic struggle.

However, the workers' action on this issue showed how alien this mode of thought was to them. A revolution stripped of its social content, even as a temporary tactic to cement the alliance with census society, was simply not worth the candle. In this, at least, the workers from the outset were in accord with the Bolsheviks, who urged the Soviet to enact the eight-hour day at once.[21]

Wages

After the revolution the workers expected 'to live in a manner befitting a workman and a free citizen', wrote the journal of the Textile Workers' Union.[22] 'The conditions of predatory exploitation that existed in the feudal system of Russia cannot exist in the new Russia', declared the Nevskii District Soviet.[23] A decent wage was thus yet another social demand of the revolution. Although the eight-hour day increased hourly wages by 20–28 per cent it did not satisfy many workers. Only a week after the agreement of 10 March, the PSFMO noted that it had not succeeded in calming the workers, that various demands continued to be made, and first of all wage demands.[24]

According to the 1918 Industrial and Professional Census, in 28 Petrograd factories that were in continuous operation in 1913–17, the average wage rose 120 per cent between 1913 and 1916. Strumilin, the Soviet economist, calculated in the 1920s that the average wage of January 1916 represented 84 per cent of the pre-war average real wage; that of February 1917—55 per cent.[25] Volobuev notes that, according to calculations of workers' organisations in 1917, calculations that initially went unchallenged by the PSFMO, the cost of living had quadrupled during the war. Hence, he concluded, the almost tripling of the nominal wage still meant a 25–30 per cent average decline in the real earnings.[26]

But this was only the average. According to the owners, unskilled male workers in February–March 1917 were earning 2.25–3.5 rubles a day. The owners of the Langezipen Factory themselves admitted in March that to live 'on three rubles is already a matter of extreme ingenuity'.[27] The plight of the unskilled workers was especially urgent, and they were pressing hard. Petrov, a worker from the Treugol'nik Rubber Factory (10 133 women and 5205 men)[28] pleaded before the Soviet on 20 March:

> Conditions of labour at the Treugol'nik Factory are lousy. Wages don't correspond to the quality of work. The women received 1.35 rubles a day—the majority are married and the wives of soldiers, and it is difficult to live on that. Men received 2.40—very low. During the revolution we put forth demands and the administration seemed prepared for concessions. But wages are no better. The women—2.35 and the men—3.35 ... Now, I'd like the Soviet to ask the EC to immediately set to work on an economic reform. Comrades, we cannot live like this any longer. The high cost of life is terrible, and a family can't live on 3.35. To calm the workers we had to tell them that reforms are being drawn up. But we don't even know whether that's true or not.[29]

At the Putilov Shipyards the connection between the revolution and the wage demands was especially clear, as the factory's delegate pointed out to the meeting. In mid-February, the economic situation had become so critical that the workers finally presented the administration with their demands, declaring:

> We'll hold out whatever the cost, because we cannot go on living like this. But it suddenly turned out that the whole of Petrograd came out for this struggle ... The government was overthrown ... Before us the question arose—to return to work or to continue the strike. The Soviet W and SD gave the order that we must begin work. We obeyed and at the same time presented our demands.[30]

Where wages had been especially low, the situation was extremely volatile. A Bolshevik worker from the state-owned Admiralty Shipbuilding Factory reported:

> You know what sort of anarchy exists there now. You know how the workers were squeezed there until now, and, having achieved certain political freedoms, they are using them to the full ... They tell the director: Either you agree to what we say, do what we demand, or get out ... One day we take a decision. Next day they learn that another plant decided something different and they demand the same ... In one day five or six changes, and each day work almost stops and not infrequently actually does stop as the

workers assemble and discuss ... Do the workers have grounds to be agitated? Yes. At the Admiralty Shipbuilding Factory a good half of the workers made 1.18 rubles for 9 hours. There is no doubt that no one can live on that wage, and as a result they are forced to work 16 hours a day and are so exhausted that any day they are ready to quit. During the war, they say, they already struck two times, and many of the leading workers were sent to the front, and now they're ready for a third.[31]

All speakers asked for one thing—the enactment of a minimum wage. The delegate from the Putilov Shipyards concluded:

And so we want a commission to be formed here to investigate the situation and enter into negotiations with the administration, which together with the entrepreneurs, under the flag of patriotism, stripped the worker naked, since they all believed that a worker is created in order that they drink his blood drop by drop, squeeze out all the juices, and then throw him overboard like a useless object. Now, comrades, it isn't so: When the workers have awoken from their sleep of toil, they demand a just wage and put forth just demands, and the entrepreneur cries—'Help, they're robbing us!' Comrades, you probably don't share their horror. You understand the situation of all the workers and you will probably tell them: No. You oppressed the workers, you fleeced them, and in the future you have to pay only that which the labour is worth.[32]

One cannot avoid the conclusion that for the workers the February Days were more than a political action directed against autocracy but equally an economic strike against capital. Immediately upon returning to the factories, the workers presented their wage demands and once again, on this economic issue, the unskilled workers were especially militant. At the Kersten Knitwear Mill (2193 women and 335 men),[33] where wages were low even for the textile industry, about 2000 workers gathered in the yard and decided on the following demands:

(1) the immediate removal of the head of the knitwear department as 'not corresponding to his appointment', 'he deals with the workers in a coarse manner'
(2) the immediate introduction of the eight-hour day and a general raise of 50 per cent, pending a review of the wage rates
(3) payment for the days of the revolution
(4) wages to be paid every fortnight
(5) defective goods to be sold to the workers at cost in limited quantities
(6) overtime to be voluntary and paid at time and a half

(7) the right to hold meetings without the permission or presence
of foremen or representatives of the administration.

The meeting decided to remain out until the demands were met in full.
Thus, an economic strike followed directly upon the political. Production resumed on 15 March after most of the demands had been won.[34]
At the Skorokhod Shoe Factory (3242 women out of 4900), work
began on 10 March after the administration promised a quick reply to
the workers' economic demands. The average wage had been 5.72
rubles for men and 2.95 for women; the workers were asking for 10
and 7 rubles respectively and for the administration to supply work
materials at its expense. When the administration agreed to only a 20
per cent rise, refusing to supply materials, the dispute went to a
conciliation chamber. Here, however, the sides remained deadlocked.
At this point the administration offered another 20 per cent and
promised 10 000 rubles for the Leatherworkers' Union. Although the
majority of the worker delegates to the chamber were inclined to
accept this offer, the mass of workers would not hear of it. On 20
March, an angry crowd of 500 gathered in front of the director's office
and refused to leave without full satisfaction of their demands. At last,
the director rang up the PSFMO, which gave him the green light to
agree to the demands.[35]
Thus, on the wage question, too, the workers showed they were not
in the mood for concessions. The appeals of the more cautious
elements of the Soviet leadership had little effect.[36] The feeling among
the workers was that it was they, not the capitalists, who had suffered
under the old régime and had made the revolution, and it was up to the
latter to make concessions and display good will.

The Press Campaign Against 'Worker Egotism'

The unity of revolutionary democracy was quite another matter to the
workers. And the test of this alliance came very soon. Already in the
second half of March, the non-socialist press (especially *Rech'*, the
Kadet paper, and *Russkaya volya*) began to accuse the workers of
pursuing narrow egotistical interests at the expense of the war effort.
The workers at once saw this as a concerted campaign of census society
aimed at turning the soldiers against them. They were naturally
alarmed.
Many factories, including some of the most radical, began to declare
their readiness to work overtime, the eight-hour day notwithstanding.
The Old Parviainen Factory (which passed a resolution for Soviet
power as early as 13 April) resolved:

Considering the seriousness of the current moment, we consider it necessary to carry on work in full. No negligent attitudes or excessive wage demands. At the same time, we must say that the socio-economic defects, such as lack of raw materials, are a serious brake.[37]

At the end of March, the factory committee of the state Patronnyi Factory prepared a special report on the plant's operations since the revolution for the soldiers of the 25th Infantry Regiment. Output was down by 2.5 per cent, but this was seen as temporary and inevitable, given the revolutionary situation.

The workers of the Petrograd Patronnyi Factory, as true patriots of their fatherland, which is going through a difficult war, and also valuing the freedom that has been won, having frequently discussed the issue of production at their general assemblies, in refutation of the false rumours being spread by unknown persons with provocational aims, have mandated the executive committee [factory committee] to declare that, while recognising the eight-hour day as the basis, the workers will nevertheless, conscious of the coming danger, by all means try to support their brother-soldiers at the front who, together with the workers, have won freedom inside Russia, freedom which the workers guard with all their might, [and will] work unquestioningly if necessary more than eight hours up to twelve hours, and if required, even more. But the workers cannot in any case take upon themselves responsibility for the fact that work will stop for lack of fuel, metals or other materials or for other reasons not depending on the workers. Dark slander is attacking the workers from the direction of the stooges of the old régime, who want to break the unity of the workers and soldiers, who want to destroy the freedom we have won with our blood.[38]

Soon the workers became more specific on the nature of these 'dark forces'. 'Comrade soldiers', began a resolution from the Aivaz Machine-construction Factory,

Rumours have been reaching us that someone is spreading the slander that the workers think only how to increase their wages and scorn the production of artillery shells, that they are busy striking. We were silent while we thought this was merely a case of idlers wagging their tongues. But now we see that by these means the landowners, fearing for their land and [the capitalists] watching over their profits, want to sow discord among us, want to weaken that union of workers and soldiers, who shoulder to shoulder overthrew

Tsarist autocracy and placed Russia on the democratic path of life.

Comrades. The enemies of democracy spread discord among us since they fear the united strength of the workers and soldiers in the Soviet W and SD. You, who have left our ranks, the lathe and hammer, and have gone to the barracks, and you comrade soldiers, declare to these slanderers that workers are applying all their energy so that work on defence proceeds at full steam ... We know of no factory in Petrograd that is striking now.[39]

In the long run, despite some initial success, the press campaign backfired, serving only to bind the workers and soldiers more closely together in opposition to census society.[40] In the factories themselves, it intensified suspicions regarding the true motives of management whenever hitches arose in production. (No doubt this was also a factor in the opposition to the 'Liberty Loan'.)

This episode revealed a considerable degree of political sophistication among the workers. They appear here not as mindless masses 'ripping off' as much as possible as quickly as possible, but as workers keenly aware of the importance of the soldiers' support and prepared to make important concessions to keep it. That this was not true in their relations with census society was, in part, due to the workers' perception of the latter's weakness. For it soon became clear that without an apparatus of repression, the power of the bourgeoisie was mainly negative in nature; it could only take the form of passive resistance or sabotage. The threat from a hostile army, on the other hand, was much more immediate.

But there was also a moral element involved, in that the revolution, in its socio-economic, and even, in part, its political aspects, was directed against census society as well as the autocracy, and to make concessions to the capitalists would have in a sense meant to compromise the revolution. The workers' class pride and traditional hostility to census society would not allow this. The soldiers, on the other hand, were a part of 'revolutionary democracy', of the people, and concessions to them did not bear the same moral significance. Besides, the soldiers had, along with the workers, made the revolution; it was felt that they had a right to make claims.

There is, in fact, evidence to indicate a rise in productivity in many factories in March and April, despite the initial disruption and the supply problems. Even N. N. Kutler, member of the Kadet Party Central Committee and a leading Russian industrialist, noted a certain 'enthusiasm for work' at the start of the revolution.[41] The Conference of Factories of the Artillery Authority in early April reported that productivity had begun to rise where the supply question was under control. At the Patronnyi Factory, which had lost almost its entire administration, production was down only 2 per cent. At the Okhta

Powder Factory, instead of the former output norm of 800 puds with 30 per cent defective output, productivity was now at 900 puds with only 15 per cent defective. At the Orudiinnyi Factory output was up 28 per cent, at Opticheskii—11 per cent, at Trubochnyi it was normal and at the Sestroretsk Arms Factory 600 rifles were being produced daily in place of the former 450. In fact, the worker delegates, for their part, attacked the Artillery Authority for poor management and demanded its abolition.[42] At the end of March, the Petrograd Committee of Medium and Small Industry also confirmed that 'in many small enterprises in Petrograd, labour productivity had not declined but has risen in spite of the introduction of the eight-hour day'.[43] Similarly, the director of the Schlusselburg Powder Factory reported to the Ministry of Commerce and Industry in mid-April that, although for many reasons the first week had been a difficult one, now

> production is proceeding in a more satisfactory fashion ... The workers in a fully conscious manner take into account the current conjuncture and as far as possible are guarding the factory from any occurrences that could harm it in any way and are energetically cooperating in increasing the output of powder and explosive materials.[44]

Rabochaya gazeta reported on the results of the investigations conducted by delegations from the front which had spoken to representatives of both workers and administration: in some cases productivity had risen; in others it had declined, not through the fault of the workers but for lack of fuel and materials.[45]

Worker – Management Relations—The Democratisation of Factory Life

To the workers, the revolution also meant the abolition of 'autocracy in the factory', the 'democratisation of factory life'. In part, this meant simply the elimination of those elements of the Tsarist state that had penetrated the factory administration.

The pre-revolutionary relationship between management and the state can only be described as symbiotic. Administrators doubled as police informers, while the police were always on call to aid in putting down strikes. During the war this partnership developed a special intimacy—activists, or for that matter anyone who dared to protest against the deteriorating conditions, faced the immediate prospect of loss of military deferment, jail or exile. Many plants had police or regular army troops stationed nearby or inside to maintain 'order'.

This state of affairs was underlined in the inquiry into the strike movement by the left fractions of the State Duma in the summer of 1916:

> Another characteristic is the length of the strikes. Usually a strike ends in a lockout, and, moreover, this lockout takes place with the closest participation and most intimate support of both the civil and military authorities ... Just as soon as the factory closes, the military authorities immediately begin to take workers into the army. For example at the Putilov Factory several hundred youths were sent to disciplinary battalions ... [Here] for lack of workers, soldiers are being sent, and often not specialists ...

This noted intervention of the military authorities in favour of the entrepreneurs, characteristic of the workers' economic movement during the war, has in no way weakened the old traditional regulation of conflicts between labour and capital in which the civil authorities have long been involved in Russia.

All the conflicts of late have been accompanied by incessant repressions. Searches and arrests do not cease even for one day. The workers are afraid to elect representatives for negotiations for fear of losing their best people ...

Sensing the weight of the civil and military authorities behind them, the entrepreneurs are conducting an exclusively insolent and provocative policy towards the workers ... The entrepreneurs during the war are making use of 'war methods' to subjugate the workers. The strongest weapon in their hands is the deprivation of workers subject to military service of the right to freely move from one enterprise to another ... The threat of the front—the last word in entrepreneurial tactics—is a threat which they in the end carry out willingly, transforming the front into a place of exile and forced labour.[46]

But there was also another side to the 'factory autocracy'. This was the despotic absolutism that characterised the Russian factory system. Now that the revolution had made the workers citizens, equals with the administrators in public life, they wanted to be treated as such in the factory, too. 'I felt as though I had grown up', recalled the Treugol'nik worker cited above. Workers accordingly demanded 'internal' authority for themselves in the workplace, a demand that did not deny the right of the administration to manage the technical and economic sides of production, but which gave the workers at least an equal voice in regulating the conditions under which work was conducted.[47]

Another consequence of the February Revolution was the awakening in the workers of a certain sense of responsibility for the correct functioning of the factory. This was especially noticeable in the state factories where the workers at the start of the revolution really felt they were the boss, but it was also present in the private enterprises. It was the result of a number of factors. In part, it reflected the new sense of citizenship, and, in part, it expressed the workers' concern for defence of the revolution. But it was also the product of latent suspicion of the administration, suspicion of technical incompetence and mismanagement, but also of counterrevolutionary sympathies, suspicions that the press campaign of the second half of March only aggravated.

Purge of the Administration

Returning from the battles of February, the workers almost immediately set to purging the factory administrations of 'undesirable elements'. At the very first general assembly of the Artillery Branch of the Patronnyi Factory, for example, it was unanimously resolved to 'filter the administration from foreman to general'.[48]

At times this purge took on a rather dramatic character. In many factories, usually after some discussion for and against the merits of the individual in question, a vote would be taken. If it was against him, the workers summarily tossed a sack over his head and drove him outside the gates in a wheelbarrow. This traditional mode of reprisal, frowned upon by the more conscious workers, was considered to be a mark of special disgrace. At the Putilov Works 40 administrators were removed in the course of three days, many in wheelbarrows.[49]

In the textile mills, the workers tended to be more magnanimous. In a scene typical of early March, the workers of the Thornton Mill assembled in one of the shops and called out the foremen, one by one, to give an account of themselves. The crowd shouted: 'Foreman of such-and-such department onto the table!', and he was pushed forward. Sweating profusely, he would try desperately to justify his actions, most often claiming that he had been merely transmitting pressure from above. After promising to change his ways, he was let go. The English foremen got the worst of it because their rudimentary Russian did not allow them to understand the goings on. As for the 30 policemen on the factory payroll and the members of the administration with known counterrevolutionary views, despite the desire of a part of the meeting to deal them a good thrashing, they were merely escorted to the local militia.[50]

As heads cooled, especially in the more skilled and organised metalworking plants, the process took on a more orderly character. In the larger factories, each shop would meet and then present its list of undesirables to the central factory committee for approval.[51] This was no mere explosion of blind rage against authority. A real attempt was made to justify charges and carefully to weigh the evidence. For example, the pattern-making shop of the Baltic Shipbuilding Factory voted on 9 March by 56 to 23 with 3 abstentions to fire the shop's manager, Sadov. But at a second meeting held two days later, where Sadov was allowed to plead his case, the question was reconsidered, ending in a vote of 46 and 12 with 7 abstentions to retain him.[52] On the other hand, once the facts had been weighed and the final decision taken, the workers categorically refused to take the purged administrators back, the rulings of conciliation chambers notwithstanding.[53]

The motives given for firing these administrators illustrate the workers' conception of the revolution in the factory. The general assembly of the submarine department of the Baltic Factory discussed the case of 'master Stesyura and his activity under the old régime'.

1. At first, the question was raised as a political one and no basis was found to accuse him.
2. Secondly, the question was posed: Did he exploit labour? This question too was examined by the general assembly and the result was the following—that he liked to press the work, but at the same time he paid more for labour than other administrators . . .
3. Is he suited to his appointment? . . . There were no major disagreements . . . and it was found that he was acquitted on the three main questions and also on the smaller questions he was found not guilty.[54]

The second question considered was in fact broader than payment for work, an area in which, incidentally, the foremen had enjoyed wide arbitrary powers.[55] It included all manner of mistreatment of workers by the administration, especially affronts to their sense of dignity. Often mentioned in this context were 'coarse relations' with the workers, use of foul language, arbitrary and oppressive use of fining, assignment to overly strenuous work as punishment, playing favourites, etc.[56] There was thus a definite moral, as well as economic, dimension involved.

The political type of accusation was the most clear-cut. The workers of the iron boiler-making shop of the Baltic Shipbuilding Factory explained their dismissal of the manager:

We find that he fulfilled what were sooner the duties of a purely police administrator than those of a foreman and shop manager striving to turn the above-named shop into a house of silence or a disciplinary department where with aching heart one could hear his replies 'I'll ship you to the front! I'll use military authority!' He sent . . . [four names are given] and others. From the above his devotion to the old reactionary régime can be seen. To this we add that his removal had caused no harm to the shop.[57]

But accusations were rarely limited to one type of charge. The following resolution of the riveting and chasing department of the Baltic Factory combines the political, economic and moral aspects, at the same time relating a sense of the intense emotions involved.

> We, the workers of the ... department, have unanimously resolved at our general assembly that each administrative individual who has received an order from us to immediately leave the plant is removed by us so that, because of his past criminal activity and in the future, he will not be able to enter the factory and therefore we ask that special attention be given to these people for in their being at the head of the department they were a bulwark of autocracy, occupied exclusively in oppressing our comrades. In pre-revolutionary times they were the 'rulers of the destinies' of the workers, many of our comrades, for a conversation about the freedom that has just been victorious, were placed on trial before higher authorities who immediately fired them and contacted the Military Commander to have them shipped to the front. Besides that, coarse relations, low economic rates in the factory's favour, and the miserably paid, thanks to them, piece of bread earned by our sweat, in our common opinion are weighty accusations against them which arouse in us not charity towards them but a sense of extreme scorn. On the basis of all the above, we ask the EC of the Baltic Factory to fire them immediately for there is no room for condescension here.[58]

The struggle for the recognition of their human dignity was not a new one for the workers. The experience of 1905 and especially 1912–14 had not been forgotten. The foreman Morozov, according to his accusers, was of an 'unconscious and unfeeling nature ... [He would] often come running up with insults, not taking into account the dignity of a person. He inflicted abuse of the foulest kind.'[59] Of the foreman Volkov the workers of the paint shop of the Baltic Factory wrote:

> This is the chief culprit of our oppression and humiliation which we have suffered over the last years ... Let us recall the first days after his arrival [.] of course not many of us experienced this but the voice of our comrades whom he mocked calls to us and begs for revenge. From the very first days of his rule when he put on his idiot's mittens of violence, he showed his base soul. In 1915 many of our comrades suffered in their self-respect and thanks to his contrivances were thrown out of the factory in the most shameless manner ... From that year began the era of our oppression. They [Volkov and his superior] forgot 1905. In 1909 he began his shameful programme of lowering rates to an impossible 8–9 kopeks, not considering the

conditions of work ... We all felt this horror all the time till the last days of the arbitrary rule.[60]

Here, too, the 'exploitation' is seen most of all as a moral issue, an affront to the workers' human dignity. And, again, the evidence shows clearly that this was no elemental *bunt*, no anarchistic rebellion against all authority, but a decisive rejection of unlimited, arbitrary power, experienced as an insult to the workers' self-respect.

The last type of charge, technical incompetence, rarely appeared by itself but usually as a back-up to other arguments. For example, the department head Lyashchenko' was a 'man poorly versed in the technical tasks of his job. He was present in the shop only two or three hours a day and some days not at all.' But he was also accused of 'limitless exploitation' and 'he replied to any request with the threat of jail, and during the war—with the front. He set up a system of spies and was careful that among his aides there be none but a monarchist organisation.'[61] The general assembly of the First Power Station unanimously decided to remove its board of directors as 'henchmen of the old régime and recognising their harmfulness from the economic point of view and their uselessness from the technical'.[62]

The Factory Committees

If the purges represented the negative or destructive aspect of the democratisation process, the positive side was expressed in the workers' demand for internal autonomy in the factories. The vehicle for this was the factory committee.

The demand for elected representatives in the factory had a long history, and, in fact, several large factories already had semi-legal 'councils of elders' before the revolution. These served to represent the workers before the administration.[63] The 10 March agreement between the Soviet and the owners legalised these committees, providing for their election in all industrial enterprises. According to the second paragraph, the factory committees had the following functions: (1) to represent the workers in dealings with government and public institutions; (2) to express the opinions of the workers on questions of public and economic life; (3) to resolve questions relating to the mutual relations among the workers themselves; and (4) to represent the workers before the administration and owners on questions of their mutual relations.[64]

Where the workers overstepped the provisions of the agreement was in the area of the rather vague third point. Virtually everywhere they raised the demand for 'control over internal order' (*vnutrennii poryadok*). This too was not a new demand. It represented the essence of the workers' conception of the new order in the factories. To them, it amounted to 'the establishment of a constitutional regime'.[65] On 13 March, the provisional factory committee of the Radiotelegraph Factory recognised 'the need for the creation of a permanent factory committee to manage [*vedat'*] the internal life of the factory ... What should the above-mentioned committee decide?' The following items were presented for the approval of the general assembly:

(1) length of the workday
(2) minimum worker's wage
(3) mode of payment for labour
(4) immediate organisation of medical aid
(5) on labour insurance
(6) on the establishment of a mutual aid fund
(7) on hiring and firing
(8) resolving various conflicts
(9) labour discipline
(10) on rest
(11) on guarding the factory
(12) on food
(13) rights, duties, elections and existence of a permanent factory committee.[66]

At the Phoenix Machine-construction Factory, the areas of concern of the factory committee included guarding the plant, regulation of wages, norms and the determination of rates, resolution of labour conflicts, the food supply, health care, and cultural and educational work.[67] Finally, a meeting of the representatives of 8000 workers of eight tobacco factories drew up the following list of demands that together represent a comprehensive statement of their conception of the new order in the factories. Besides purely economic demands, these included:

(2) to abolish overtime and authorise it individually in each case with the permission of the central organ
(3) to destroy the black book of the entrepreneurs
(5) to oblige the administration to polite address with the workers
(7) to oblige the administration to deal with the workers through their representatives
(8) to remove from the factory elements undesirable to the workers
(9) to conduct the hiring and firing of workers only with the agreement of the workers' committee
(10) to abolish searches and transfer the duty of protecting the integrity of the material to the workers themselves and their representatives

(12) to abolish fines; choice of means of influence to fall to the factory committee

(20) to elect elders at work by the workers themselves.[68]

Thus, on the one hand, the factory committees were intended to correct the worst pre-revolutionary abuses of authority: arbitrary firings, the hiring of 'foreign elements' hiding from the draft, playing favourites, arbitrary assignment to wage categories and payment for work, arbitrary and despotic use of fines, etc. The other side of this coin was the collective assumption by the workers of those prerogatives now taken out of the competence of management. These functions constituted the 'internal life' of the factory, control over which, the workers felt, rightfully belonged to them as autonomous human beings and citizens. None of these demands were intended to deny the basic right of the administration to manage the technical and economic sides of production. Nor did the workers in practice deny this right at this stage of the revolution.

Nevertheless, in retrospect, the attitudes that lay behind these demands can be seen to form a basis out of which such a denial could grow, given the right conditions. The purge of administration itself, for example, implied the right to abrogate the rights of the administration, through dismissal, in case of failure to adhere to the workers' concept of a constitutional system in the factory or even on grounds of technical incompetence.

In March this potential generally lay quietly hidden under the surface. The slogan of the workers' control nowhere was raised in private industry. But there were already faint hints of what lay ahead. As noted, suspicions regarding the true intentions of management were already quite widespread. The Minister of Trade and Industry admitted in March that the workers of the capital 'suspect the administration of holding up the production of goods for defence'.[69] These suspicions were politically based. The workers had not forgotten the close cooperation between the factory administration and the Tsarist state. Lockouts had been a familiar part of the capital's labour scene and had been used as readily against political as against economic strikes.[70]

On 22 March, the representatives of the factories of the Moscow District of Petrograd, meeting to discuss the 'bourgeois press campaign', resolved to address the workers of the capital

with the suggestion to call meetings to clarify the causes of the industrial dislocation in their districts and then [to call] a city-wide meeting of representatives of all districts to clarify and publish these causes of the industrial dislocation and to expose those who are preventing the elimination of this dislocation.[71]

It is obvious whom the resolution had in mind.

Similar suspicions were aired at the 20 March session of the Soviet. The representative of the Metallicheskii Factory stated:

> We are getting declarations that although there is work in certain shops, for unknown reasons this work is not being set in motion. We are told—its turn hasn't come yet and the shops are idle. We had a meeting of elders at our factory and they reached the conclusion that they elected a commission of three which is to investigate whether there aren't abuses on the part of the administration in favour of the old régime and the Germans, and if it turns out that the work can begin, then immediately to demand of the administration that it be done. Maybe the administration won't want to submit, so it is desirable that it be issued from the Soviet W and SD that a commission be chosen immediately from the factories of all Petrograd, as earlier there was one from the War–Industry Committees. True, that commission was bourgeois, and there was only a small group of workers in it, but it is desirable that now such a commission be created with a view to control and that it conduct an inspection of all the factories in order to make sure there are no abuses on the part of the administration in holding up work. Are the declarations of the administration correct that there is no metal and coal?[72]

In effect, this is already a call for workers' control—control in the Russian sense of observation and inspection. But it is important to note that the speaker was asking for control by the Soviet, centralised control, and this because he felt the Soviet would have greater power than the factory committee in dealing with the administration. There was no concern here for any special rights of the local factory committee: it was a practical question of the correct functioning of the plant. Workers' control was neither in its embryonic nor in its more developed stages predominantly a movement for 'industrial democracy' as an abstract right in itself, as something intrinsically desirable. In this sense, the movement was not motivated by anarchist ideas, although the anarchists enthusiastically supported it. To the workers, workers' control meant watching over the administration in order that the interests of the workers and the revolution be protected. If a centralised body—the Soviet or a workers' state—could do it better, there was no objection.

At the same meeting, a representative from several small enterprises recounted how upon returning to work the workers found no materials. A search also turned up nothing. A few days passed, and they finally went to the respirator department where they found a small amount of tin that sufficed for their needs.

But they could have done that two days earlier, i.e. we could have worked three days. But instead of bothering themselves with it, through carelessness or maybe with the aim of holding up production, they did not ask about it in the respirator department ... Such a great shortcoming is their fault in that they don't want to bother about it in time. In view of this I would also ask that they be obliged to conduct matters properly.[73]

The motives of the workers are evident here: concern for production stemming from concern for their livelihood and for defence of the revolution against the external enemy—all this on the background of suspicion of administrative negligence or counterrevolutionary sympathies.

Already in early April one can find isolated cases of direct intervention by the factory committees into selected areas of management, mainly the shipping of goods and materials. At the Kebke Canvas Factory, the committee reported to the general assembly on the situation at the plant where production had come to a total halt. The meeting resolved to ask the Soviet to investigate. The workers claimed that production was being held up despite initial assurances from the administration of the existence of orders worth ten million rubles and at least a year's supply of raw materials. When questioned, the administration was evasive. Meanwhile, it was learnt that canvases were being hastily packed and the loaders offered a special bonus. The administration would only say it was a matter of military security. Moreover, when the trucks came, instead of loading the canvases that had already been prepared, others were taken right off the machines. As a result of all this, the factory committee ordered that no canvases should leave the grounds and had all telephone communications from the factory cut.[74]

At a meeting of the PSFMO on 7 April, it was claimed that the administration did indeed have documents from the air force, though why it had refused to show them to the factory committee was not explained. The meeting noted similar occurrences at a few other factories, including United Cable and the Paramanov Leather Factory.[75]

But such cases of direct intervention were still very rare. Nor did the workers formulate a generalised right of 'control'. They merely reacted to the situation, as they perceived it. In other words, these were defensive reactions, not the assertion of a right for its own sake.

Still, in the foregoing, one can already see the beginnings of the movement for workers' control. It was totally spontaneous at this point, coming entirely 'from below'. The vast majority of the factory committees in March and April were led by Mensheviks and SRs, and the Bolsheviks had not yet embraced the slogan.

The situation in the state enterprises was different and presents a special interest for what it reveals of the workers' view of their relationship to management. In many of these factories at the start of the revolution the workers, through their elected representatives, either fully took over management or actively participated in it, along with the remnants of the former administration. However, after a few weeks they retreated, yielded all executive powers, declaring their refusal to assume responsibility for production. Only the right of 'control over the administration' (i.e. observation) was claimed.

Typical was the pattern of events at the Patronnyi Factory. According to the factory committee's report to the 265th Infantry Regiment,

> On receiving the order of the Soviet W and SD on the renewal of work beginning March 7, the workers met on the morning of March 6 in their general assembly and in view of the fact that there was no one of the higher ranks at the plant and that they could not have helped but know of the Soviet W and SD's summons on starting work at the plant since it was published in all the papers, the workers at the general assembly decided to begin work independently from March 8.
>
> At the general assembly on March 7, after a preliminary discussion of the question on the shop level, it was decided not to take back the majority of officials and to begin work on the morning of March 8.
>
> To decide current and at times very complex and responsible matters in the factory, a provisional executive committee was elected from representatives of the shops ... After the agreement reached with General Orlov on the election of the factory administration and the arrival of Major-General Doronin, elected by the workers to be director of the factory, the last functions of management will be liquidated ... The provisional executive committee of the Petrograd Patronnyi Factory, having fulfilled the task placed upon it as best it could, is now reorganising itself on a new basis, having transferred all executive authority to the administration of the factory, the director Maj.-General Doronin elected by the workers, and retains for itself the functions of an observing and consultative organ.[76]

The takeover here is portrayed more or less as a matter of necessity. However, the refusal to readmit the administration might indicate a more positive assertion of right, besides the fact that the administrators had all been, literally, servants of the old régime. The director of the Okhta Powder Factory, for example, reported that the workers felt they 'should and can manage all the affairs of the factory'.[77] Somewhat later, Patronnyi's factory committee admitted that 'at first, the tasks of

the factory committee were unclear and it was forced to move groping-
ly. It took upon itself not only the functions of control but also the
duties of administration. Such cases occurred, of course, also at other
plants.' In the end, however, the committee decided to limit itself to
'internal order' and as for the rest—only control, in accord with the
position taken by the Conference of Factories of the Artillery Authority at the start of April.[78]

The protocols of the general assembly and factory committee of the
Admiralty Shipbuilding Factory shed light on the causes of this retreat.
Initially, it was decided that the factory committee had the right of
control, but this right was interpreted so broadly as to effectively
include management. For example, the 'technical commission' was to
examine the need to improve the equipment of the factory and make
repairs, the formulation of conditions for taking on and giving production orders, questions of the size of the administrative staff, etc. The
'control-financial commission' was to be in charge of the movement of
all orders from the moment the offer was made, the subcontracting of
orders, incoming and outgoing factory funds, cash on hand, etc. On 15
March, the committee was given the additional task of purchasing all
metals, instruments, etc. required by the plant.[79]

However, less than two weeks later, the factory committee decided
to restrict its functions to control, in the sense of observation, though
retaining the right to remove administrative personnel through a
conciliation chamber, and on 7 April the general assembly resolved
that the election of administrative personnel by the workers was
undesirable.[80] The factory committee noting 'the difficulties involved
in conducting the affairs of the factory committee in view of the
complexity and indefiniteness as well as the novelty of the situation',
laid out the entire state of affairs before the workers on 27 April:

> Given the confused circumstances that existed at the time of its
> creation and the difficulties in adapting this institution for manage-
> ment and control, the committee was placed in a contradictory
> position—for in giving orders to the corresponding organ of the
> administration, it would thus limit itself in the sphere of broad
> control and also inhibit the initiative of the director of the factory,
> thus harming the efficiency and orderliness of execution. Practice
> and common sense told us that it is necessary to transfer the function
> of management to the factory's director and thus to unite the entire
> staff into a single unitary organisation. The committee retains the
> right to control all of its actions up to and including removal, through
> the conciliation chamber, of both the factory director and individual
> management personnel and also the initiative in the reorganisation
> and reduction of their numbers.[81]

It seems, therefore, that in the state factories the workers did initially decide to take over management. To them, the democratic revolution meant that the state factories now belonged to the people and that they should run them. Similar attitudes existed on the railroads, where 'the majority of railroad workers saw the February Revolution as a popular revolution and they, therefore, could not picture it without their close and active participation. This was especially so on the question of management. 70 per cent of the railroads belonged to the Tsar. He fell. Naturally, the railroads now belonged to the people. The workers, as part of the people, should be entrusted with them. Such ideas of primitive democracy were widespread among the railroad workers.'[82] Such attitudes were also common among the employees of the Ministry of Posts and Telegraph. Here there undoubtedly was a syndicalist element.[83]

However, the workers in the state factories, as opposed to those on the railroads or in the Post-Telegraph Union, soon reached the conclusion that they did not want, at least at this stage, to run the factories. They decided this because they felt technically unprepared. Worker management was something for socialism, and that still lay in the future. Moreover, in the given conditions of economic crisis, the factory committees understood that their chances of failing and being discredited were very great. The Instructions on the Activity of Factory Committees issued by the Conference of State Enterprises of Petrograd on 15 April stated this clearly: 'Not desiring to take upon ourselves the responsibility for the technical and administrative organisation of production in the given conditions until the full socialisation of the economy, the representatives of the general factory committee enter the administration with a consultative voice.'[84] What is clear from the foregoing, at any rate, is that the workers did equate workers' management, in one form or another, with socialism.

At the same time, despite this retreat from management, the workers in state enterprises remained more radical than those in private industry on this issue. They asserted their right of control in an overt and positive manner, independently of the specific conditions in the factory (although, it is true, in many cases the state factory administration went into hiding immediately after the revolution). On the other hand, as noted earlier, no such right was claimed in private industry nor was control instituted, except in the few isolated cases where the workers saw a direct threat to their factories.

As for the entrepreneurs, they were not about to countenance any interference with the prerogatives of management. Back in 1912 the Petrograd industrialists issued their famous 'Convention of June 1912', binding on all members of the PSFMO. Paragraph 5 called 'not to allow permanent representation of the workers in the form of deputies, elders, etc.'; paragraph 6: 'Not to allow intervention and mediating participation on the part of trade unions, societies and in general of organisations outside the factory'; and paragraph 7: 'Especially impermissible is interference in the hiring and firing of workers, in the establishment of wages and conditions of hiring and in the working out of rules of internal order'.[85] Despite various liberal pronouncements since then, this remained the practical position of the Petrograd industrialists, who even tried to establish fines for non-observance of the convention by members of the Society.

No doubt, under the impact of the revolution, and out of necessity (they could no longer lean upon the Tsarist state apparatus), their tactical stance underwent some changes. Many felt that in the given situation, it was in their interest to deal with an organised working class. Judging by the West European experience, they wanted to believe that organisation would exert a restraining influence on the workers. The director of the Nev'yansk Mines in the Urals wrote to his manager from Petrograd on 9 March:

> I consider it superfluous to linger on these [events of the February Revolution] but I will only point out that the first act of this revolution, unprecedented in the history of the peoples of Russia, had a purely political character. On this platform, full unanimity and unity of all strata and masses of the people, who toppled the shameful old government into dust with such dizzying speed, were possible. But now the second act is opening—in this act a socialist platform is being put forward. Of course, there can be no unanimity and unity on this platform. There is no doubt that under the influence of socialist ideas and propaganda at the factories many excesses are arising, directed chiefly at the participation of the workers masses in the management of affairs.
>
> At the Izhorskii Factory [a state enterprise] such an excess has already taken place, and a soviet of workers of 50 people was elected to manage the factory, including six engineers, who, having removed the director of the factory, Admiral Voskresenskii, began to run it. The soviet held out for several days and now they have already returned to the normal management of the factory.
>
> In regard to this, at a closed meeting of the Council of Congresses of Mining Industrialists of the Urals, opinions were exchanged, and the conclusion was reached to go towards meeting any desires of the workers that related to their organisation (election of elders, conciliation chambers, etc.) but under no circumstances to allow intervention into management of the factory, and that it is necessary to firmly and stubbornly defend this position.[86]

The entrepreneurs were obviously as suspicious of the workers' intentions as the workers were of theirs. Although the letter might appear rather liberal and even in tune with the workers' aspirations, in actual fact the workers' conception of 'internal order' and the owners' understanding of 'management' overlapped considerably. All the elements for a spiralling sequence of reactions and counterreactions were at hand: the workers, suspicious of the administration (and often not without cause), would feel compelled to intervene; upon which the owners, feeling themselves vindicated in their suspicions of the workers' socialist intentions, would take measures, mostly economic, and especially lockouts, against the workers; upon which the workers would be spurred to even deeper intervention, and so forth. Of course, the situation was in reality even more complex because the workers believed that the entrepreneurs' policy of sabotage and lockouts was politically motivated. Soon, it would be impossible to separate the political from the economic aspects of the struggle.

The parallels between the workers' attitudes towards the state and the attitudes of workers in state factories towards management are very striking. In both cases, through their representatives the workers initially assumed full power, only to relinquish it shortly to the representatives of census society, in the first instance, and to the factory administration, in the other, in return for 'control'. The workers were not prepared to run either the state machinery or the factories. They decided, rather, not to participate at all in the administration but to exert control from the outside, partly from fear of being compromised. In both cases there was no revolt against authority as such, but a rejection of absolute authority in favour of a 'constitutional' régime.

But these 'constitutions' were not the outcome of negotiations between the workers and census society or the factory administration. They were, in fact, the workers' own programmes, their independent conception of the revolution. As long as census society and the representatives of the owners in the factories adhered to these constitutions, the workers were quite willing to leave executive power in their hands. And this is where the seeds of the future conflict lay. For the workers' current hopes notwithstanding, the coming weeks would convince them that census society would not and could not go along with their conception of the revolution.

Alongside these parallels between the economic and political spheres, one can also see a certain lack of correspondence in the degree of militancy and radicalism in each of these areas. It was in the state enterprises where the transformation of worker-administration relations went furthest. Yet, politically, these turned out to be among the most moderate workers. Similarly, it was the unskilled workers who displayed the greatest militancy in the wage struggle after the revolution.

On the other hand, one observes no extraordinary radicalism among the metalworkers of the Vyborg District in the sphere of worker–management relations. The demands for soviet power that issued from here were not accompanied by calls to take over the factories or even for workers' control of production.

Nevertheless the very strong interconnections between the economic and political spheres, both in the workers' consciousness and in the objective reality itself, were evident from the very start. It was the desire of the moderate socialist leadership of the Soviet to keep the two separate that, in fact, underlay the first conflict between it and the worker rank-and-file. In the coming weeks these interconnections would grow into a virtual merging of the two spheres with all threads uniting in one overriding demand: 'All power to the soviets!'

6 From the April to the July Days

On 18 April (1 May, New Style) the Russian workers celebrated May Day for the first time in conditions of political freedom—indeed, by Lenin's own testimony, the broadest political freedom of any of the belligerent countries. It was early spring, and also the spring of the revolution. The hearts of the demonstrators were brimming with hope and enthusiasm, and spirits soared.

In keeping with the spirit of February, May Day was not merely a day of labour demonstrations and meetings but a national holiday, a holiday of the revolution. In Petrograd, the number of demonstrators exceeded even the turnout for the 23 March funeral for those who had fallen in the insurrection. 'In general', recalled Sukhanov, 'the entire city, from large to small, if not at some meeting, was out in the streets.'[1] The Menshevik-Internationalist *Novaya zhizn'* remarked how different the day was in Petrograd from May Days abroad, which were demonstrations of the proletariat against the bourgeoisie. 'The [Russian] proletariat can say with legitimate pride that on that day all of democracy of the country was to a greater or lesser degree an active participant of its proletarian socialist holiday.'[2]

Of course, 18 April could not claim quite the same sense of national solidarity that had marked the first days of the revolution. The campaign against the workers' alleged egotism in the non-socialist press had already created a wedge of bad feeling. Still, it seemed that much had already been accomplished and that the alliance with census society was working. Few suspected that May Day would be the last event of the revolution to bear an all-national stamp, that on the very same day events were being set in motion that would bring down the curtain on this 'honeymoon phase' of the revolution.

The April Days

It was noted earlier that the workers' 'revolutionary defencism' was premised upon the assumption that the government, prodded by the Soviet, would pursue an active peace policy and in the meanwhile conduct a purely defensive war. But almost immediately, the workers

111

were given grave cause for concern. On 7 March, the official government organ pledged to spare no effort to provide the army 'with all that is necessary to pursue the war to a victorious conclusion'.[3] Less than a week later, Minister of Foreign Affairs, P. N. Milyukov, stated in an interview that 'we need a decisive victory'.[4] Meanwhile, the non-socialist press stubbornly insisted that the entire nation was now more than ever united around this goal of victory.

Such claims notwithstanding, the nation was far from united around this goal. The general assembly of the Dinamo Factory declared:

> The people and army went into the street not to replace one government by another but to carry out our slogans. And these slogans are: 'Freedom', 'Equality', 'Land and Liberty' and 'an end to the bloody war'—for us, the unpropertied classes, the bloody slaughter is not necessary.[5]

Although the 14 March declaration of the Soviet 'To the Peoples of the Entire World' calling them to struggle against the annexationist policies of their governments was met with enthusiasm, statements by representatives of the government and the attitude of the non-socialist press continued to agitate the workers. *Rabochaya gazeta* printed the following report from the Pechatkin Paper Mill:

> On March 19 a general assembly took place at which a series of reports from the factory council of elders and others from the P[etrograd] O[rganization] of the RSDWP [Menshevik] were heard.
> The meeting, having discussed the question of the attitude of the proletariat to the war, unanimously passed the following resolution:
> We the workers of the Pechatkin Mill, greet the Soviet of W and SD for its internationalist position in relation to the war.
> But we consider it totally insufficient on the part of the Soviet of W and SD in its striving for peace to limit itself to the publishing of manifestos.
> For a speedy end to the war it is necessary immediately to undertake pressure upon the PG in order that it, submitting to the will of Russian democracy, also declare its rejection of annexations and reparations and its readiness at any time to enter peace talks on the conditions declared in the Manifesto of the Soviet of W and SD.
> At the same time, the meeting protests against the slogan 'War until complete victory' that is being unfurled now on the banner of the PG and the entire bourgeois press: for under this slogan hide the annexationist aspirations of the capitalist class of Russia and the whole world.
> The path to peace is not a bloody war but the revolutionary pressure of the popular masses of Europe on their predatory ruling classes and governments.[6]

Under pressure from the Soviet, the government finally issued a declaration to the citizens of Russia on 27 March which rejected all annexationist aims, yet, curiously enough, pledged Russia's determination to fulfil all her treaty obligations with the Allies (treaties that, in fact, determined the new division of the world upon Allied victory, Russia receiving, among other prizes, Constantinople and the Dardanelles).[7]

All the same, the Kadet Party's Central Committee and its leader Milyukov continued to speak out for the annexation of the Dardanelles.[8] As a result, the Bolshevik demand for the publication of all secret treaties began to gather considerable working-class support, despite the workers' 'defencism'. A meeting of 3000 workers of the Skorokhod Shoe Factory declared, after hearing a report from their district soviet delegate:

> We support the [district] soviet's demand that the PG immediately publish all treaties and that the PG propose peace terms and convene a peace conference. We do not want to find ourselves in the position of conducting an annexationist war.[9]

Again, after prodding from the Soviet, Milyukov agreed to transmit the 27 March declaration (intended originally for domestic consumption) to the Allied governments but on the condition that it be accompanied by a note of clarification. This note was sent on 18 April and became public through the newspapers on 20 April. It affirmed Russia's determination to carry on the war in full agreement with the Allies, to fulfil all treaty obligations. It also claimed that the revolution had merely strengthened the popular will to bring the war to a victorious conclusion.

The publication of this note caused a spontaneous explosion of popular indignation in the form of workers' and soldiers' meetings and demonstrations on 20 and 21 April. On the whole, these were not directed against the PG or dual power as such but at forcing the resignation of Milyukov and, somewhat less insistently, that of the Minister of War, Guchkov. There were, however, relatively small working-class groups with banners reading 'Down with the PG' and 'Power to the soviets'.[10]

One need not dwell here upon the events themselves. *Rabochaya gazeta* gave the following account of 20 April.

> Petrograd reacts unusually sensitively and nervously to the burning political issues of the day. Milyukov's note, published yesterday, called forth great agitation on the streets. Everywhere were groups of people, meetings, which have of late become usual sights, but in immeasurably larger numbers. Everywhere, at street meetings, in trams, passionate, heated disputes over the war take place. The caps

and handkerchiefs stand for peace; the derbies and bonnets – for war.

In the working-class districts and in the barracks, the attitude towards the note is more defined and organised. A sharp protest is being expressed against the politics of annexation, against the challenge to democracy that the government has made in its note.

Already in the morning, the Finland Regiment came out. Carrying red flags bearing the inscriptions: 'Down with annexationist politics', 'Milyukov and Guchkov into retirement', and so forth, they moved toward the Mariinskii Palace, where the PG sits in session . . .

After the Finlyandtsy move the other regiments. Towards evening, workers' demonstrations make their appearance. The banners, for the most part, are old ones, left over from May Day. But there are also new ones, and they protest against the policy of annexations, demand peace without annexations or indemnities, greet the Soviet of W and SD. A part of the demonstrators moves to the building of the Morskoi Korpus on Vasilevskii ostrov, where the general assembly of the Soviet is in session.

From time to time counter-demonstrations appear. Small, disorderly crowds of petty bourgeois [*obyvateli*—literally, inhabitants; at any rate, not workers or soldiers] among which one can also see officers, but especially many women. They run along Nevskii Prospekt with placards and shout: 'Long live the Provisional Government', 'Down with Lenin'.

By evening the atmosphere becomes even more excited. And just as the mood that reigns in the working-class districts and in the barracks is sympathetic to the Soviet of W and SD, so does an attitude hostile towards it predominate on Nevskii Prospekt.[11]

The next day the demonstrations recurred, but on a much larger scale and with more serious consequences. Again, *Rabochaya gazeta* reported:

Yesterday on the streets of Petrograd the atmosphere was even more agitated than on April 20. Everywhere were small meetings, everywhere demonstrations. In the [working-class] districts a whole series of strikes took place . . .

The inscriptions on the banners were of a most varied nature, but all the same, one noted a common feature: in the centre, on Nevskii, Sadovaya and others, slogans in support of the PG predominate: in the outskirts—the opposite. There, decisive protests against the foreign policy of the PG and its inspirer Mr Milyukov reign undividedly . . .

Clashes between demonstrators of the different groups are frequent. The initiators are defenders of the PG, who often charge at the banners protesting against Milyukov. The demonstrators of the other side repulse them, but this often takes the most unfortunate forms. There are many rumours of shootings. But who is to blame—that has still to be clarified.

After midday, when the Executive Committee published its order to the soldiers not to go into the streets armed, one began to observe curious scenes where soldiers try to persuade their comrades to refrain in general from participation in the demonstrations, whatever their character [armed or otherwise]. Often the soldiers also appealed to civilians for calm . . .

In the evening the situation in the streets became more acute. The gunfire was very strong.[12]

As the report notes, upon learning of the Soviet's order, the soldiers generally refrained from demonstrating, entrusting resolution of the conflict to the Soviet leadership. The workers, however, did not take so passive or trusting a position and came out in even larger numbers than the previous day. As usual, the Vyborg District was in the van. But there were also many workers from less skilled factories, including several thousand from the Petrograd Trubochnyi (Pipe) Factory, from the Putilov Works, and even two or three textile mills.[13] All strata of the working class were united in their opposition to an imperialist war.

On 21 April, the Kadet Party organised counter-demonstrations in support of Milyukov. Several workers and soldiers were killed or wounded in the clashes—the first blood to be shed since the insurrection. By all accounts (official hearings were held) the shooting was begun by provocateurs in the midst of the 'proper public'.[14] One of these clashes involved textile workers. According to Perazich:

On April 21 the women of these mills [Novaya Bumagopryadil'nya, Kozhevnikovskaya and part of Okhtenskaya Bumagopryadil'nya] moved with the demonstrators onto Nevskii on the odd-numbered side. The other crowd moved in parallel fashion on the even side: well-dressed women, officers, merchants, lawyers, etc. Their slogans were: 'Long live the PG', 'Long live Milyukov', 'Arrest Lenin'. At Sadovaya a clash occurred. Here a hail of curses descended upon our workers: *Bezulochnitsy!* [trollops] Illiterate rabble! Filthy scum! P. Romanova could not hold back: 'The hats[15] you're wearing are made from our blood!', and a fist fight broke out. The bearer of the Novaya Bumagopryadil'nya banner was knocked off her feet and the banner torn. The same occurred to the Kozhevnikovskaya banner. In response, our workers tore some of the opponents' banners and in the scuffle tore off the fancy hats and scratched the faces of the bourgeois women. At that moment, a detachment of sailors approached, led by an orchestra, and the Kadet demonstration retreated. After this, with the remainder of the red banners, the workers moved to Vasilevskii ostrov to the Morskoi korpus, where the Soviet was in session. From there our demonstrators were accompanied by a detachment of Putilov workers to Ekaterinov Prospekt.[16]

These clashes made a deep and lasting impression. 'That day opened the eyes of everyone. The repressed hatred towards the bourgeoisie intensified', recalled a Vyborg worker.[17] The cleavage in Russian society, papered over in February, was beginning to show through. According to the letter of a Putilov worker printed in the SR *Delo naroda*, it was the clashes that finally brought the factory out on 21 April. At a meeting that afternoon, attended also by workers of the neighbouring Treugol'nik Rubber Factory,

> The mood wavered, some speaking for a street demonstration, others advising against it. It was decided to wait for a decision from the Soviet. But before that decision could arrive some workers returned from the centre with news of clashes, the tearing of banners and the arrests. A leaflet summoning to demonstrate in favour of Milyukov was also read. The mood suddenly shifted. 'What?! They're chasing us off the streets, tearing our banners, and we're going to watch this quietly from a distance? Let's move to Nevskii!' The vote supported this overwhelmingly.[18]

Here, besides indignation over the betrayal by the government, one can see at work the powerful factor of class pride, with its corollary—class hatred.

The 'April Days' strengthened the workers' desire for their own armed force. The general assembly of the Skorokhod Shoe Factory, roundly condemning the 'imperialist scheme of the government', and 'considering the counterrevolutionary designs of the bourgeoisie, which is attempting to use armed force against the workers', decided to form a Red Guard of 1000 and asked the Soviet for 500 rifles and 500 revolvers.[19] On 23 April at a meeting of factory delegates on the organisation of Red Guards, one speaker, referring to that 'regrettable day', argued:

> The bourgeoisie attacked on the streets on April 21 ... One can conclude much from that. The Soviet put too much trust in the Kadets. The Soviet doesn't go out into the streets. The Kadets did. Despite the Soviet, the workers went into the street and saved the day. If we have a Red Guard, they would take us into account... At the head of the districts would march red guards. Then they wouldn't tear down our red flags.[20]

An indication of the broad support for a workers' armed force is the city conference of Red Guards that met on 28 April with delegates from 90 factories employing some 170 000 workers.[21] On the other hand, the moderate Soviet leadership qualified it as unnecessary and even harmful in view of the fact that the soldiers were revolutionary and might see in the Red Guard a threat directed against them.[22] Yudin, representing the EC, told the conference: 'As a true friend of the working class I must tell you openly that our worker lives in ignorance. One can hold a rifle in one's hand when one has a strong head.' This raised such a storm of indignation that the conference even voted to deprive Yudin of the floor. In reply, the conference asked the Soviet to reconsider its position. After all, had not the Soviet itself distributed arms to the workers in February? It might well find itself faced with the necessity of disarming the workers, it argued prophetically. At any rate, the EC's opposition apparently put a temporary halt to this attempt at a city-wide organisation, although work continued on the factory level.[23]

But if on the psychological and social levels the April Days did much to restore the pre-revolutionary class polarisation of urban Russian, and especially Petrograd, society, this was not at the time translated directly into politics. Judging from the resolutions of factory meetings, from the voting in the Soviet and the workers' general continued support for the policy of the Soviet's moderate leaders, the predominant reaction was to reaffirm, in yet stronger terms, the earlier position on dual power. Demanding the resignation of Milyukov and Guchkov, the workers asked the Soviet to tighten its control over the government, to press it harder on foreign policy, and they reaffirmed their support for the Soviet in this task.

A meeting of 2000 workers at the Siemens and Gal'ske Electrotechnical Factory demanded 'firmer control' over the government and 'to remove those who stand for an annexationist policy, Milyukov and Guchkov in particular, and to put in people who will guarantee a more democratic defence of the interests of the broad popular masses'.[24] At the Baltic Shipbuilding Factory, the workers demanded the repudiation of the note and expressed their 'full confidence in the Soviet, and we are sure that the Soviet, basing itself upon our trust and the support of organised revolutionary democracy, will be able to force the PG to take into account the wishes of the revolutionary people and army'.[25] What the workers had in mind was most directly expressed in the resolution of the Voronin Cotton Mill: 'All power must belong to the Soviet, and the PG must execute its will.'[26] This was a reaffirmation of the position of February.

Some, in effect, offered the bourgeoisie a last chance. A meeting of the workers of the Nevskaya Nitochnaya Mill declared that 'the act of the PG was no error but a conscious plan to dupe the people ... The

Soviet must watch every step of the PG and force the PG to publish the secret treaties and call all warring states to end the war ... If there is any new anti-revolutionary step by the PG, take all measures up to taking power.'[27] The workers at Dinamo called to replace the entire government if it refused to remove Milyukov and Guchkov.[28]

Once again, most of the demands for a break with census society came from the Vyborg machine-construction plants (and a few others in other districts[29]), i.e. factories where at least a good part of the workers may have already been hostile to dual power. The general assembly of the Optico-machine-construction Factory resolved that

> The PG by its composition does not represent the population of Russia. Representing a bunch of capitalists and landowners who made up the Fourth State Duma, having seized the power won by the people, Milyukov and Co. have unmasked themselves. We declare that we do not want to shed blood for the sake of Milyukov and Co. in cooperation with the capitalist oppressor of all countries. Therefore, we find the Milyukov–Guchkov Co. not corresponding to their appointment and recognise that the only power in the country must be the Soviets of the WS and PD, which we will defend with our lives.[30]

However, now for the first time, workers from other sectors besides metalworking, though still rare, began to speak for the soviet power. The Nevskii Shoe Factory, for example, called to 'reorganise both the EC of the Soviet of W and SD and also the Soviet itself, which are not able to take a decisive revolutionary class stand for a break with bourgeois policy, and for their replacement with representatives who stand for a revolutionary path of struggle, for full transfer of power to the hands of the proletariat and peasantry'.[31] Similar positions were taken by the Needleworkers' Union[32] and the Delegates' Council of the Upholsterers' Section of the Union of Woodworkers.[33] (Both industries, as noted, were relatively skilled.)

The Vyborg District Soviet, for its part, resolved merely 'to give a decisive rebuff to this betrayal of the interests of democracy. Inform the Soviet of this, calling it to decisive action, promising our full support.'[34] This may have been a veiled call to take power, veiled because the district soviet did not want to oppose directly the central Soviet. Or perhaps there was still not a majority here for soviet power.

In any case, for the great mass of workers the April crisis did not produce an immediate qualitative shift in political attitudes. For the most part, those who now called for soviet power had already been inclined in that direction. What the majority of workers had in mind in responding to the note was expressed by a Putilov worker in reply to a student's question whether the Soviet had authorised the demonstration: 'No. No permission from the Soviet. We don't want to make a civil war but we'll show the bourgeoisie that they have to take us into account.'[35] Most workers still believed that they could force their will on census society and were, therefore, unconvinced of the need for a break with it and for the civil war that might follow.

Fear of civil war remained a significant factor in the workers' continued support for dual power. 'We fully support the tactics of the Soviet', resolved the general assembly of the Leont'ev Textile Mill,

> directed at maintaining the unity of the revolution and at the energetic rebuff of any attempt to divide the revolutionary forces. The meeting rejects the anarchistic calls of Lenin to seize state power that can only lead to civil war, which in the given moment would threaten to ruin the cause of freedom, which is far from secured.[36]

Relatively few, as yet, were swayed by the Bolshevik argument 'that there was no sense in fearing a civil war. It had already arrived, and only as a result of it would the people achieve their liberation.'[37] Most agreed with the SR leader Stankevich who stated on 20 April at the Soviet:

> So what do we do now? ... Certain people decide it very simply: it is necessary, they say, to overthrow the PG and arrest it ... Why, comrades, do we have to 'come out'? ... At whom should we shoot? Against the masses who stand behind you? Why, you do not have a worthy opponent: against you no one has any power. As you decide, so it will be. It is not necessary to 'come out', but rather to decide what to do ... Decide that the PG should not exist, that it should resign. We will inform them over the telephone, and in five minutes they will hand in their resignations. By seven o'clock it will not exist. What is the purpose here of violence, demonstrations, civil war?

This speech was met with 'stormy applause' and 'cries of enthusiasm'.[38] To these workers the conclusion was simple: rally ever more resolutely round the moderate Soviet leadership so that it can all the more easily force the government to tow the mark.

The crisis was finally 'liquidated' with the government's agreement to dispatch a new explanatory note to the Allies reiterating the original 'Declaration to the Citizens of Russia' and stressing that Milyukov's 'sanctions and guarantees of firm peace' actually meant arms limitation, international tribunals, etc. This 'clarification', of course, totally contradicted the original note. Yet both stood, as the note was never repudiated. Nor, for that matter, were Milyukov or Guchkov forced to resign, although they both left the government within a week or so.

This solution was accepted by the Soviet's EC on 21 April by a vote of 34 to 19. It also passed in the plenum of the Soviet by a large majority. Despite the alarm, the defencist majority of the Soviet seemed to be riding higher than ever on the wave of popular support.

The First Coalition

It was quite natural at this point that the representatives of census society should raise the question of a coalition. The crisis had demonstrated dramatically that the government had neither the authority nor, failing that, the physical resources to keep the masses in line. The Soviet, on the other hand, was more or less in full control of the workers and soldiers, yet shared no responsibility for government policy. Accordingly, the government, with the non-socialist press following suit, began to press for the formation of a coalition with representatives of the Soviet. Kerenskii threatened to resign if the Soviet refused.

The EC at first was totally opposed to the idea, voting unanimously on 26 April against participation in the government. But on 28 April, a joint conference of the ECs of the Petrograd and Moscow Soviets barely missed reversing this. Guchkov's resignation on 30 April as Minister of War forced a reorganisation of the government and added urgency to the situation.

Until now, Tsereteli, the undisputed leader of the Soviet majority, had opposed a coalition. His party's paper, *Rabochaya gazeta*, putting forth the traditional Social-Democratic position, maintained that socialists in the government would soon find themselves compromised in the eyes of the masses, the targets of 'anarchist demagogues' (i.e. the socialist left) and would quickly lose all influence among the workers.[39] Another argument was that one could more effectively pressure the government from the outside; once on the inside, such pressure would be difficult to exert. Nevertheless, on 1 May, Tsereteli spoke for a coalition, and it passed in the EC by 44 to 10 with 2 abstentions. Opposing were the Bolsheviks, Menshevik–Internationalists and Left SRs.[40]

In the ensuing negotiations, Milyukov was forced out by his colleagues in the government, despite posturing by the Kadet CC threatening to recall all its ministers. As a result, six representatives of the Soviet, a sizeable minority, entered the government. On 13 May the Soviet plenum voted overwhelmingly full confidence in the new coalition government. February's formula of conditional support was now abandoned. Trotsky's resolution opposing the government gathered a mere 20–30 votes.[41] *Izvestiya* explained the EC's new position. First of all, the government was unable to govern and save the country from the approaching ruin because no one obeyed its representatives and it was distrusted by the masses. On the other hand, it was impossible at this time for the Soviet to take power alone as this would unleash a civil war, and the Soviet already had enough enemies. The 'broad masses' would not follow the Soviet in such a move. Finally, with Soviet representatives in the government, it would be more decisive in carrying out the programme of revolutionary democracy.[42]

At least on the surface, the Soviet's action seemed in accord with the will of the majority of workers (although the opposition was clearly larger than the 20–30 votes cast for Trotsky's resolution—the recall campaign was only just beginning). The workers who had supported dual power, that peculiar form of political alliance with census society, saw the Soviet's action mainly as a means of asserting firmer control: with the Soviet's people inside the government, the census ministers would be totally under the Soviet's thumb. There would be no more room for manoeuvres such as the Milyukov note.

But while the Soviet majority pledged full confidence in the coalition government as a whole, the workers in the factories typically sent greetings and expressed support only for the socialist ministers. Thus, the workers of the Ust'-Izhora Shipyards sent their 'warm greetings to the socialist ministers',[43] while the general assembly of the Wireless Telephone and Telegraph Co. Factory promised 'full support for our comrades in the government'.[44] Finally, the Zigel' workers, 'having heard a report on the coalition from our representatives to the Soviet ..., pledge full support for the Soviet and its representatives in the PG ... We are sure they will carry out their work honestly before the people.'[45] Even the factories that followed the Soviet in expressing support for the coalition government as a whole did not fail to make clear that real legitimacy lay only with the Soviet and its representatives in the government. A meeting of 7000 workers at the Admiralty Shipyards resolved

> to support the PG and to organise around the Soviet of W and SD, which must serve as the centre of revolutionary democracy, consciously and unswervingly striving to increase socialist influence over the organs of power. We approve of the entrance of our comrade socialists into the government. We welcome their intention to carry out the financial programme developed by the economic department of the Soviet of W and SD.[46]

But once again, the main opposition to the coalition came from factories that had already spoken out against the dual power. The thrust of their position was that the socialist ministers would only serve as a screen for the continued machinations of the bourgeoisie, that the only solution to the crisis of power was a soviet government.[47]

There were, thus, two divergent interpretations of the Soviet's action. The minority of workers, convinced that census society was opposed to the programme of revolutionary democracy, maintained that the representatives of the Soviet would become hostages of census society and the result would be a blunting of the revolutionary policy of the Soviet. The majority, on the other hand, saw the coalition as the logical extension of their position that cooperation with census society should not be rejected but that control by the Soviet should be reinforced. These workers believed that the formation of a coalition would inject radicalism and decisiveness into the PG, and this was certainly how their leaders presented it to them.

But despite the apparent continued support for the Soviet leaders among the large majority of workers, the two were in reality far apart, though this was not immediately apparent. For if the workers believed that the Soviet's representatives had entered the government primarily to ensure the execution of the Soviet's will, the Soviet leadership, in fact, moved first and foremost to keep alive the alliance between democracy and census society, an alliance they were convinced was crucial to the survival of the revolution. 'It is necessary by all means to keep the liberal bourgeoisie—the Kadets—in the government', argued *Rabochaya gazeta* emphatically.[48] But such reasoning was alien to the great majority of workers. For them, what was crucial was first of all to defend the revolution, or rather their conception of the revolution and its tasks. Should the alliance between revolutionary democracy and census society prove an obstacle to this, it would have to go. That this was indeed the predominant way of thinking became exceedingly clear in the subsequent two months, during which the idea of soviet power gradually seized the consciousness of the majority of Petrograd's industrial workers.

The Break With Census Society

In the weeks following the April crisis, the euphoria of March was forgotten amidst the growing sense of political cul-de-sac and approaching economic doom. February's guarded *rapprochement* between the working class and bourgeoisie gave way to an increasingly bitter polarisation in the social, economic and, finally, political spheres. In the following pages, I will first document these developments and then offer an explanation of their dynamics.

Perhaps the most striking indicator of the shift that occurred in May and June is the voting in the Workers' Section of the Petrograd Soviet, made up of representatives of the capital's wage- and salary-earning classes (excluding managerial personnel). Immediately after the April crisis, the Petrograd Bolsheviks, having rallied to Lenin's 'April Theses', launched a campaign in the factories for new elections that met with widespread response. On 1 July the Petrograd Bolshevik leader Volodarskii informed the City Conference that the party now had a majority of the worker delegates to the Soviet.[49] Two days later, less than two months after Trotsky's anti-coalition resolution had received a trifling 20 to 30 votes, a majority of the Worker's Section demanded the transfer of state power to the soviets.[50] A majority of Petrograd's workers had opted for a break with the bourgeoisie.

On closer examination, certain patterns emerge. The largest and earliest Bolshevik gains were made among the metalworkers and first of all in the machine-construction factories. In the two districts with the largest concentration of metalworkers (in relative and absolute terms), Vyborg and Vasilevskii ostrov, already in May the soviets had left socialist majorities. The same is true of the soviet of the small Kolomna District, whose workers were almost all employed in three large shipyards.[51] Elsewhere, the district soviets remained defencist until at least after the July Days.

At the Sestroretsk Arms Factory elections on 3 May gave the Bolsheviks an overwhelming majority and all three seats to the Petrograd Soviet.[52] The Phoenix Machine-construction Factory, which had originally elected two Mensheviks and one Bolshevik, by early June had exclusively Bolshevik delegates.[53] The general assembly of the New Baranovskii Machine and Pipe Factory spent five hours in mid May heatedly debating the mandate for their delegates and ended by overwhelmingly endorsing the Bolshevik position.[54] In June the workers of the Nobel Machine-construction Factory recalled their SR delegate for failing to follow the Bolshevik mandate as published in *Pravda*.[55] At the Putilov Works the first resolution for soviet power was passed on 9 May by the 1250 workers of the new engineering shop.[56]

Typical of developments among this stratum of workers was the following report sent to *Pravda* from the Vulkan Foundry and Machine-construction Factory:

The Vulkan Factory was under the intense influence of the Mensheviks. Noted orators would come to the general assemblies of the workers. Mensheviks, members of the Soviet EC would pay visits. Despite this, their work did not yield the desired results. The Menshevik current did not grow but, on the contrary, declined. On the other hand, the Bolshevik current from the start began to win a firm position for itself. This was evident not only from the expressed opinions of individuals but also through the speeches of worker comrades and their common demands, and little by little it turned into the strong dissatisfaction of the workers with their Menshevik representatives in the Soviet of W and SD. And so it was decided to hold new elections.

Before the elections the Bolshevik faction and the United Mensheviks [Internationalists] decided to work jointly and began pre-election activity. From that moment onward, our work went smoothly and quickly. The comrade workers united around the slogans expressed in the mandate to the representatives to the Soviet of W and SD. At the pre-election meeting, the talented speakers, Kamenev and Lunacharskii, once and for all rallied almost all those present, and the above-mentioned mandate of ours was voted by the entire meeting. As a result of the new elections, the overwhelming majority elected all four delegates from the Bolshevik and the united faction.[57]

Lunacharskii wrote of this meeting: 'I now know how it is possible in the course of half an hour to leave not the slightest trace of the most hollow defencism.'[58]

Two characteristic traits of the situation among the skilled metal-workers emerge from this. As Lunacharskii indicated, these workers were by now more than ripe for the change. Secondly, the shift in party allegiance was very largely from Menshevik–Defencist to Bolshevik, and to a small degree, to other internationalist parties.

In contrast, 'conciliationist' attitudes held much firmer sway among the less skilled workers, though even here they were beginning to erode, especially where economic conflicts arose to serve as catalyst (see below, pp. 142–5). Moreover, where party allegiance did change in the less skilled factories in this period, it was typically from the SR party to the Bolsheviks. At the Petrograd Pipe Factory, with little more than 10 per cent skilled workers,[59] from the start of the revolution 'the SRs had enormous influence and carried away membership dues by the sackful, ... [while] the Menshevik–Defencists enjoyed less success'.[60] New elections here in June yielded the following results: SRs—8552, Bolshevik–SD Internationalist Bloc—5823, and Menshevik–Defencists—1067.[61] The Internationalists were making inroads into SR territory but were still unable to carry a majority.

The SRs also dominated the textile industry, where few supported the call for soviet power before July.[62] The Kersten Knitwear Mill (87 per cent female, largely semi-literate recent arrivals from the village) was represented exclusively by SRs in the Soviet until mid-September when new elections gave the Bolsheviks 965 votes and the SRs 1340. The Mensheviks did not even run a list.[63] At the Treugol'nik Rubber Factory (two-thirds female), despite the growth of Bolshevik sympathies, the SRs often had the upper hand at general assemblies before July.[64] Among the workers at Petrograd's railroad workshops the political struggle was similarly played out largely between the Bolsheviks and SRs.[65]

The fact is that by the end of June there was little sign of any Menshevik–Defencist presence among the industrial workers, except for the printers. In a few factories the Menshevik–Internationalists were popular, especially on Vasilevskii ostrov, with its institutions of higher learning. But on the whole, even these left Mensheviks had few supporters. When the question of an electoral bloc with them was raised at the Bolshevik City Conference on 20 July, only two delegates were in favour. 'We must be careful about a bloc', warned one speaker, 'since the Menshevik–Internationalists are so unstable and they are so insignificant numerically that a bloc has little meaning. If they are consistent internationalists they should break [with the Menshevik–Defencist organisation].' A delegate from the Vyborg District noted that here 'there are almost no Menshevik–Internationalists, maybe a few hundred'. 'They are too few to help us, and there is no sense in helping them', added another.[66]

The first speaker hit directly on the main reasons for Menshevik–Internationalist weakness: they failed to take a clear and consistent stand on the question of power, never really espousing the idea of a soviet government that had become so close and comprehensible to the workers. Moreover, their refusal to break organisationally with the defencists (closely connected with their stand on state power) compromised them in the eyes of many workers.

The virtual disappearance of the Menshevik–Defencists from the factories and the concomitant rise of the Bolsheviks, along with the only relative decline of SR influence are explained by the fact that the shift to support for soviet power came largely, though not exclusively, from the more skilled urbanised sections of the working class. This was the Social-Democratic constituency, the main battleground of its two wings. And by the end of June the battle had been largely played out.[67] On the other hand, the largely Bolshevik–SR struggle among the unskilled stratum was far from decided, though the Bolsheviks were definitely gaining on the SRs.

To the factory masses, the Social Democrats were a workers' party, while the SRs, with their 'Land and Freedom' banner, were seen as a peasant or people's party. Indeed, as opposed to the SRs, the SDs had extremely weak ties with the villages and especially the Mensheviks evinced downright fear of the peasantry. Voitinskii, a Bolshevik turned Menshevik with much experience in 1905 as an agitator in the factories of Petrograd, recalled that

the main ace up the sleeve of the SRs was their agrarian programme which they willingly laid out before the workers. At these meetings they would ask the Social Democrats: What will your party give the peasantry, the provider of the Russian land? On the questions of terror and land the sympathy of the meeting was clearly on the side of the SRs. But the masses still followed the SDs because they already saw it as their party and they liked its name: 'Russian Workers ...'[68]

Rabochaya gazeta, commenting upon the big SR victory (62 per cent) in the June 1917 municipal elections in Moscow, noted that 'the masses follow the simple slogan—"Land and Freedom", especially those who have not broken with the village'.[69]

The soviets were not the only forum to register a shift towards soviet power and the Bolsheviks. In the elections to the twelve district dumas (municipal government) at the end of May, of a total of 784 910 votes (about 75 per cent of all eligible voters), the Bolsheviks received 159 936 (20.4 per cent), the moderate socialists 439 858 (56.0 per cent), the rest going mainly to the Kadets (see Table 6.1).[70] The Bolshevik showing was impressive, especially considering that most of their support came from the working-class districts. In the Vyborg

TABLE 6.1:   *Petrograd district duma election returns (number of votes cast)*

District	Bolshevik	%	Moderate socialist[a]	%	Kadet	%	All parties[b]	%
Admiralty	2983	15.8	11105	58.7	4503	23.8	18931	100.0
Aleksandr-Nevskii	8737	12.8	49891	73.0[c]	9116	13.3	68318	
Kazan'	2219	10.1	9253	41.9	9382	42.5	22077	
Kolomna	6035	14.9	23724	58.4	10241	25.2	40626	
Liteinyi	5085	8.6	30583	51.5	22507	37.9	59423	
Moscow[d]	6758	9.7	41517	59.4	21667	31.0	69942	
Narva	18202	17.1	73293	68.9	12625	11.9	106392	
Petrograd	30348	22.6	72750	54.2	29323	21.8	134345	
Rozhdestvenskii	2944	5.0	37671	63.5[e]	18126	30.5	59358	
Spasskii	4945	13.2	20210	53.8	10885	29.0	37581	
Vasilevskii ostrov	37377	34.3[f]	49293	45.2	19299	17.7	108975	
Vyborg	34303	58.2	20568	34.9	4071	6.9	58942	
Total	159936	20.4	439858	56.0	171745	21.9	784910	100.0

[a] Includes Mensheviks, SRs, Trudoviks and Popular Socialists, the latter two with about 1 per cent of the vote.
[b] Not included in the breakdown are the minor non-socialist parties with about 1.7 per cent of the vote.
[c] The Mensheviks and SRs ran separately here, the former taking 10.6 per cent of the vote, and the latter 60.5 per cent.
[d] Known to be incomplete.
[e] The Mensheviks and SRs ran separately here, the former taking 32.1 per cent of the vote, and the latter 15.4 per cent.
[f] This was a Bolshevik–Menshevik–Internationalist bloc. As the majority of the Menshevik organisation was internationalist here, the defencists did not run.

Source: based on W. Rosenberg, *Liberals in the Russian Revolution* (Princeton: Princeton University Press, 1974) p. 162.

District, the most homogeneously proletarian district, they received an absolute majority—34 303 (58.2 per cent), as opposed to 20 568 (34.9 per cent) for the moderate socialists and only 4071 for the Kadets. In the other two districts with a significant amount of industry, Petrograd and Narva (though far less homogeneously proletarian than Vyborg), the Bolshevik vote was 22.6 per cent and 17.1 per cent respectively. Elsewhere, their showing was well below the city average.[71]

But perhaps the most dramatic success for the proponents of soviet power was the First Petrograd Conference of Factory Committees (30 May–3 June), attended by 568 delegates representing 367 factories employing some 337 000 workers.[72] The resolution on the struggle against the economic dislocation concluded that 'the coordinated and successful execution of all the above measures is possible on the condition of the transfer of power into the hands of the Soviet of WS and PD'. It gathered 297 votes. The moderate socialist and Menshevik–Internationalist resolutions calling for 'state regulation' without defining the nature of that state (but in any case clearly not a soviet one) received a total of 85 votes. The anarchists characteristically ignored the state but obviously wanted a break with census society. Their resolution received 45 votes. Another 44 abstained. Thus, 63 per cent of the delegates present voted for soviet power; 73 per cent, if one includes the anarchist vote.[73]

However, a note of caution is in order. Of all their organisations, factory committees were the closest to the workers, both in terms of continuous daily contact and frequency of elections. But they were elected primarily, though not exclusively, with economic considerations in mind. It also seems likely that most delegates to the conference were elected not by the factory collectives but by the committees themselves. Thus, the 73 per cent vote at the start of June was not necessarily an accurate reflection of the distribution of the workers' political attitudes. What is clear, however, is that those actively involved in factory committee work were strongly inclined towards soviet power.

Before proceeding to an analysis of its causes, one last manifestation of the political shift should be mentioned—the demonstration of 18 June. Without entering into the details here, suffice it is to say that the Bolshevik Central Committee decided to call a demonstration on 10 June in response to pressure from the factories and certain garrison units. However, the Soviet Congress, then in session, got wind of this and fearing a repeat of the 'April Days', banned all demonstrations. (Tsereteli insisted that the Bolsheviks were planning a *coup d'état*.) In search of an alternative, the Soviet majority decided to sponsor a demonstration for 18 June as a show of unity of revolutionary democracy and its support for the soviets. To avoid any discordant notes, the EC proposed only slogans acceptable to all soviet fractions: general peace, speedy convocation of the Constituent Assembly, democratic republic, etc. The issue of state power was studiously avoided.

The demonstration, in fact, was a resounding success for the Bolsheviks. In a crowd of between 300 000 and 400 000, all accounts agree that only a small minority carried the Soviet's neutral slogans, not to speak of slogans in support for the PG.[74]

This is how Sukhanov, an eyewitness, described it:

> 'All Power to the Soviets', 'Down with the Ten Capitalist Ministers'. Thus did the vanguard of the Russian and the World Revolutions, the workers and peasants [the soldiers] of Petrograd, firmly and forcefully express its will ... The situation was totally clear and unambiguous. Here and there the chain of Bolshevik banners and columns was broken by specifically SR and official Soviet slogans. But they were drowned amidst the mass; they appeared as exceptions, expressly confirming the rule. And again and again, as the insistent call from the very bowels of the revolutionary capital, as destiny itself, like the fateful Birnam Wood, they came toward us: 'All Power to the Soviets', 'Down with the Ten Capitalist Ministers' ... [75]

Not all workers participated. Only 800 of the 15 000 workers at the state Obukhovskii Steel Mill in the Nevskii District came out. This was true in general of the Nevskii District, which remained an SR stronghold until September. But abstention itself indicated the doubts that were besetting even the most firmly defencist workers. Unwilling to break with the alliance, they were nevertheless unable to give their 'conciliationist' leaders active support when called upon.

Rabochaya gazeta tried to explain away the Bolshevik success, claiming that the Bolsheviks were the only ones to take the demonstration seriously. 'Every little Bolshevik group had a banner.' What this failed to explain, however, is why the supporters of the Soviet majority remained indifferent to a Soviet-sponsored demonstration? The paper concluded sourly: 'It would have been better not to have held the demonstration ... , to have let the Bolsheviks demonstrate alone.'[76]

Pravda noted how far the political situation had evolved since March:

> What strikes one in surveying the demonstration is the total absence of the bourgeoisie and its fellow travellers. In contrast to the day of the funeral ... when the workers were swallowed in the sea of philistines and petty bourgeois, the demonstration of June 18 was a purely proletarian demonstration; its main participants were workers and soldiers. The Kadets already on the eve of the demonstration declared a boycott, proclaiming through their CC the necessity of

'abstaining' from participation—they literally hid. Nevskii, usually bustling and filled with people, was on that day absolutely clear of its usual bourgeois habitués.[77]

Izvestiya, though the official organ of the Central Executive Committee (TsIK) of Soviets[78] and of the Petrograd Soviet, had to agree that 'the bourgeoisie and philistines, scared to death, were almost not to be seen on that day'.[79] The polarisation had gone far indeed.

Underlying Causes of the Shift to Soviet Power

The groundswell of support for soviet power was based upon the conclusion, embraced by increasingly broader circles of the working class, that census society and 'its' government (the socialist ministers were seen as mere captives) were counterrevolutionary. Alarm over the growth and outspokenness of the forces of counterrevolution in the foreign and domestic political spheres as well as in the economic came to dominate the consciousness of Petrograd's workers in this period.

The Political Counterrevolution

On the eve of the demonstration of 18 June, the workers of the Russko-Baltiiskii Wagon-construction Factory by an 'overwhelming majority' passed the following resolution:

> At our general assembly on June 9 we discussed the appeal of the Central Committee of the RSDWP (Bolshevik) to all workers and soldiers of Petrograd for a peaceful demonstration against the counterrevolution that is raising its head and we found this summons timely and corresponding to the interests of the toilers.
> Now that the necessity of a demonstration against the counter-revolutionary bourgeoisie has been recognised finally by the All-Russian Congress of Soviets of W and SD too [!], and since the call to demonstrate is supported by the CC RSDWP, we also, as on June 9 have decided to join that demonstration.
> We demand the most decisive measures be taken against the Black Hundred forces, that the State Duma and State Council, those centres around which counterrevolutionaries of all sorts and hues are grouping, be immediately dispersed.
> We demand the removal from the PG of the ten ministers of the bourgeoisie, appointees of the Third and Fourth Dumas.[80]

It is obvious that these workers had a very different conception of the aims of the demonstration than did its moderate socialist sponsors.

Not without interest also is the resolution's emphasis on the approval
of the Bolshevik CC. In fact, many factories refrained from demonstrating on 10 June only because the Bolshevik CC decided to respect
the ban of the Soviet Congress (see below, p. 158). The fears of the
Menshevik leaders were materialising: their 'conciliationism' *vis-à-vis*
the 'class enemy' was compromising them in the eyes of the workers.

To the workers it was obvious: if the bourgeoisie was counterrevolutionary, its representatives had to be eliminated from power,
leaving only the socialist ministers, the representatives of revolutionary democracy. The answer, in other words, was soviet power. A
meeting of 2000 workers of the Old Parviainen Machine-construction
Factory decided on 8 June to 'recognise that the only correct path to
forestall the advancing counterrevolution is to take state power into
the hands of the All-Russian Congress of WS and PD'.[81]

It was, in fact, the workers' concern over the 'insolence' of the
counterrevolution that had persuaded the Bolshevik PC to call a
demonstration in the first place. In the debate on its advisability,
Stukov, a PC member from the Kolpino District, stated:

> An objective evaluation of the moment gives us hope for success. A
> demonstration on the widest possible scale is necessary because, on
> the one hand, the counterrevolutionary movement is growing; on
> the other hand, we have to oppose it with the organisation of
> revolutionary forces ... As concerns the workers of Kolpino, they
> are downright dismayed, [asking] how long the party will put off
> joining battle with the counterrevolutionary movement.

Tomskii, the trade union leader, noted that 'the atmosphere of class
antagonism is extremely heavy—just take a look in the trams. We
cannot take for granted that the demonstration will be peaceful.'[82]

The most galling symbol of census society's counterrevolutionary
turn of mind was the resurrection of the State Duma, to the workers a
discredited relic of the old régime, whose distorted representation had
made it a tool of the propertied classes. Less than a week after the
April Days the State Duma held an anniversary session, at which the
leaders of census society denounced the soviets in unadorned terms,
bringing the audience to raptures. Most widely reported in the socialist
press were the words of the monarchist Shul'gin, who expressed his
'serious doubts' about the course of the revolution, decrying the fact
that the 'honest and gifted PG' lacked 'fullness of power'.

> It has been placed under suspicion. A guard has been posted next to
> it, to whom it is said: Look out! They are bourgeois. Therefore,
> watch them closely, and in case anything happens, know your duty.
> Gentlemen, on the 20th we were convincingly shown that this guard

knows his job and carried out his duty honestly. But it is a big question whether those who posted this guard are acting correctly.

Turning to the leftist agitation critical of the government, he echoed Milyukov's question of 1916 addressed to the autocratic regime: 'Is this stupidity or treason? Stupidity, but taken all together, it is treason anyway.'[83] The ovation was deafening. 'Clearly they had been hurting!' remarked Sukhanov:

> True, in essence there was nothing new here in relation to what the bourgeois papers were repeating daily. Still, a public declaration of this in front of people, at a large gathering of like-thinkers, in the face of the victorious enemy—this filled to overflowing with enthusiasm the bourgeois souls.[84]

The State Duma continued to meet in 'private session' throughout May and June. The Chairman of the Fourth Duma, Rodzyanko, went so far as to imply that the State Duma was the sole source of legitimate power in the state.[85] 'Keep yourselves prepared', he appealed to its members, 'for soon the time will come for your intervention into the life of the country.'[86]

Meanwhile, with increasing urgency the factories demanded the abolition of the 'State Duma and State Council, those centres around which counterrevolutionaries of all sorts and hues are grouping'. The Petrograd Union of Woodworkers mandated its delegate to the Third All-Russian Conference of Trade Unions to demand the immediate dispersal of the State Duma and Council and the immediate arrest of all open counterrevolutionaries.[87] And according to *Izvestiya's* account of June 18: 'Again and again the banners: "Proletarians of all lands, unite!", "Confidence in the Congress of S and WD!", "Cease-fire!", "Down with the State Duma and State Council!", "All power to the soviets!", "Down with the counterrevolution!".'[88]

Nor was it only the State Duma. In May, at the Congress of the Kadet Party, the main census party in the coalition, Milyukov was given a standing ovation for his declaration that 'possession of the Straits is the most essential and vital necesssity for our country'. And he continued:

> We have been told that one cannot call forth a revolution. That is not true. I think one can call it forth when it is necessary for the welfare of the fatherland. But if one can call forth a revolution, then one can also stop it if that is necessary for the welfare of Russia.[89]

Novaya zhizn' remarked: 'The physiognomy of the party is now clear: hatred of the red rag.'[90]

It is on this background that one must see the workers' reaction to the 'Durnovo Incident'. The dacha (for some—'palace') of this former Tsarist Minister of Interior, bloody architect of the defeat of the 1905 Revolution, stood next to the Metallicheskii Factory in the Vyborg District and had been occupied after February by local workers' organisations, its shady park becoming a favourite recreational spot for the workers of this grimy district. The building's entire bottom floor, however, was taken over by anarchists, armed to the teeth. On 7 June, the Minister of Interior ordered all unlawful occupants to vacate the premises, but hastily re-edited the order to include only the anarchists—28 factories in the district had struck in the meanwhile. The Soviet Congress finally had the order totally rescinded. However, during the demonstration on 18 June, the anarchists raided the local jail and brought back to the dacha seven of their comrades. Early next morning government troops raided the building, killing one anarchist in a gun battle, arresting 70 other occupants (including members of Metallicheskii's factory committee and union activists), and leaving the place in a shambles.[91]

On learning of this, the entire Vyborg District struck, and the rest of the capital awaited only the signal to come out in demonstration against the government.[92] The Soviet EC responded by setting up a committee to report back in 24 hours. On 19 June, the Soviet Congress discussed the EC's conduct and approved its handling of the affair. The workers, however, were not so satisfied.

> Workers from the Petrograd factories, from different parties, appeared to express their attitudes to the events of the night and marched onto the tribunal one after the other. In a direct and unadorned manner they bitterly reproached the government for the raid on the dacha, for the senseless murder. Some were indignant, others laughed at the grandiose military operation organised against a band of people who had never shed a drop of blood, even now, defending themselves from this military pogrom.
>
> The Congress listened silently and sullenly. Maybe the workers were not correct, but they, in one voice, without respect to party affiliation, were live testimony to the fact that an impassable chasm had opened up between the workers of the capital and the coalition majority.[93]

The workers of the Aivaz Machine-construction Factory left no doubt about the nature of this chasm:

> Despite the pressure of the entire Petrograd proletariat on the Soviet of W and SD to take measures to suppress the rising head to reaction, the inactivity of the Soviet, on the one hand, and the

cooperation of the bourgeois government, on the other, have given the counterrevolution the opportunity to make great strides forward.

In the day of the greatest solidarity of the proletariat, the government mobilised the new 'revolutionary gendarmerie' for a violent operation against anarchist groups at the Durnovo dacha. Instead of an open struggle through word and reason against these opponents of principle who disorganise the proletariat, the government resorted to mass arrests without trial or investigation, calling forth a violent counterreaction that divides the forces of the proletariat.[94]

'We recognise that the tactics of our comrade anarchists are impermissible and harmful', admitted the resolution of the New Lessner Machine-construction Factory,

> but the causes for the creation of such conflicts have their root in the counterrevolutionary policies of the bourgeoisie behind the back of the Socialist ministers. This policy, based very nearly upon the old foundations, gives birth to agitation in the masses. It is possible to eliminate these phenomena only by the transfer of power to the soviets of w and sd (example—Kronstadt. There the anarchists have made no seizures and will not try to).[95]

One of the 'counterrevolutionary policies of the bourgeoisie' alluded to in the revolution that raised a storm of worker protest in the spring of 1917 was the so-called 'unloading' (*razgruzka*) of Petrograd. Though moving at a snail's pace on state economic regulation, the government began work as early as April on a plan to evacuate Petrograd's industry to the provinces, arguing that food and raw materials were more easily obtained there. The workers were immediately suspicious. Besides its economic unsoundness[96] (on which there was widespread, if not unanimous, agreement in soviet circles), the plan appeared to have strong political overtones. To revolutionary democracy, the Petrograd workers were the initiators and the mainstay of the revolution; but they were a sore in the eye of census society, a sore that was in need of surgery. As the Prime Minister, Prince Lvov, lamented at one of the State Duma meetings,

> All Russia has totally sold herself to that idol, Petersburg, which even under the old régime sucked the juices from the people and continues to do so. Russia is being sacrificed to that loud-mouthed insolence, that chaos which is called Petersburg.[97]

At any rate, there were no doubts in the workers' minds about the main intention behind the plan. A meeting of 700 workers of the Kozhevnikovskaya Textile Mill having heard and discussed the report on the unloading of Petrograd, protests against the malicious intentions of the factory and mill owners and our coalition government. We find that the factory and mill owners intend by this unloading to exile by stages part of the revolutionary proletariat beyond the Urals, so that it will be easier [for them] to assume the leadership of the counterrevolutionary movement.[98]

At other factories, it was suggested that it would make better economic sense to rid the capital of its speculators, bureaucrats and other 'idle strollers along Nevskii Prospekt'.[99]

In fact, the Bolsheviks won their first major victory in the Workers' Section of the Soviet on this issue. According to *Izvestiya's* account of the 31 May session,

> In the ensuing debate, representatives of the Central Bureau of Petrograd Trade Unions, the Union of Metalworkers and the Bolsheviks and United SDs [Internationalists] sharply attacked the coalition government and the EC in particular, subjecting the latter to harsh criticism, pointing out the need to transfer power to the hands of the soviets, to demobilise industry immediately, etc. In the plan to unload these speakers saw only a definite move on the part of the bourgeoisie in the interests of the struggle against the political and social aspirations of the proletariat. The Central Bureau of Trade Unions proposed a resolution in the same spirit ... The EC's resolution received 144 votes; that of the Central Bureau—173.

The Bureau's resolution stated that, not 'unloading', but an end to the war and a genuine struggle against economic ruin were needed and that 'a real struggle against it is possible only through regulation and control of all production by state power in the hands of the Soviet of WS and PD'.[100]

Under intense working-class and soviet pressure, the plan was discreetly shelved, for the time being.

Foreign Policy

Soon after the April crisis the government began preparations for a summer offensive. In this connection Kerenskii moved to rescind many of the rights won by the ranks in February: officers were again given the authority to use force against insubordinate troops under battle conditions, while the elected soldiers' committees lost the right to remove commanders or to interfere with battle orders. On paper, at least, the power of the mostly counterrevolutionary officer corps was restored.

The workers, still largely 'revolutionary defencist', saw in these measures a threat to the revolution, and some factories even expressed sympathy for the soldiers being disciplined for insubordination. The general assembly of the Nevskii Shoe Factory indignantly protested against the disciplinary disbanding of military units:

> The insubordination of these regiments is a consequence of the soldiers' justified anger over the tactics of offensive. The ruinous tactic of annexations could not but meet with a rebuff on the part of conscious soldiers. We express our solidarity with the soldiers of the disbanded regiments.[101]

Also alarming was the government's announced intention to send part of the capital's garrison to the front in disregard of the February accord between the Soviet and the Duma Committee that the garrison remain intact to protect the heart of the revolution.

In fact, under the impact of the government's policies, the workers 'revolutionary defencism' was fast dissolving. It had been premised upon the government's active search for a general peace, but after the April crisis any peace offensive was drowned in the preparation for the military offensive. Meanwhile, the Allies replied to the government's appeal for a general peace and the rejection of annexations and reparations by emphasising the need to 'overthrow Prussian militarism', 'just reparation for losses' and the restoration of Russia's military might. Inside Russia, it was no secret that this offensive was being undertaken under the most intense and varied pressures from London, Paris and, not least, Washington.[102]

In the light of all this, it is not surprising that Kerenskii's attempts to portray the offensive as merely a tactical, but not political, question[103] did not convince the workers. To them the offensive was an unjustified termination of the *de facto* ceasefire that had reigned at the front since February. Given the Allies' rejection of the Soviet's peace policy and the government's at best ambiguous acceptance of it, the offensive could only hurt the chances of peace by severely damaging the international authority of the Russian Revolution as an example to be emulated by the other peoples who wanted to end the slaughter. Even *Rabochaya gazeta*, which supported the offensive, admitted that the slogan 'immediate general ceasefire' was 'very popular'. A mass meeting of workers and soldiers on the Plains of Mars broke into applause at every mention of 'ceasefire'.[104]

Foreign policy was a prominent topic at all factory meetings, where the debates more and more concluded with the demand for soviet power. A joint meeting of the tool and pattern-making shops and the iron and copper foundries at the Putilov Works in early June sent its greeting to the Soviet Congress, adding:

We hope that foreign policy, which now stands frozen on the issue of peace without annexations, ... will at once start to move off that spot ... and we similarly hope that the All-Russian Congress will decide the fate of the power of our coalition PG and that the Congress will now declare that power should be transferred to the hands of democracy.[105]

On 15 June, both shifts at the Old Parviainen Machine-construction Factory resolved unanimously that

the politics of conciliation with our capitalists and through them with the capitalists of the world [are] ruinous for the cause of the Russian and International Revolutions, for the cause of the world unification of the proletariat.
  We call on all our comrade proletarians and semi-proletarians of the village to a decisive break with the policy of imperialism and conciliation with imperialism—a policy directed at reducing the Russian Revolution to the role of executor of the desires of international capital. The Russian Revolution, which calls the toilers of the wide world to struggle against capitalism, must give a worthy example of this struggle ... Down with the power of the capitalists! Long live the revolutionary proletariat and peasantry! Away with the politics of powerlessness, politics of conciliation with worldwide plunderers! Peace for the whole world! Peace to the hovels, war to the palaces! ... Neither a separate peace with Wilhelm nor secret treaties with the English and French capitalists. Immediate publication by the Soviet of truly just peace conditions. Against the policy of offensive. Bread. Peace. Freedom.[106]

In an ironic replay of the April scenario, when the May Day celebrations coincided with the dispatch of the Milyukov note, on 18 June, while the workers were in the streets demonstrating their lack of confidence in the coalition, demanding soviet power, the government launched the offensive. The Soviet plenum (Workers' and Soldiers' Section) of 20 June approved it by 472 votes against 271 with 39 abstentions.[107] But considering that the largely conservative garrison was heavily overrepresented in this body and that the Soviet Congress the previous day had lent the full weight of its authority to the offensive, this vote appeared as a victory for the internationalists. To a growing majority of Petrograd's workers, the offensive was nothing less than a stab in the back of the revolution. 'We declare', went the resolution of the New Lessner Machine-construction Factory (one of many similar resolutions),

that a blow has been dealt to the Russian Revolution and the International by this offensive, and the whole responsibility for this policy lies with the PG and the party of Mensheviks and SRs supporting it ... We need not an offensive at the front but an offensive against the bourgeoisie inside the country for the transfer of power into the hands of the Soviet of W and SD.[108]

The Economy

The appearance in the second half of April of the demand for economic regulation marked a definite deepening of the social content of the revolution, until then largely concerned with destroying the remnants of the old régime and attending to the grievances it had bequeathed. For the workers, economic regulation was a new issue born of the new conditions created by the revolution. But in this instance too, it was intimately bound up with the growing perception of the bourgeoisie as counterrevolutionary. For surely the most concrete and immediate manifestation of the counterrevolutionary mood of the capitalists, for those workers who shared this view, was their perceived sabotage of the economy—on the national level, in their opposition to attempts at state economic regulation, and on the local level, in their growing 'loss of interest' in production and the alarming tendency to cut back and ultimately close down. Nor did the workers see this as merely an economic tactic; it was at least as political, aimed at weakening and disorganising the proletariat, the vanguard of the revolution. 'Of late', wrote *Novaya zhizn'* in early May,

one observes a curtailment of production in a whole series of enterprises. So far this phenomenon had manifested itself only in medium and small enterprises, but all the same it is beginning to alarm the worker masses. The advanced workers are beginning to ask if there is not any relationship between their new economic gains and the curtailment of production that follows.[109]

This was the period when the flight of capital first became noticeable. *Novoe vremya*, which no one had ever accused of harbouring anti-capitalist sentiments, reported in June that owners were selling their plants, transferring the cash abroad and taking off after it in fulfilment of the old Russian proverb, 'where my treasure is, there lies my heart'.[110]

In Petrograd's largely British-owned textile industry, the entrepreneurs, alarmed at the course of the revolution, had taken to liquidating their current accounts and shipping to nearby Finland finished and semi-finished goods and even, where they could get away with it, raw materials and machine parts. Some mills were already on a reduced week. The Textile Workers' Union journal *Tkach* reported a case where management told the workers it had to curtail production because of insufficient raw cotton, while these same raw materials from the mill were being loaded onto barges for destinations unknown. Another textile entrepreneur, Charles Munken, left for Finland in May to buy spools and ended up in England, soon to be followed by his partners and the English managerial personnel, whose last administrative act was to empty the safes. Even Percy Thornton, who enjoyed a rare liberal reputation among Petrograd's capitalists, was threatening to pack it in.[111]

Before the revolution, and even in the early spring of 1917, the leaders of census society had tended to attribute the economic problems to Tsarist misgovernment and the effects of the war. Now, all this was forgotten. Kadet CC member and prominent businessman, Kutler, painted a most gloomy picture at his party's congress: the economic mechanism was destroyed by the workers' ousting of various managerial personnel. Productivity had fallen 20 to 40 per cent. Anarchy and disorganisation ruled. But the main problem, he lamented, were the 'inordinate demands' of the workers, 'making management of the enterprises impossible'.[112] Commenting on this speech, *Rech'* ominously predicted: 'Two or three weeks will pass, and the factories will start to close one after the other.'[113]

As for state regulation of the economy, this hardly got off the ground, mainly due to the opposition of the capitalists. In mid-May the Soviet EC approved an economic plan calling for broad state regulation of production, distribution and finance. Two days later, A. I. Konovalov, Minister of Trade and Industry (himself a wealthy Moscow industrialist), resigned 'in view of the impossibility of working productively in the given conditions'. In his letter to Prince Lvov, he explained that he had no quarrel with the Minister of Labour (Skobelev, Menshevik–Defencist member of the EC) on most issues, not even on financial reforms or labour relations. But he was 'sceptical about the form of public control and the measures of economic regulation proposed by the Minister of Labour'. There would be hope of averting the crisis he advised, only if the 'PG demonstrated, at the least, truly full authority, if it at least entered upon the path of restoring discipline that had become lax and showed energy in the struggle against the excessive demands of the extreme Left'.[114] Put bluntly, his alternative to economic regulation was to rein in the workers. At the Congress of War-Industry Committees, he again railed against the 'excessive demands of the workers' and warned: 'If in the near future a sobering of minds does not occur, we will witness the closing of tens and hundreds of enterprises'.[115]

Now, Konovalov was no arch-reactionary. Avilov, a left Menshevik, described him as 'a very conciliatory figure and on the extreme left of the industrial-commercial class, . . . a favourite of the Moscow capitalists . . . . who knows this group well'. If Konovalov was unwilling to give up *laissez-faire*, there was no hope for the rest of his class.[116] And sure enough, the keynote of the All-Russian Congress of Representatives of Trade and Industry (1–2 June) was opposition to any form of state economic control.[117]

Why this opposition to a measure that had been accepted by the capitalist class of other warring countries? Ryabushinskii, another member of the haute bourgeoisie and also a 'leftist' explained:

> In Europe, the state, in intervening into the sphere of national [economic] life, receives full control, to which we do not object. But we fear that such control is impossible in Russia in terms of its usefulness for the state as a whole as long as our government continues to be in the position of being controlled itself.[118]

To put this in non-Aesopian language, the Soviet and revolutionary democracy had too much power in the state for the capitalists to allow it to intervene in the economy, since such regulation could be exerted to the detriment of the interests of capital.

Interestingly enough, virtual unanimity reigned in soviet circles, from right to left, in their evaluation of the economic policies of the bourgeoisie. *Rabochaya gazeta*, whose platform was an alliance between the working class and census society and which certainly had no interest in painting the capitalists black, summarised its view of the situation in an editorial that is worth quoting at length:

> In the industrialists' camp there is animation. The brief stupor which seized them in the first days of the Revolution has passed. Now no trace remains of their recent confusion and panicky tendency to make concessions. In the first month of freedom the united industrialists offering almost no resistance, granted the workers' demands. Now they have decisively passed to the defensive and are quick making ready for an offensive along the entire front ...
>
> They are not deciding immediately to declare open war on the workers. The volcanic soil for the Revolution is still too red-hot, the working class still too threatening in its bursts of revolutionary enthusiasm for the industrialists, at least in the given moment, to decide on a frontal assault in order to smash the enemy with a counter-thrust.
>
> But the intensification of the general course of economic ruin, the advancing spectre of mass unemployment, the social fright of the possessing classes—all this will create a favourable ground for carrying out the entrepreneurs' plan for the offensive. And having decided not to advance openly 'down the middle', they are attempting an encircling movement around the flank in order to attack the enemy from the rear. Of late, more and more frequently one hears of an 'Italian strike' [slowdown strike] practised by the entrepreneurs

now here, now there. The plants are not being repaired, worn parts are not replaced, work is conducted in a slipshod manner. The entrepreneurs shout at all crossroads that the 'excessive demands' of the workers are not realisable and are directly disastrous to the enterprises. They generously propose, or at least pretend to propose, that the government lift from them the unbearable burden of running the enterprises.

In other cases, they cut back on production, dismiss workers under the pretext of lack of metal, fuel, orders, the competition of imports. We have before us a different means of struggle—the hidden lockout.

In the Labour Department of the Soviet of W and SD one daily encounters facts that confirm the existence of a definite plan of the industrialists.[119]

This was the same analysis shared by growing numbers of the working class itself. Zhivotov, delegate from the 1886 Power Co. to the First Conference of Petrograd Factory Committees in early June, asserted:

For us workers it is clear that the bourgeoisie is organising a counterrevolution against democracy and especially its vanguard, the working class ...

It has conducted its counterrevolutionary offensive very skilfully, and, at first glance, imperceptibly, disorganising production, aggravating the economic dislocation and the scarcity of goods. It is even prepared to call forth hunger, riot and anarchy in order later to set up a dictatorship and with the aid of the military to do away with anarchy and at the same time with the Revolution, because to them it is anarchy.

You have to be blind not to see this counterrevolutionary work. Sabotage in the Donbass, in the textile industry, in a whole number of Petrograd factories requires the organised intervention of the working class in the form of the immediate establishment of workers' control, which alone can put an end to the counterrevolutionary ideas of the capitalists ... It is naive to think that the PG will set up control over its own capitalists ... Undoubtedly in the near future life will put forth this demand for workers' control over production, but it will be fully realised not in bourgeois government but in a government of revolutionary democracy.[120]

The conclusion was clear: a government whose task was to control the counterrevolutionary capitalists could not have in it representatives of that same capitalist class. It had to be a government exclusively of revolutionary democracy, i.e. a soviet government. Zhivotov's words were echoed by other worker delegates, such as Tseitlin from the Kersten Knitwear Mill, who took the 'conciliators' to task:

> Foreseeing unemployment, we can't allow it to ruin us. You [Skobelev, Dan and other moderate socialist speakers] say that we can't take power into our hands now because the masses aren't organised. But when they're hungry, we won't be able to do anything. We need to create such a government that will avert hunger—to create those organs mentioned in the resolution. We need a strong centre of factory committees that will be the ministry of labour of the proletariat. It, of course, will act more decisively than that of Skobelev. We need to regulate production, arrange its demobilisation. In this the workers must show initiative in this direction, not pinning hope on those sitting in ministerial chairs. Where will the money come from? Take it from our marauders who hypocritically cry out about the 'Liberty Loan', which remains on the placards. We should take the money and not act like artists, begging on the streets for a 'Liberty Loan' of pennies from the bourgeoisie. We have to look at things as they are, not like the conciliators with the bourgeoisie tell us they are. We must demand categorically. With conciliations you'll get nothing.[121]

Dan, speaking for the Soviet EC, totally opposed this line of thought: 'To say the workers should take on themselves the direction of production means that the workers should take state power. And I protest that such a conference should raise any sort of political questions.'[122] But he protested in vain. The very logic of the situation drove the workers most involved in issues of production to call for soviet power. This logic did not escape even the most moderate of the Soviet leaders. When the Economic Department of the Soviet, consisting of Groman and other mostly moderate Mensheviks, presented its plan for state economic regulation to the EC, Skobelev exclaimed: 'You want to seize power!'[123] Skobelev understood only too well that even this mild programme would be unacceptable to the census partners in the coalition; it could be carried out only if their opposition was overcome, i.e. by eliminating them from power.[124]

The two-thirds vote for the Bolshevik-sponsored resolution at the Factory Committee Conference was, thus, no accident, even if it was not an accurate reflection of the strength of support for soviet power among the worker masses as a whole. Work in the factory committees forced even those with 'conciliationist' sympathies to the left.[125] A Bolshevik worker from the Admiralty Shipyards recalled:

> At the First Conference of Factory Committees I was a delegate along with a Menshevik and an SR. My opponents voted with me on

all the basic questions ... Our [i.e. Bolshevik] resolutions were passed. One of my opponents tore up his card at his party meeting and joined our party several days later.[126]

Of the three types of issues—foreign and domestic political and economic—in which workers perceived the counterrevolutionary face of census society, it was the latter that appeared to play an especially important role in the limited political radicalisation that did occur among the unskilled workers before July. For the majority of these workers the issues discussed in the preceding pages were still too abstract to make much of an impact, including even the issue of economic regulation, as most factories had still not been directly touched by the incipient economic crisis. However, once a serious economic conflict did arise in their particular factory, it often served as a catalyst to political radicalisation, though this was not an automatic process by any means.

As noted earlier, the unskilled workers tended to be much more militant in economic questions than in political ones. Describing the conflicts that began to arise in the textile industry over the issue of declining production, in which the workers saw concealed sabotage, Perazich, a Bolshevik, observed that

in some mills the local Mensheviks and SRs had managed already by that time [before July] to compromise themselves sufficiently in the eyes of the worker masses with their speeches in defence of the owners' rights. So it was, for example, at James Beck, where a group of Mensheviks and SRs from the former followers of Gapon lost all credit in the eyes of the [women] workers, who would raise a hue and cry if Manulin, Galybin or E. Tikhon would try to ascend the speaker's platform. But at the same time these workers would listen with approval to the demagogic speeches of other Mensheviks, not from their own plant, who came from neighbouring mills. In general, our masses at that time were still quite benighted politically and followed the Mensheviks and SRs. At Thornton, when the left SR Marusya Spiridonova spoke in that period for the slogan 'All power to the Soviets', they did not let her continue and shouted: 'Get down ... Hard labour convict ... Murderer!'[127]

(This was at a time when over in the Vyborg District workers were tearing down the banners of 'conciliationist' agitators.[128])

In early June, at the Bolshevik PC, Slutskii, a delegate from the strongly SR Nevskii District, noted the same phenomenon:

Listen to what the workers say after the meetings at which they applauded orators standing on the platform of the Soviet of W and

SD. In so far as the question touches their essential needs—rates, inflation, raises, the evacuation—if these issues have touched this stratum, then the agitation in the masses is great.

In other words, for these workers to become interested and angry the issue had to be very concrete—on the whole economic—and it had to be directly experienced. Drawing a parallel with peasant political consciousness, Slutskii continued:

The same can be seen also among the peasants: in politics the peasants are able to orient themselves very poorly. But as far as the solution of the land question is concerned, they are radical. Take only the sixth point of their resolution [May 25, at the First All-Russian Congress of Peasant Representatives] where they say clearly that one must kick out the appointed government commissars.[128]

The classic case of an economic conflict having a directly radicalising effect was that of the Putilov Works, whose 30 000 workers were a microcosm of the Petrograd working class.[129] During the 1912–14 period, the Bolsheviks became undisputed leaders of this factory which was in the van of the escalating economic and political movement. According to management, the factory struck 102 days in 1913 and 145 in the first half of 1914, mainly over political issues.[130] During the war, however, although the Putilov workers sent a majority of Bolsheviks to the second stage of the War-Industry Committee elections, they were no longer at the militant front of the workers' movement. A police report from February 1916 observed that

from the start of the war a sharp turn occurred among the workers, and patriotic sentiment got the upper hand over socialist sentiment. Over time, the patriotic sentiment declined significantly, but justice requires one to note the unconditional loyalty and restraint of the Putilov workers, who did not participate in such traditional time-honoured labour demonstrations as May 1 and January 9.

For the entire previous year, the report continued, attempts by the Bolsheviks to draw the workers into the movement failed to yield results.[131]

The reasons for this turn must be sought in the changed social composition of the Putilov workers during the war. About 6000 pre-war workers were drafted, while the total work force more than doubled as the factory expanded massively into ordnance production. There were no less than 10 000 unskilled labourers (*chernorabochie*) by 1917.[132]

However, after their failure to persuade the workers to demonstrate on 9 January 1916, the Bolsheviks changed tactics, playing down politics in favour of economic demands. The results were soon in coming. Indeed, on the very date the report was written, the factory was on strike over economic conditions.[133]

In the first three months after the February Revolution, the Putilov Factory remained among the more politically moderate in the capital, with the exception of the more skilled shops, like tool-making, which supported the demand for soviet power early on. The first election to the Petrograd Soviet in the factory sent only 9 Bolsheviks out of 45 delegates. In the first months 'innumerable defencist resolutions' were passed.[134] On the other hand, in the economic sphere, the Bolsheviks had much more to feel happy about. In local elections to the Metalworkers' and Woodworkers' Unions they did surprisingly well, and in the 14 April factory committee elections, 6 party members and 7 sympathisers were elected, a majority of the 22-member committee.[135] Clearly, the workers preferred the more militant activists when it came to their economic interests.

The change in political attitudes of the majority of the workers began at the end of May, and the catalyst was the festering 'conflict of 7 March', involving new wage rates approved by the director on 19 April, that were to be introduced retroactively from 7 March. But as the weeks went by the difference was not made up. The administration remained silent. Slowdown strikes began. Finally the board of directors announced that the director had overstepped his authority and had no right to make any such promises. The workers sent delegations to the various ministries (the factory had earlier been sequestered by the state) but to no avail. A strike was set for 8 June, but the Bolsheviks persuaded the workers to wait. On 13 June the Menshevik leader Gvozdev, Vice-Minister of Labour, promised he would fight to obtain the workers' demands, which he admitted were justified. However, at the insistence of the board of directors he agreed to postpone a decision once more until the PSFMO and the Metalworkers' Union completed talks.

This further delay so enraged the workers that they marched in the 18 June demonstration under the banner: 'Comrades, we have been deceived! Prepare for battle!'[136]

Was this deception a reference to the economic dispute at the Putilov Works or to the entire policy of the coalition government *vis-à-vis* the working class? In fact, it was both. Gessen, delegate to the Bolshevik PC from the Narva District (location of the Putilov Works), reported on 20 June:

In the Narva District there has been a sharp shift in mood in our favour, as the new elections have shown at which Bolsheviks were elected. The Putilov Factory, which determines the mood of the whole district, has decisively adhered to our position with the passing of Trotsky's resolution. The militant mood of the Putilov Factory has deep economic causes. There the question of a wage rise is acute. The workers' demands on rises have not been satisfied since the very start of the Revolution. Gvozdev came to the plant, promised to satisfy the demands that have been put forward but did not carry out his promise. At the demonstration of June 18 the Putilovtsy also carried this placard: 'We have been deceived!' This morning the factory decided to strike. The Union of Metalworkers proposed that the strike be postponed for three days to notify the other factories. The Putilovtsy agreed to work these three days, but certain shops decided on a slowdown strike. The masses consider the strike to be political. The workers decided to arm themselves by Wednesday. Earlier, the Putilovtsy were not at the head of the movement; now they are pushed there by economic causes.[137]

The SR paper reported on 20 June: 'The mood is tense. There are meetings in all shops, and calls for an immediate armed demonstration, not only in defence of the [economic] demands, but also against the general direction of the PG's activity.'

And what of the still very significant working-class minority that continued to support the coalition government? As noted earlier, these were largely unskilled workers (though their numbers, too, were slowly shrinking) and the worker 'aristocracy'. Among the former, there was a marked increase in militancy over economic issues in this period (inflation had already eaten up much of the gains of March[138])[139] but for the most part this was not directly translated into politics. Nevertheless, the abstention of the 'conciliationist' workers from the 18 June demonstration indicated that here too consciousness had not stood still.

What is striking about the more active and politically conscious elements that still supported the coalition is that they, like the moderate leaders of the Soviet, did not so much disagree with the left's evaluation of census society as they felt that soviet power was not a viable solution. One of the few Menshevik delegates at the Factory Committee Conference in early June, Tkachenko, from the Electric Lighting Co., put it this way:

Zinoviev [speaker for the Bolshevik Party] already sees in the attempts of the West European workers at protest batallions coming to storm the bastions of capitalism. He told us of our age-old hatred of the capitalists, of the millions they have made from our blood, of the insults of our enemy exploiters that we suffer on our hides every hour of every day. He said that the socialist ministers are being led around by the bourgeois plunderers and told us to expect nothing from them. But ... he did not show us who in the final victory will accompany us in the struggle for power. Workers alone cannot hold power without the peasantry. You all know who the peasantry said they would support at their congress ... Let us not forget that we live in a period of the bourgeois-democratic revolution under very difficult conditions. We must act cautiously and not take steps that are too risky, so that we don't add problems that we won't be able to solve to the already existing ruin ... The workers by themselves will not be able to cope with the tasks of control and distribution without the cooperation of all democracy and against the open opposition of the big bourgeoisie and intelligentsia. Fear total isolation from the rest of democracy. For once we are alone, we will be smashed, and over our bodies the captains of industry will climb onto the ship and seize the helm of power.[140]

Tkachenko offered no positive arguments in favour of the coalition; he merely argued that if the soviets took power the working class would find itself isolated and would go down to defeat. *Novaya zhizn*'s correspondent at the Food Supply Conference in May reached a similar conclusion. He found a left and a right faction and a majority of centrists, who

do not believe in the capitalists but are afraid of any decisive measures directed at the liquidation of property privileges. The path of Russia's future development appears to them as a struggle against insurmountable obstacles; now and then they point to the 'greyness' and ignorance of the masses, their tendency to anarchy, the absence of firm government, the obstinacy of the merchants and industrialists.[141]

Similarly, resolutions in support of the moderate Soviet leadership never referred to any achievements of the coalition. The most positive note sounded was the call for unity—against the Bolsheviks who are depicted as splitters. On 16 June the printers of the Otto Kirkhner Bindery and Printing House, after a lengthy debate on slogans for 18 June, resolved:

We consider that the Bolsheviks are making a gross mistake in their evaluation of the current moment, which calls for the unity of the forces of revolutionary democracy, and that they are harming the cause of the Revolution by introducing disorganisation into the midst of the working class. We propose that the whole Petrograd Proletariat demonstrate on June 18 against their capitalist class who are the main culprits behind this war which drags on.[142]

Here the capitalists are also seen as the enemy, but soviet power is opposed to the need for unity.

Given that the main remaining basis for their support of the coalition was essentially negative[143] (and fear was always a major element in the psychological make-up of women and peasant workers), it is not surprising that most of these workers failed to come out on 18 June. In fact, the local defencist leaders were put in a very embarassing situation—they did not have any affirmative slogans they could put forward. On 20 June at the Bolshevik PC the delegate from the Moscow District reported: 'The SRs are still very strong. The Soviet's marking time and our [cancelled] June 10 demonstration saw a shift in the workers' mood in our favour ... Before the eighteenth the SRs were totally disoriented, not knowing what slogans to put forward.' And in the Nevskii District, 'until the demonstration we were, or at least we seemed, very weak. The Mensheviks and SRs were thrown into confusion and did not put forth their slogans. Before the demonstration they were busy scaring the people, and few went out.'[144]

In less than four months the political attitudes of all in Petrograd had undergone a major transformation. Does one explain so sudden and drastic a shift in terms of the fickleness of disoriented and unstable masses, uneducated to the ways of democracy, as Western historiography has traditionally sought to do? I have tried here to argue that what occurred in these four months was rather a process of clarification, a deepening of consciousness on the basis of the unfolding of events.

Besides the evidence I have cited above, I am supported in this by the views of contemporary observers on both the right and the left of the socialist camp. Comparing 18 June to 23 March and 18 April (May Day) Lenin wrote:

Then, it was a universal *celebration* of the first victory of the Revolution and its heroes, a glance thrown backward by the people at the first most successfully and swiftly completed stage toward freedom. May First was a *holiday* of the aspirations and the hopes tied up with the history of the worldwide labour movement, with its socialist ideal.

Neither demonstration set as its goal to show the *direction* of the further movement of the Revolution, and they could not have shown it. Neither posed to the masses the concrete, specific and burning questions of whether and how the Revolution should proceed.

In this sense the eighteenth of June was the first demonstration of *action*, a clarification—not in pamphlet or newspaper, but through the masses—clarification of how the various classes act, want to act, will act in order to carry the Revolution further.[145]

Izvestiya, which unlike Lenin was the big loser on 18 June, concurred:

> The characteristic difference between the present demonstration and those of March 23 and May 1 was the abundance of banners and the precision of slogans. If the former unity no longer exists, now at least everyone is more acutely aware of what he is struggling for and what the next tasks of the struggle are.[146]

7 The Struggle for Power in the Factories in April–June

The issue of economic regulation, one of the focal points of the intensifying political struggle around the demand for soviet power, found its analogue in this period in the unfolding struggle for power in the factories under the banner of workers' control.

The conflict at the Langezipen Machine-construction Factory is a case in point. At the end of April, the Senior Factory Inspector for Petrograd Guberniya reported:

> Guards posted by the workers on April 27 refused to allow the administration to leave before the end of work. As a result, the factory director was forced to remain in his office until 4:00 p.m. The workers of this factory suspect the administration of holding up defence production. Accordingly, the issue is being discussed by a mixed commission of the Soviet of W and SD, the Society of Factory and Mill Owners, the Union of Engineers and the Central War-Industry Committee.[1]

The conflict came to a head on 2 June when the director announced his intention of closing operations, citing a 33 per cent decline in output, 10 million ruble losses on state orders, and lack of funds, all due to the eight-hour day, a 50 per cent decline in labour productivity, constantly rising prices, and finally, shortages of fuel and raw materials.

At the request of the workers, the Central Soviet (CS) of Factory Committees (elected at the conference in early June) enquired into the company's ownership. Although the director refused to cooperate, it was finally ascertained that the original owner had been the Azov-Don Bank, but it had transferred its stocks to a certain Zhivotov, who in turn transferred them to the Siberian Bank of Commerce, which registered them in the name of Kislyanskii. However, by this time, the director informed the workers that he had quite unexpectedly 'come across' 450 000 rubles, borrowed from an acquaintance, and production would go ahead full speed.[2]

But in the interim, the workers had set up full control over management. On 5 June, the factory committee reported:

The situation of late at the factories of the Langezipen Co. Inc., i.e. 1) the refusal of the factory administration to recognise the control commission of the workers and employees 2) the violation by the administration of the decision of the conciliation chamber of May 6, 1917 on the amount of wages for employees and 3) the latest declaration of the administration on the closure of the plant—have placed us before the necessity of taking the following measures: 1) No goods or raw materials may be shipped out from the factory without permission of the factory committee, and also manufactured goods ready for shipment must be registered by the factory committee and are stamped by it. 2) All orders of the factory committee are binding on all workers and employees, and no order from the administration is valid without the sanction of the factory committee. 3) No papers or correspondence relating to the factory can be destroyed without the factory committee reviewing them. 4) To carry out the above tasks the elected control commission will begin to fulfil its duties from today. 5) The firemen and guards are duty-bound to keep watch over the factory's buildings against fire.[3]

Two weeks later, this control commission asked the government to hold up payment of dividends pending a full state investigation. The commission itself began work on a counter-report to that of management and requested that the Ministry of Labour obtain for it the necessary documents. Finally, it turned to the CS of Factory Committees for aid in drawing up regulations and working procedures for the factory committee.[4]

Izvestiya described this conflict as characteristic of a 'whole series of declarations on closure by the owners' that had been reaching the CS of Factory Committees. The paper observed that despite the variety of reasons given, in most cases they boiled down to lack of funds and financial losses. 'However, at the first attempt of the workers' organisations to verify the reasons offered by the entrepreneurs, very often the most complex and crafty machinations aimed at a lockout by the capitalists are uncovered.'[5]

What is characteristic in the Langezipen conflict is the workers' perception of their actions as essentially defensive, aimed at forestalling a further decline in production or a total shutdown, which they suspected—in this case clearly not without foundation—were the result of passive, or even active, sabotage on the part of the administration. Thus, the 5 June declaration states that the owner's intention to close 'placed us before the *necessity* of taking ... measures'. The overriding motivation was to safeguard the workers' livelihood, their factory and, in the last analysis, the revolution, as the assembly of the Voronin and Co. Cotton Printing Factory forcefully pointed out:

On hearing the report of the systematic decline in production at the factories of Voronin and Co. ... [we resolve that:] The observed decline in production of late at the factories of Voronin and Co. is the conscious activity of the industrialists, aimed at bringing the country to ruin and thus destroying the freedom won by the great Russian Revolution. Taking into account the seriousness of this hidden counterrevolution, the general assembly mandates the factory committee, together with the committees and employees of the other factories belonging to the given company, to elect a control commission which must control the activity of the company in its production of goods. In so far as a desire to disorganise production in the enterprises is discovered, inform the Soviet of W and SD and the PG.[6]

An estimate of the proportion of conflicts in which the workers' suspicions were justified is beyond the scope of this study. However, an investigation by *Torgovo-promyshlennaya gazeta*, the newspaper of the industrialists, in the spring of 1917 found that of the 75 plant closures in Petrograd since April, 54 had been motivated by the desire to break the workers' pressure and 21 by supply difficulties.[7] According to *Den'*, a non-socialist paper, 'If in some cases these closures are motivated by lack of raw materials, in many others the aim is to intimidate the workers and the Provisional Government.'[8] At any rate, these suspicions had firm basis in a sufficient number of cases[9] almost automatically to raise doubts in the workers' minds whenever a serious problem arose. Perhaps more importantly, the workers viewed these conflicts against the background of both the government's plan to 'unload' Petrograd and the long history of recourse to lockouts by Petrograd industrialists as a favourite means of struggle against the workers' political as well as economic demands.

The defensive or reactive nature of workers' control explains why the demand did not really come into its own until May when the situation had become sufficiently serious. Even so, control in the sense of access to documents and comprehensive monitoring of management was still very rare in this period. A Soviet study of 'instances of control' for May and June in 84 Petrograd factories (employing 230 000 workers) found that only 24.5 per cent of all cases involved any sort of control over production, with another 8.7 per cent over finances and sales. For the rest, 24.6 per cent had to do with 'control over conditions of work', 24.1 per cent with hiring and dismissals, and 7.5 per cent with guarding the plants—all areas previously subsumed under the March demand for 'control over internal order'.[10]

In other words, workers' control was a practical demand born of the new situation in which the workers found themselves. As V. M. Levin, a Left SR member of the CS of Factory Committees, stated:

No party programme foresaw the intervention of the working class into the bourgeois economy with a bourgeois government [in power]. Now all recognise its necessity. True, they were forced to this in order to avoid finding themselves out on the streets.[11]

In fact, it was only on 19 May that the Bolshevik PC issued its first call to the workers to establish control, and the wording of this appeal is significant: 'In response to a series of declarations from factory committees on the need for control and its establishment, it was decided to recommend to the comrade workers to create control commissions in the enterprises from workers' representatives.'[12]

There is no doubt that the movement for workers' control originated from below, from the factories. 'When the factory committee arose', wrote the committee at the Putilov Works,

it was given neither a programme of action nor a charter by which to guide its work. As the functions of the the committee developed, its practical instructions became the basis for its guiding principles. In this way, the factory committee had the best teacher—life.[13]

The same is true of the initiative for city-wide and national organisation of workers' control. Osipov, a worker from the Benois Factory, told the First Factory Committee Conference:

At our factory, the boss announced that there isn't any money and he is throwing 500 workers out ... The factory committee of Benois answered with a resolution sent to the ministries showing that production is being conducted in an irregular manner and demonstrating the incompetence of the entrepreneur. We showed figures that production is rising, but that there are neither materials nor money. Yesterday, workers from the factory spoke to Pal'chinskii [acting Minister of Trade and Industry]. He sent them to the Military Authority. They said they couldn't help. It shows that we cannot work alone—only the proletariat as a whole.[14]

Even the idea of a city conference appears to have come from below,[15] and its timeliness was demonstrated by the fact that the Central Soviet was swamped with appeals for aid immediately upon its creation by the conference.

The practical nature of the movement also explains why workers' control developed so unevenly. In June it ranged from full control, as instituted at Langezipen, to merely searching for additional supplies. It was noted at the Second Conference in August that some factories still did not even have factory committees.[16]

Since the most pressing problem initially was fuel and raw materials, supply questions were the first and most widespread area of worker intervention into administrative functions. In fact, a workers' conference on fuel and raw materials preceded by some weeks the First Conference of Factory Committees,[17] and many factories had sent out workers' delegations to the Donbass and elsewhere to facilitate and speed up the delivery of supplies.[18]

The Factory Committee of the Rozenkrantz Copper Foundry described its early activity in the following manner:

> Our first steps were to struggle for better wage rates, and we achieved this. Then we took decisive measures to enlarge the work force. The factory was very poorly supplied with fuel, and only a trip by representatives of the factory committee fixed this. The factory committee had to put pressure on the administration for the speedy execution of orders. On the other hand, there were whole piles of [finished] orders that our clients refused to accept. The factory committee took the regulation of this matter upon itself and achieved favourable results. We observed that the furnaces in the foundry were stopping due to a lack of bricks, and only thanks to the intervention of the factory committee did we obtain what was needed.[19]

This report illustrates how the workers saw themselves being forced into action to compensate for the lack of initiative of management or, as Levin put it at the Conference, its 'Italian strike'.

> Strangely, after the first weeks of the revolution, in one factory after another there was no fuel, raw materials, money. More important, the administration took no steps to secure what was necessary. All saw that this was an Italian strike. The factory committees sent representatives all over in search of fuel to other factory committees, to railroad junctions, warehouses, etc. ... As a result of their activity, oil and coal, orders, money were found. Why, it is no secret that an end to the economic dislocation is not only not in the interests of capital, but contradictory to them. To end the dislocation would mean to strengthen the young growing organisms of our revolution—and no one knows how that revolution will end up: at the least, in the deprivation of capital of a part of its rights; at the most, who will say that from a Russian revolution it will not become a world revolution?[20]

The workers, on their part, were by no means averse to cooperating with management and even to making considerable sacrifices, as long as they believed that management was acting in good faith. In mid-July the management of the Baltic Wagon-construction Factory announced its intention of closing down automobile production because of its unprofitability. When the factory committee produced figures that put this assertion into question, management offered to continue production if the workers would guarantee the profitability of operations. The workers agreed but put forth a condition—workers' control over production and all accounts—which management rejected as 'unprecedented'.[21] The workers were willing to cooperate and more but they refused to be used.[22] At the August Factory Committee Conference, Antipov, a 23-year-old Vyborg worker, explained why he opposed worker participation in public economic bodies alongside the capitalists.

Can our comrades achieve anything by participating in conferences with the industrialists? It would be possible to liquidate the ruin by such means if the owners were really unable correctly to manage production. But here it is a question of an absence of desire on the part of the owners, and we will not be able to force them by means of these conferences. They are making no concessions, and therefore we have no reason to go to them.[23]

Perhaps the most forceful expression of the real motive behind workers' control—concern for production—issued from the committee of the Schlusselburg Powder Factory, whose chairman, Zhuk, was, significantly, an anarchist. It will be recalled that the manager had praised the workers in March for their conscientiousness. At the First Factory Committee Conference, however, Zhuk brought evidence of the administration's desire to close down. He then read his committee's declaration, which took note of the sorry state of industry and the often negligent attitude of management and continued:

Tarrying not a single moment, the toilers must organise a better management . . . and not trust the owners. The workers themselves must elect specialists in each area so that work will begin to move ahead at full throttle and every kopek will be accounted for. In these elections the workers should be guided not only be personal sympathies for individual managers, engineers and foremen, but also by the latter's experience and knowledge. Not one hour of wasted work: all time only for useful labour![24]

There is not the least trace of the anti-specialist attitudes that appeared during the civil war.

As for anarchist influence in the movement at large, the vote at the conference showed this to be minimal, and this is confirmed by the very limited number of takeovers before October. The above-mentioned study found that only 1.4 per cent of the cases involved actual workers' self-management. But even these followed the generally defensive pattern, occurring when the only alternative was passively to accept closure. And even so, the workers turned to the state for aid and demanded it sequester the factory. There was no thought of setting up any sort of workers' cooperative.[25]

But, as noted, cases of takeover were very rare in this period, the main thrust of the movement being for 'control', in the sense of monitoring and observation. No claim was put forward for actually running the factories. 'We demand control over production from the ministries', stated Levin at the August Conference.

> But here we meet on their part with indecision and reluctance to act; and on the part of the industrialists—with anger and fear for their property. Many consciously or unconsciously confuse the concept of 'control' with 'seizure of the mills and factories', although the workers are not at all conducting a tactic of seizure, and if such did occur, then only in exceptional and isolated cases.[26]

This is not to say that there were not already voices raised for full takeover of management. But these were decidedly a small minority. When the Central Bureau of Petrograd Trade Unions met on 11 May to discuss the coming Factory Committee Conference, according to *Novaya zhizn'* some union representatives defended the view that the workers should demand the socialisation of production, and that the factory committees should carry it out. But the other group of representatives, 'incomparably larger, spoke for control of production. They argued that one has to consider the objective possibilities and not one's subjective desires.'[27]

In at least one textile mill, agitation by some union activists for takeover seemed to have had an effect on the rank-and-file. At the end of May, after management had rejected the workers' wage demands, they voted to take over the mill. However, the factory committee threatened to resign if this occurred. On 3 June, another general assembly was held, and some tough questions were put to the workers: Where will you get money for wages? Will the technical personnel agree to work? The workers had no satisfactory answers, and, in fact, many now explained that their earlier decision had been misunderstood, that they had really only had control in mind. Only a few continued to demand a takeover, but the majority voted to go to conciliation on the wage issue, and the matter was closed.[28]

This exception really proves the rule—that the workers, especially when the issue was posed on a practical footing (and, of course, the factory committees were closer to this practice than the worker masses), were only interested in seizing the factories as a last resort, as an alternative to closure. But just for that reason, this incident was an indication of things to come, when conditions would become truly desperate and the rank-and-file would begin to push their reluctant factory committees, awed by the enormity and complexity of the task, to assume more and more of the tasks of management. But in May and June this was not yet the case.

Even on an abstract, theoretical level, the workers did not identify control with socialisation. As Naumov stated at the First Conference of Factory Committees.

> We, as Marxists, must look on life as always moving forward. The revolution continues. We say—our revolution is a prologue to the world revolution. Control is not yet socialism and not even the taking of production into our hands. But it already passes outside of the bourgeois framework. It is not socialism that we propose to introduce. No. But having taken [state] power into our hands, we should direct capitalism along such a path that it will outlive itself. The factory committee should work in that direction. That will lead to socialism ... Having strengthened our position in production, having taken control into our hands, we will learn in a practical manner how to work actively in production and in an organised fashion we will direct it towards socialist production.[29]

Similarly, the factory committee of the Putilov Works declared that through its activity

> the workers are preparing themselves for the time when private ownership of the factories and mills will be abolished and the means of production, along with the buildings erected by the workers' hands, will be transferred to the working class. Therefore in doing this small matter, one must continually keep in mind the great and principal aim towards which the people are aspiring.[30]

Without doubt, then, workers' control was seen as a step towards socialism, a school for socialism, but the ultimate goal at this time was still quite distant.

This period witnessed the emergence of two parallel and mutually reinforcing power struggles—one in the state, the other in the factories. But whereas in the factory arena the workers were still at the stage of 'control', they had already gone beyond it in the larger political arena, demanding direct management of state affairs by revolutionary democracy through the soviets. Both struggles, however, were conceived by the workers as primarily defensive responses to the onslaught of census society against the democratic revolution of February. It would still be some time before they realised that the very logic of their struggle for the democratic revolution was fast leading them towards a new one of a very different social and political character. The July Days would be a major, if painful, step towards this realisation.

8 The July Days

The Workers and the Soviet Majority

The almost universal support for the slogan 'All power to the soviets' by those who wanted to end the alliance with census society indicates that, despite the political disagreement, the workers still viewed the moderate socialist leaders as part of 'revolutionary democracy', as 'comrades'. Since these people were still a majority in the Soviet, the slogan obviously implied that the workers were willing to entrust state power to them. In fact, the basic idea behind the 18 June demonstration had been to impress upon the moderate Soviet leadership that the workers wanted them to take power. At this stage, any idea of breaking with the 'conciliationist' elements of democracy—the Soviet majority and the majority of peasants, soldiers and democratic intelligentsia that supported them—was something most workers could not even contemplate, as it would have meant almost complete isolation of the working class and a civil war against nearly impossible odds. Belief in the coming Western European revolution was strong, but it could not be counted upon too heavily in a calculation of forces.

Thus, the shift away from support of an alliance with the census society in May and June was premised upon the assumption on the part of the workers that the leaders of the Soviet would ultimately heed their demands. The idea of taking power against the Soviet majority was not even entertained.

Nevertheless, among the Vyborg metalworkers and some of their like-minded comrades in other districts, anger at the 'conciliationists' was fast reaching the boiling point. This became clear from the workers' reactions to the Soviet Congress's ban of the proposed demonstration on 10 June. One of the congress delegates sent out to dissuade the workers filed the following report:

> Vyborg District. June 10. 1) Nobel Factory 2) Old Parviainen 3) New Parviainen 4) New Lessner [all machine-construction]. Everywhere the attitude is sharply hostile to the Congress of Soviets of W and SD, 'dragging itself after the bourgeoisie and [which] is petty bourgeois in essence'. Nowhere do they intend to demonstrate on the tenth, but not because the Congress of Soviets is calling for this but only because the CC of the RSDWP [Bolshevik] is suggesting not to demonstrate today.

The impression is such that one can expect a 'coming out' in the nearest future, if the [Bolshevik] CC calls for it. At the Nobel and Old and New Parviainen Factories I was able to speak only with the council of elders [factory committee], since it was not possible to hold a meeting as work was in progress. At the N. Lessner Factory there was a workers' meeting, but it was impossible to speak since they would not let me finish.[1]

According to *Novaya zhizn'* also,

The attitude to the orators, Congress delegates, is hostile ... They did not want to hear the orators and interrupted them with shouts: 'We are not comrades to you.' It was decided not to demonstrate until a new call by the CC RSDWP [Bolshevik].

At certain metalworking factories in the Vasilevskii ostrov district the hostile workers interrupted the congress orators with shouts of 'bourgeois'.[2] One orator sent to the Putilov Works, where the atmosphere was very heated over the economic conflict, reported:

Near the shops where work was in progress I was met by about 300 people. They met the automobile in an extremely hostile manner. 'There were already two before you; there's no sense in your coming to disturb people. As it is, we barely managed to keep them at work. And then you come and take people from their work, etc.' There were no meetings at the factory. Work was in progress.
   Declarations of the workers in relation to the All-Russian Congress: 'Some characters arrived from the boondocks to teach us; we already know everything without you. We won freedom here with our own blood, and where were you?'
   They would not let me speak and asked me to leave. The car left amidst whistles and angry rumbling. A Bolshevik who made a speech waved his revolver. Our visas were demanded, although in the great state of agitation they forgot to look at them. The attitude to the Soviet W and SD is hostile, a series of ironic remarks about the army at the front and Kerenskii.[3]

This same hostility was vented in several factory resolutions. After hearing a report on the Conference of Factory Committees, the workers of the Optico-machine-construction Factory resolved: 'We welcome the correct path of struggle against the adventurism of capitalism upon which our representatives have embarked, despite the various disgraceful ruses of the ex-socialists.'[4] This was already very strong language, a move away from the view of Soviet leaders as 'nevertheless comrades' towards seeing them as class traitors, accomplices of the counterrevolution. The general assembly of the Aivaz

Machine-construction Factory, reacting to the government raid on the Durnovo dacha, resolved to protest

> against the inactivity of the Soviet in the struggle against the counterrevolution and demand that the Soviet authoritatively affirm the rights of all revolutionary groups to free revolutionary activity and take decisive steps to end the world slaughter. The meeting declares that while power is in the hands of the bourgeoisie and while it, under the cover of the Soviet, is digging the grave of the proletarian revolution, the workers will not hesitate before any means of struggle for the victory of the cause of the people.[5]

Again, fighting words, unthinkable a few weeks earlier. On 19 June the workers of the Baranovskii Factory warned the Soviet: 'We are horrified by the thought, which involuntarily creeps into our consciousness, that this blow was directed consciously, having turned your eyes from reality.' They called on the Soviet to re-examine its policy and promised support 'if the latter will express our will and carry out our desires'.[6] Here was the old formula of conditional support, but now addressed to the Soviet itself![7]   But these expressions of opposition and outrage should not necessarily be taken as signs of readiness to act against the moderate leaders. The July Days show quite conclusively that the 'conciliators' had not yet been written off as counter-revolutionaries. In the last two cited resolutions especially, one can sense the workers' hedging.

This very issue was, in fact, raised at the 20 June session of the Bolshevik PC, when it had become clear that the 18 June demonstration had produced no concrete results. Discussing the great agitation in various districts, some spoke in favour of rejecting the 'parliamentary means of struggle', i.e. trying to win a left majority in the soviets. They argued that the Congress and the Petrograd Soviet had in effect sanctioned the raid on Durnovo, proving their readiness to use force against the left and effectively ruling out the parliamentary, legal path of struggle.

The majority, however, did not support this. Echoing other speakers, Naumov (who, incidentally, was on the left) argued: 'We should present the Congress with an ultimatum: either take power, or we do not guarantee what will happen. We must direct the movement into an organised channel.'[8] The question was, thus, still being put to the Soviet. Latsis, party organiser for the Vyborg District, wrote in his diary on 20 June: 'At the PC and CC the idea is to prevent a demonstration, but if it happens to assume the leadership and direct it toward pressuring the soviets to take power.'[9] The Bolsheviks were not about to initiate action but they would use the threat of it to pressure the Soviet leadership into taking power.

A delegate from the Vyborg District offered his appraisal of the workers' position:

> I'll tell you how the workers of the Nobel Factory reacted to the events. When the question arose at the meeting—What, then, should we do?—the workers replied: The situation is complex. We have to wait, to clarify what forces we have, and be on the ready. The question of parliamentarism is a serious one. When the masses are straining to come out, we have to explain to them against whom exactly they are going. Why, we can't come out against our own comrades who haven't yet understood that which we know. We have to tear those comrades away from the politics of conciliationism with the capitalists and push them towards the politics of a break ... Our task is to go to the workers and soldiers who still haven't understood that and we will call them to understand us ... When our comrades have understood us, we'll rise up face to face with the enemy of our class and join battle.[10]

Given these attitudes among even the most radical workers, the July Days could be nothing but a repeat of 18 June, at least on the part of the workers. On the other hand, the reaction of the Soviet leadership, the government and census society would indeed be something new; for the workers—shockingly new.

The Demonstrations of 3–4 July[11]

The 18 June demonstration achieved none of the demonstrators' goals. Just the contrary. In the interval between 18 June and 3 July, the deterioration of the political and economic situations continued unabated. The 'insolence' of the counterrevolution, as the workers put it, was becoming more and more intolerable: the raid on Durnovo,[12] the offensive at the front, patriotic demonstrations accompanied by physical assaults and arrests of workers and soldiers for refusing to remove their caps, or for no reason at all.

On the economic plane, the major government initiative was the following message of the socialist Minister of Labour to the workers:

> Comrade workers, remember not only your rights, not only your desires, but also the possibility of their realisation; not only your welfare, but also sacrifices in the name of consolidating the revolution and the victory of our ultimate ideals.[13]

Not a word about economic regulation or the policies of the industrialists. A few days later a member of the Tsvernin Factory committee wrote to Skobelev: 'Having read the appeal of the Minister of Labour to the workers, I consider it necessary to report on our factory.' The directors had decided to dismiss half of the work force and place the other half on a three-day week, citing lack of orders and raw materials at their client factories. The workers sent representatives to these factories and found all but one to be working at full steam. 'From this, it is obvious that it is not the workers who undermine industry but these same Roms and Kitel'bergs [the directors]. Therefore we ask our respected comrade Minister Skobelev to take decisive measures against such phenomena up to and including arrest.'[14] It is difficult to miss the intended irony in the address 'our respected comrade Minister'.

The ripening wage disputes coupled with growing intransigence on the part of the owners were also important elements of the immediate pre-July situation. Although the Putilov dispute is the best known, conflicts had arisen in many factories as the workers struggled to retain their level of real wages in face of the galloping inflation.[15]

The food situation, though not desperate, was again worsening, for the first time since the winter. On 26 June bread rations were reduced by 15 per cent; the same for meat and butter on 1 July. An entry in Latsis' diary for 2 July reads: 'A meat speculator was caught, and the crowd wanted to mete out its own justice.'[16]

The offensive produced in the workers a bitter sense of betrayal. But among a part of the garrison the anger was perhaps even more intense, as various units, including the extremely militant First Machine-gun Regiment, learnt they were about to be disbanded and sent to the front.[17]

Deeply alarmed at the course the revolution was taking and exasperated at the obstinacy of the Soviet leadership, the workers needed little coaxing to lay down their tools when the factory whistles sounded on 3 July. ' "Finish up! Into the yard! Into the yard!" We already knew what this meant', recalled Metelev, a Bolshevik worker in a Vyborg District factory.

We knew to put away our tools, dress and go to the general assembly. Among the workers no one thought to stay in the shops after these shouts—that would be worse than strike-breaking. We could only think that this was the result of some extraordinary political event.

Representatives of the machine-gunners and some other factories were waiting. On the way, we heard that the regiment was ready to move, part of the automobiles, mounted with machine-guns, had gone downtown, and the Lessner and Erikson workers were already in the streets.

Excitement. Everyone wanted to hear something new, something good. Hearts beat excitedly. A speaker appealed to await exact instructions from the Bolshevik CC, but this caused an even louder racket and the stubborn demand is repeated to open the factory gates. To argue: Why? Where? Against Whom?—this was totally superfluous. Everyone knew the meaning of the demonstration. It had been ripening for a long time ... Ten abreast we filed out onto Sampsionevskii Prospekt. The Red Guards went ahead. All power to the soviets! Then the unarmed men, women and youths ... Hope beat in the hearts of the workers, hope that already soon the dawn would come, the great dawn which would light up with its social light all the corners of their dark and slave-like life.[18]

Over in the Petergof District, in the cannon shop of the Putilov Works, rumours had been circulating since the morning of a meeting to be held in the street. The workers learnt of the resignation of the 'capitalist ministers' on the previous night[19] and of the government's intention to send more troops to the front. 'On hearing this, the workers' mood turned militant', recalled the Putilov worker, Efimov, a Bolshevik. At about 2 p.m. a delegation from the Machine-gun Regiment arrived, asking for a meeting, but the Bolshevik-dominated factory committee opposed this.[20] 'The workers, burning with impatience, gathered in front of the main office, shouting: Start the meeting!' At that moment a soldier entered and confirmed the reports that they had already been ordered to the front but that the soldiers had decided 'not to fight the German proletariat but against their own capitalists'. By now, about 10 000 workers had gathered and hearing this, began to shout: 'Down with this kind of minister!' When the machine-gunners announced that they were coming out at 4 p.m. with machine-guns mounted on lorries, the crowd roared: 'Let's move'. The factory committee argued for the need to act in a more organised fashion, but the workers had already begun to assemble in the street.

Efimov ran to the Bolshevik district committee, where the consensus was that they 'could not leave the workers to the whims of fate; and so we'll go with them'. By this time they had learnt that the whole city was moving. 'We assembled and left. At the Narva Gates there was such a throng, it seemed as if no one was staying behind. The women shouted: Everybody has to go. No one should stay behind. We'll take care of the homes.'

The huge Putilov column did not arrive at the Tauride Palace, seat of the TsIK, until 2 a.m. Camping down in the park, they declared their intention to stay put until the TsIK took power. The latter replied that the matter would be taken up 'today or tomorrow', but the workers insisted on a definite answer. However, at 4 a.m. they began to file back to the factory. At 10 a.m., after meetings, they dispersed to their homes.[21]

A number of observations can be made about the first day of demonstrations. In the first place, the initiative undoubtedly came from below: not only did the TsIK expressly forbid a demonstration, but all political parties opposed one. The workers had to force the hand of their (by now, mostly Bolshevik) leadership. And if the machine-gunners provided the spark, the mood among the workers was already red hot. The workers were also the more organised and disciplined element. Most active on 3 July were the more working-class districts—Vyborg, Petergof, Vasilevskii ostrov.[22]

On 4 July, after considerable wavering, the Bolshevik CC issued a call to continue the demonstrations, stressing the necessity of maintaining their peaceful character. The vast majority of factories voted to participate, the exceptions being those still under SR influence in the Nevskii District, Okhta and Moscow Districts as well as most textile mills and printing houses. Despite the TsIK's ban, between two-thirds and three-quarters of the capital's industrial workers participated. On the other hand, the soldiers by now were already wavering, with some of yesterday's demonstrators deciding to stay inside. Of the 100 000 men in the garrison, about one half came out on the fourth.[23]

In retrospect, the 'July Days' seem a paradox within a paradox, the essence of which was expressed by the anonymous worker who, shaking his fist at the SR Minister of Agriculture, Chernov, shouted: 'Take power, you son of a bitch, when they give it to you.'[24] Here were workers and soldiers marching in their thousands to demand that the TsIK leadership, already quite compromised in their eyes, take power. This TsIK, apparently more willing to commit political suicide than to take power, states that it alone will decide the composition of the new government at a forthcoming plenary session (the resignation of the Kadets ended the first coalition), thus acknowledging itself as the supreme power in the land. And yet this same TsIK describes the workers and soldiers clamouring for soviet power as counter-revolutionaries. And when 'loyal' troops arrive to put down the insurgents demanding soviet power, their commanders solemnly declare that the Soviet is the only authority the army will obey and unconditionally serve, that the TsIK alone will decide the fate of the revolution.

The workers had one goal: to be rid of the 'ten capitalist ministers' and to press the Soviet to take power. To this end they ignored the Mariinskii Palace, seat of the government, going directly to the Tauride Palace. There was no intention of using violent means, except for self-defence against the 'philistine' and bourgeois crowds in the centre. Among the demonstrators were women and children. The Kronstadt 'raiding party' was led by an orchestra, an unusual battle formation indeed. In fact, the entire affair was marked by the rather naïve conviction of the demonstrators that the leaders in the TsIK would be unable to resist their moral pressure.

The workers' attitude towards the moderate Soviet leadership was clearly very ambivalent, but this ambivalence was rooted in what to the workers seemed a highly contradictory state of affairs: the Soviet, the political organ of revolutionary democracy, which held all real power, was using it to support 'bourgeois' policies which were aiding the counterrevolution. Nevertheless, at this point, before the lessons of July had sunk in, there could be no question of moving against the Soviet or 'our comrade socialist ministers'. Given this state of mind, all the workers could do was to hope that with a little more prodding the Soviet leadership would see the light.

On 4 July, one of the four workers representing 54 factories who were allowed to address the TsIK, stated:

It is strange when one reads the appeal of the TsIK: workers and soldiers are called counterrevolutionaries. You see what is written on the placards. The same question was discussed in all the factories. These are decisions taken by the workers. You know these resolutions. We are threatened with hunger. We demand the resignation of the ten capitalist ministers. We trust the Soviet but not those whom the Soviet trusts. Our comrade socialist ministers have taken the road of conciliation with the capitalists, but these capitalists are our blood enemies. We demand that all the land be seized immediately, that control over production be instituted immediately! We demand a struggle against the hunger that is threatening us.[25]

'We trust the Soviet, but not those whom the Soviet trusts.' Or perhaps: we want and need to trust the Soviet, but it does not seem to want to let us because it stubbornly continues to yield its positions to our enemies.

Of course, there were various shades of this attitude. At this same session, an excited Putilov worker suddenly leaped onto the platform, rifle in hand.

Comrades! Must we, the workers, endure betrayal for much longer?! You have gathered here, you reason, you make deals with the bourgeoisie and the landowners. You busy yourselves with the betrayal of the working class. Then know that the working class will not endure that! We Putilovtsy are here 30 000 strong, all to a man. We will achieve our will! Absolutely no bourgeois! All power to the soviets! Our rifles are in our hands. Your Kerenskies and Tseretelis won't fool us.[26]

This sounds very determined and threatening. But when Chkheidze handed him a note stating merely that the TsIK was currently discussing the matter and that he should tell his comrades to return to their factories, the bewildered worker simply walked off. To shout and threaten was one thing; to take any sort of decisive action against the Soviet was still quite another. Even Metelev who was in the very thick of it, mentions no calls to use force against the TsIK.[27] He himself, delegated by the workers, patiently waited out the night inside the Tauride Palace and, totally dejected, was forced to leave at dawn by the arrival of the 'loyal' troops.[28]

By the evening of the fourth, the streets around the palace had emptied and the movement, for all practical purposes, was at an end. The two days saw perhaps 400 dead and wounded, the victims of clashes between the demonstrators and provocateurs. Underworld elements had also been active looting shops.

After the demonstrators had returned to their homes and barracks, the situation took a drastic turn. While Tsereteli addressed the TsIK on the night of 4–5 July, the assembly was thrown into a panic by the sound of marching boots. Dan calmed them down. 'No danger. These are regiments loyal to the Revolution and have come to defend its legitimate organ, the TsIK.' Sukhanov recalled:

> At that moment in the Ekaterinskii Hall, a powerful refrain of the Marseillaise was struck up. In the hall—enthusiasm. The Mamelukes were radiant. Jubilant, they cast dirty looks in the direction of the Left and in an effusion of sentiment grasped each other by the hand. Standing bareheaded, they sang the Marseillaise.

'A classic scene of the start of counterrevolution', Martov (Menshevik–Internationalist leader) spat out. But in fact, as Sukhanov observes, there were really no need for the troops, since no one threatened the TsIK.[29] Nevertheless, the troops had arrived, some from outside the capital, others from garrison regiments that had opposed the demonstration. This influenced other units that had been neutral or undecided.

But more important in the sudden shift in the correlation of forces were the rumours and then the publication in the morning newspapers of documents alleging complicity between Lenin and his associates and the German General Staff. This 'leak' by the Minister of Justice was particularly calculated to influence the garrison.[30] For the workers, a 'debauch of counterrevolution' was about to begin.

The Aftermath

The July Days resulted in a sudden shift in the political correlation of forces away from revolutionary democracy (and especially its left wing, the working class) in favour of census society. The immediate cause of this was the TsIK's sanctioning of repressions against the workers and the left socialists. Although the beginnings of the Soviet's loss of influence over the government can be traced back at least to April, the repression that followed the July demonstrations marked a watershed. For it became clear that henceforth the TsIK would not and could not call on the support of the politically most active and conscious segment of revolutionary democracy. This turn of events, on the other hand, greatly encouraged census Russia, which now moved to the offensive in an effort to recoup the losses of the first months of the revolution.

But this is only one side of the story. For not only were the workers objectively unable to push further for their goal of a non-census government, they were also subjectively in no way prepared to do this, since it now entailed the violent overthrow of the TsIK along with the government and, in fact, the possibility of a civil war within revolutionary democracy. Unwilling to proceed, they were forced back into defensive positions until they could rethink their assumptions about the nature and course of the revolution.

In order fully to appreciate the workers' reactions to the July Days, two aspects of the new situation must be especially emphasised: the unprecedented scale of the bloodshed of 3–4 July and of the repressions that followed, and the complicity of the Soviet leadership in the latter. This first real taste of civil war shook the workers to the core and initially left them in a state of shock. But soon a different emotion began to push to the fore, a deep and growing rage directed not only at census society but more and more at the 'conciliationist' leaders of revolutionary democracy. The two emotions—fear and rage— continued to coexist, each struggling for the upper hand. For most workers, this struggle would be resolved only in October itself.

On 3 July, most of the casualties resulted from clashes between armed demonstrators and provocateurs among the hostile crowds and in the buildings that lined their route. On 4 July, however, regular government troops began to fire, often at point-blank range, on the workers' columns,[31] and soon ordinary citizens began to get into the act. D. Afanas'ev, a worker at the New Lessner Factory, related what was by no means an isolated incident:

At the Tauride Palace the Putilov workers declared they would stay until the Soviet took a decision one way or the other. When I learnt of the Soviet's decision not to decide under pressure from the street, I went to a relative who lived nearby. The next day I went home with two comrades and argued with anyone abusing the Bolsheviks.

At Shukin Market we came across a well-dressed nurse in the middle of a crowd saying that Trotsky and Lunacharskii were arrested, that Lenin and Zinoviev were in hiding, that they had

taken money from Wilhelm, etc. She called to mercilessly kill the
Bolsheviks. We ask: Who gave you money to slander the Bolsheviks
and the workers? We argued for ten minutes exposing the lies. Then
about twenty merchants, probably butchers, arrived and started to
curse the Bolsheviks—Beat the Jews and the Bolsheviks! Into the
water with them!—and the crowd thrashed us soundly. One comrade ran away, the other died in the hospital two weeks later from
the beating, they took away my *nagan* [pistol] and threw it into the
canal and began throwing stones.

Six sailors arrived and dispersed the crowd, pulled me, all bloody,
out of the canal. I dragged myself homeward but could not keep
myself from cursing two *burzhui* [bourgeois, well-to-do) who, talking among themselves, called Lenin a provocateur. I called them
provocateurs. They took me to the Aleksandr-Nevskii Militia Station, where there were already many arrested workers. I was there
until July 7. Three Don Cossacks and two sailors gave me something
to eat and freed me. I was sick for about a month.[32]

On 14 July the general assembly of the Langezipen Factory resolved
unanimously to

bring to the attention of the TsIK of the Soviets of W and SD that a
worker of the Langezipen Factory, T. Sinitsyn, was killed at the
Vologda Station for verbally defending the Bolsheviks. We draw the
attention of the TsIK of W and SD to the fact that this is the total
destruction of freedom of speech and a victory of the
counterrevolution.[33]

Reports poured into the TsIK of 'excesses' taking place in the city. In
certain districts crowds pushed their way into the trams seeking out the
'Leninists'. Once again, the jails of Petrograd filled up with 'politicals'.

On the night of 4–5 July government troops ransacked the premises
of the Bolshevik CC and PC. In effect, nearly the entire top stratum of
the party was taken out of action for the whole of July and most of
August. But the middle and lower levels were also hard hit—during
the month of July the PC reported it had been unable to conduct any
agitational work to speak of.[34] The Bolsheviks' newly purchased
printing shop was totally demolished, and *Pravda* shut down along
with a number of provincial Bolshevik papers. The Minister of the
Interior was empowered to close any publications calling for insubordination to military authorities or to violence and civil war.[35] Yet,
however critical the Bolshevik press had been of the government,
appeals to violence and civil war at this time were indeed far from party
policy.

The government also immediately began to disarm the workers as well as the military units that had participated in the demonstrations.[36] At Sestroretsk outside the capital, the local soviet had been long running things, much to the disgust of the non-socialist press that continued to rail against this 'Sestroretsk Republic'. But the time for revenge had come. A full-scale military operation was mounted including several hundred Cossacks, Junkers and six armoured trucks. The commander was even empowered to shoot all resisters and raze the town. But there was no resistance. After indiscriminate searches in workers' homes, the expedition left, taking with it the entire factory committee and leaving the premises of the workers' and Bolshevik organisations in shambles.[37]

On 11 July, *Novaya zhizn'*, which had not yet closed, printed an editorial entitled 'Blossoms' (from the Russian proverb: These are only the blossoms; the berries are yet to come).

> The counterrevolution is making great strides, not by the day but by the hour. Searches and arrests—and what arrests—the secret police of Tsarist Russia did not permit itself such insolent conduct, the likes of which the bourgeois youth and Cossack officers have of late undertaken in an effort to 'restore order' by Petrograd.

Other repressive measures not relating directly to the workers that should be mentioned are the reintroduction of the death penalty at the front, an act of immense symbolic meaning to the workers, the dissolution of the Finnish Parliament, whose Social-Democratic majority had voted for internal autonomy, and the attempted dissolution and arrest of the CC of the Baltic Fleet for disobeying an order to send ships to the capital during the July events.[38]

Where did the TsIK stand on all of this? Although it protested against 'excesses' and somewhat restrained the government's repressive zeal, for example, by obtaining the release of the delegation of the CC of the Baltic Fleet and refusing to grant Kerenskii his wish to declare the Bolsheviks totally outside the law,[39] the fact is that after the Kadet ministers resigned on 1 July, the TsIK's ministers actually formed a majority in the government (6 against 5). Moreover, the second coalition, formed on 7 July, was in fact, if not officially, a 'soviet government': the Prime Minister as well as the other key ministers were members of the TsIK (including Tsereteli as Minister of Internal Affairs), and this cabinet had, in fact, been formed solely on the decision of the socialist ministers, officially adopting the TsIK's programme as its own. 'Formally, a dictatorship of the PG has been declared', wrote *Rabochaya gazeta*, 'but in fact the TsIK of W and SD is participating in this dictatorship'.[40] In fact, Tsereteli, leader of the

TsIK, declared in response to Martov's protests: 'I take upon myself responsibility for these arrests.'[41] The TsIK also approved the introduction of the death penalty at the front.

This apparent assumption of direct control by the TsIK of the government, in fact, was merely a prelude to new and more far-reaching concessions to census society. For after a brief scuffle between the centre–left of the TsIK, on the one hand, and Kerenskii and the political leaders of census society on the other, a third coalition was formed which included five Kadets. For the first time, the government announced no programme, nor was the TsIK's approval even sought. Tsereteli himself admitted this was a major surrender of the Soviet's power when he told the Petrograd Soviet that 'the workers are a large part of the population. But they are not the whole country, and we must march under the banner of an all-national platform. The power of the revolutionary organisations must be limited.'[42]

In sum, whatever the actual sentiment in the TsIK, Tsereteli succeeded in obtaining its approval at every crucial step. In the final analysis, the TsIK proved unwilling to use its still considerable authority to restrain the government or to prevent the further erosion of the Soviet's power.

The workers' reactions to all this were complex and varied widely, especially between those who had participated in the demonstrations and those who had abstained.

A relatively small segment of the workers, apparently mainly from the Vyborg District, actually attempted a counter-offensive. On 5 July, there were a number of political strikes and even efforts to renew the demonstrations.[43] Metelev recalled Vyborg Red Guards and worker youths stuffing bombs into their pockets and boots and crossing the river in boats to the aid of the Kronstadt sailors besieged in the Peter-Paul Fortress.[44] According to Latsis, 'The Vyborg [Bolshevik] district committee instinctively raised the entire district to its feet. I personally made the rounds of the factories and asked to keep the Red Guards at the ready. A plan for the defence of the district was even drawn up.' However, the Executive Committee of the Bolshevik PC narrowly rejected Latsis' plan for a general strike. Lenin, himself, already in hiding, heatedly opposed this idea.[45]

These scattered and fundamentally defensive responses of the most militant segment of the working class really only confirm that the dominant mood was far from militant. The prevailing reaction among those who had demonstrated was rather one of shock and dismay. They were caught totally off-guard by this outcome. Not only had an originally peaceful demonstration resulted in what in 1917 appeared as massive bloodshed, but the political tables had completely turned overnight, and it was anyone's guess as to how it would all end. For the first time, the workers understood the full extent of their isolation in society.

On 5 July, some factories in the Vyborg District had started up, but 'not all workers have come. Those at the lathes cannot get back into the routine. "My hands shake from emotion", say the workers. "My hands won't obey me." ' Despite the decision of the various parties, in many places the factory committees had to let the workers go home after lunch because they were so on edge.[46] On Vasilevskii ostrov, among the women, fear was the dominant emotion.[47]

Then the depression set in. 'We felt inexpressibly sad', recalled Metelev.[48] Naumov described the mood at Lessner:

At the factory the workers are morose. They don't believe the slander, but all the same not all are sufficiently armed to repulse the poisonous fumes of slander seeping into the shops ... Not a day passes without some new 'revelation'. Instead of them giving us the opportunity to express our point of view, our views are passed on in their words in a distorted manner, and repression, repression everywhere.[49]

A certain fatigue began to set in. Some observers noted a tendency to draw back from politics. In the Narva District, 'the mood of the worker masses is sluggish, apathetic. This especially strikes the eye at the Putilov Factory ... This is to be explained by the fatigue from the exertion of the last days.'[50] At the Factory Committee Conference in early August, Skrypnik noted a 'temporary apathy into which they [the broad worker masses] have fallen as a result of fatigue'.[51]

As always when threatened from without, the workers began to assert a powerful desire for unity. Unable to break with the Soviet majority, the workers seemed to cling to the hope that now, at last, the moderate socialists would join with them against the onslaught of counterrevolution. 'Among the workers', noted Latsis, 'the question is being raised of joining with the SRs and Mensheviks on the basis of the estimation that now the eyes of all have been opened to the counter-revolution and the need to rally in struggle against.'[52] Such attempts at overcoming party differences did, in fact, occur at many factories, including Metallicheskii, New Parviainen, Orudiinyi, Promet, Dinamo and others.[53] (All, as it turned out, failed.)

Nor did the desire for unity stop at the factory level. Speaking for the Bolshevik fraction at the 10 July session of the Petrograd Soviet, Fedorov called for unity of all revolutionary forces against the danger from the right, and when Dan presented the TsIK's resolution appealing for support for the new government (which had officially adopted the TsIK's programme, with the socialist ministers promising to report to the TsIK at least twice weekly), only about ten votes were cast against it, with a full one-quarter of the plenum abstaining.[54] As Sukhanov noted, to the Bolshevik abstainers, 'the hated Kerenskii already seemed preferable to much else that could still happen'.[55]

There is little doubt, then, that at least initially the workers along with a good part of Bolshevik organisation remained wedded to the tactic of pushing the TsIK to the left. This was also reflected in factory resolutions which now took on a rather defensive tone, passing over in silence the issue of state power, and limiting themselves to protests against the repressions and demands that the TsIK take some action. The general assembly of Old Parviainen, for example, condemned the rising tide of counterrevolution in the strongest terms but now merely concluded that 'unity of all revolutionary forces is needed in order to repulse counterrevolutionary acts against the Soviet of S and SD and the further development of the revolution'.[56]

But this picture is still incomplete. For as serious as the demoralisation was, the surrender of political initiative and the drive for unity in no way involved the abandonment by the workers of their resolve to replace the coalition with a soviet government. The retreat was merely tactical and the demoralisation did not touch the workers' fundamental goals nor their conviction of the counterrevolutionary nature of census society. One need only note that the Bolsheviks were able to hold on to the allegiance of practically all the workers who had supported them up before the July Days, and this in face of the most intense and virulent defencist agitation that strove to pin the blame for the bloodshed squarely on the Bolsheviks.

Korotkov, a Bolshevik worker at the Admiralty Shipyards, described the scene he found at the plant when he was released from jail a few days after the demonstrations:

> We found a meeting in progress. The SRs had come with their 'big guns'. The workers' mood was depressed. The SRs wanted to exploit this in order to let the Bolsheviks have it. When they demanded that the instigators of the demonstration at the factory be surrendered, individual voices were even heard: 'Into the Neva with Pakhomov, Korotkov and other Bolsheviks'. They failed. Pakhomov answered well, calling them cowards covered with the workers' blood. After him the workers would not let the SRs speak and said firmly that they [the big guns] had better not set foot again in the factory. And the workers kept their word in this.[57]

Similarly, the local Bolsheviks reported from Kolpino:

> The Izhorskii Factory [located some distance from Petrograd] took part in the demonstration according to the resolution of the Workers' Section of the Soviet of W and SD. This participation took the

form of sending a delegation to the Tauride Palace (25 people) and [the factory] stopped work ... From the moment the demonstration was liquidated, the mood turned clearly not in our favour. Accusations, the authors of which were the SRs, were levelled at us that we allegedly duped the workers by saying that the factories in Petrograd were striking. (They referred to the Nevskii District.[58]) On the evening of July 5 the SRs called a meeting of five or six thousand which gave us the chance to turn the mood around again in our favour. After this, attempts to try our comrades for allegedly reporting falsely on the events in Petersburg totally fell through. There were cases of resignation from the party but they bore an individual character. On the other hand there were cases (also of an individual character) of transfers from the SRs. In general the mood has settled down and has become relatively calm, and if there were small excesses, they were against the SR leaders.[59]

The situation was the same at the Putilov Works.[60]

The Bolsheviks also did well in elections that were held soon after the July Days in a series of factories, including the overwhelmingly female Treugol'nik Rubber Factory, where they won two-thirds of the seats, finally displacing the SRs.[61] As a result of all this, Volodarskii was able to tell the Bolshevik City Conference on 16 July that 'judging by the information coming in from the districts, the mood is good everywhere'.[62] Perhaps not quite everywhere, but, even where it did not yet favour the Bolsheviks, it was in the process of changing.

One of the most graphic and moving expressions of the mood in the factories among the July Days participants is a letter endorsed unanimously on 11 July by the workers of the cannon shop of the Putilov Works. Its authors are anonymous, but the style bears the unmistakable imprint of the self-taught worker-*intelligent*. On both counts, it merits being cited at length.

Citizens!

Like an ancient oak amidst the forest, the great Putilov Factory stands amidst the nation's industry, shaking the earth with the heavy blows of its hammers. Workers from all corners of Russia are here, and working, they think their thoughts. Amidst the whistling of saws and howling of wires, under the depressing gaze of gun carriages and cannons, gloomy thoughts creep into our minds. In their toil, as in a hard labour penal regime, the mothers and fathers who bore us die. We also are dying here in bleak estrangement from that envied happiness, from that prosperity and culture which, not far from us, separated by the rich [*zhirnyi*] monument of old, the Narva Gates, the rich, carefree, 'educated' minority enjoys.

Where, then, is justice? Where are the results of the blood and lives of the fighters who fell in the Revolution? Where is the new life? Where is that paradise-like, joyous, green-red bird that so temptingly flew over our land and disappeared ... as if to deceive?

Citizens! This was not the first time the Putilovtsy shed their blood in the interests of the working class. Remember January 9 [1905] and refrain from those indiscriminate accusations that are being heard now on the streets of Piter. In those days, 3–4 July, we went with the clear hearts of loyal sons of the Revolution, and we went not against the Soviet of W and SD, but to support it. That is why on our banner was written: All Power to the Soviets! That is why certain of us in the aim of self-defence took their arms with them. On January 9 the loyal servants of the House of Romanov shot us. Now it has been established with accuracy that the first shots, and also part of the shots fired in return, were organised by provocateurs—enemies of Russian freedom, enemies of the workers.

Citizens! The renewed life does not want to wait. With the iron logic of all the events that have occurred, it inexorably pushes the revolutionary people into the streets, forward, and often the street decides the matter. But to our grief, we are alone and we lack sufficient organised forces. The developed workers are too scattered and often live not by the interests of the class as a whole, but in numerous factions and sects that also do us harm. We are left to ourselves. The 'Soviet of Workers' Deputies' seems to have begun to do without workers and, isolating itself by its composition, loses itself more and more in tedious work of an administrative nature. The Provisional Government has already congealed in dead bureaucratic forms.

In just such a light did the economic and political situation appear to us workers on the eve of the events of 3–4 July.

Citizens! Look trustingly at the black smokestacks rising from the ground. There, at their foot, the same kind of people as you, creating new values you need, suffer and agonise in a bondage of perfected and fierce exploitation. There, slowly, consciousness is ripening. In our hearts, hate is being stored, and the tender conditions of another life for all humanity are being lovingly written on the bloody banner. Away with fratricidal discord!

All citizens to the active support of the 'Committee for the Salvation of the Revolution',[63] that final effort of the forces of freedom – repeating the words addressed to the workers: 'Neither under the boot of Wilhelm nor backward under the vile yoke of Nicolas the Bloody.'[64]

The almost unbearable tension between the promise of February and the dismal reality of July cries out from these words. Hatred for the 'rich, carefree, "educated" minority' grows along with the workers' determination to create the new life for which they have sacrificed so much. Yet the overall tone is sad, even apologetic. The Soviet and the government are not spared the workers' wrath, but the letter offers no alternative. 'To our grief, we are alone ... We are left to ourselves.' And so, 'Away with fratricidal discord!' Unity in face of the counter-revolutionary offensive—this was the only slogan the workers could put forward, for the present.

This letter is an appeal to the rest of revolutionary democracy and especially to the workers who were blaming the demonstrators and the Bolsheviks for the bloodshed of the July Days. Not having participated in the events, these workers were at first easily persuaded by the aggressive campaign of the moderate socialists. 'The blood lies on the head of those who called out armed people', it was declared in the TsIK. 'This action was a knife in the back of the Revolution.'[65] The Bolsheviks are 'friends of Nicolas and Wilhelm', declared *Izvestiya*.[66]

In the Nevskii District the reaction was especially strong. On 10 July, a delegate from the district to the Bolshevik PC reported:

> The factories did not take part in the demonstration and worked continuously. The mood as regards the Bolsheviks has a pogrom tinge. The SRs are taking an active part in fanning this mood. With their participation, a list of Bolsheviks is being drawn up at the Baltic Factory with repressive intentions. The district committee is threatened with a pogrom by the crowd milling about in the street. The workers for the most part are being fed by rumours and they read the boulevard press. A meeting that took place yesterday at the Obukhovskii Factory was unsuccessful for us. Our main opponents were the SRs.[67]

The two largest factories, Nevskii and Obukhovskii, passed resolutions condemning those 'irresponsible people and parties that consciously or unconsciously conducted a policy that disorganises the forces of the Revolution'.[68]

The delegate from the Porokhovskii District painted a similar picture:

> The workers milieu of our district represents a standing swamp. After the days of 5–6 July this expressed itself clearly. The Bol-sheviks are being vilified and persecuted. We, six people, were thrown out of the factory with the blessing of the [district] soviet. Our soviet and the Mensheviks are working for the benefit of the counterrevolution. They are behaving in a vile manner.[69]

Only two textile mills had demonstrated in full force. Perazich, with considerable understatement, notes that the campaign being conducted by the non-socialist press and supported at meetings by the defencists, 'in places, for a time, confused our workers'.[70] At the Thornton Mills the Bolsheviks were thrown out of all elected offices when they refused to repudiate their party.[71]

A general assembly of printers on 7 July placed full responsibility on 'the left wing, which is a significant irresponsible minority trying to impose its will on all of revolutionary democracy'.[72] The Bolsheviks even had trouble getting their newspaper printed because 'the workers refuse to print a Bolshevik paper'.[73] In one state-owned plant, according to one printer, 'it reached the point where a non-party worker who shared the opinions of the Bolsheviks was put on trial before the general assembly in order that his military deferment be revoked and he be sent to the front'.[74]

But this reaction, strong as it was, proved merely a brief interlude in the seemingly irresistible swing of the workers to soviet power. By September, even the strongest 'conciliationist' strongholds would have begun to crumble.[75] And it is hard to see how it could have been otherwise. The 'irresponsible' Bolsheviks and their supporters had been defeated in July, but this did nothing to alleviate the problems facing the workers. In fact, each passing day seemed to bring the victory of the counterrevolution nearer. The coalition would have to be replaced by soviet power.

But that was the rub. After the July experience, could soviet power still be seen as a viable political goal? And if not, what was the alternative?

Conclusion: Four Months of Revolution—Results and Prospects

The working class emerged from the July Days divided and confused. The divisions reflected the uneven pace of political radicalisation between March and July. For although a majority of Petrograd's industrial workers had by now embraced soviet power, the extent of support for this demand varied greatly among the different strata. The confusion stemmed from the blow the July Days had dealt to the workers' perspective of the revolution. The situation seemed to call for a reorientation of revolutionary strategy, but this entailed consequences that the workers were reluctant to accept.

Most heavily involved in the radicalisation were the skilled urban workers, the most politically aware and active segment of the working class. Here virtual unanimity reigned on the urgent need to break off the alliance with census society. The exceptions were the 'worker aristocracy', printers, skilled workers in some of the state factories, small property-owning workers of the Nevskii District, who were also generally of one mind, but in support of the coalition. Very little had been seen or heard of these workers since April, and their absence on 18 June dealt an unexpected blow to the moderate socialists. But their reaction to the July demonstrations was extremely hostile. On the other hand, a shift to the left had already begun among the unskilled workers, still largely tied to their peasant origins and most of whom had been awakened to political life for the first time in February. But only a minority participated in the July Days, and the ensuing bloodshed and repressions put a temporary halt to the growth of Bolshevik influence here.

The seeds of the split between the main mass of skilled workers and the moderate socialists had, in fact, been there from the start. The former's support for the alliance with census society had been entirely conditional, the product of the all-national character of February; while the latter's advocacy of the alliance was, in practice at least, virtually unconditional, in accord with the view that the democratic revolution could not survive without the bourgeoisie and that a socialist revolution in Russian conditions was even more out of the question. The small group of 'irreconcilables', who even in February refused to support the 'bourgeois government', argued on the basis of the history of census society's (and particularly the industrialists') hostility to the revolutionary movement and to labour's specific aspirations. While this sharply antagonistic view of Russian society had become an integral part of the political culture of the entire stratum of workers, most in February felt that the stakes were too high not to give the bourgeoisie's newly professed devotion to the revolution a chance.

Viewed against this background, the subsequent radicalisation can be accounted for quite adequately without resort to such factors as anomie, anarchistic instincts run amok with the breakdown of legitimate authority or chiliastic moods and demagogic manipulation. These can explain neither the initial support for the alliance with census society nor the vastly disproportionate radicalisation among the skilled workers. Just as the early support for dual power was based upon an assessment of the situation in February and the risks involved in various courses of action, so too the shift to soviet power was grounded in experiences of the subsequent months that called for modification of this assessment. Even the 'irreconcilables' recognised that the mass of workers needed contemporary proof that the bourgeoisie could not be entrusted to administer the revolution, no matter how closely 'controlled'.

The contribution of Bolshevik agitation was first and foremost to make certain that the actual policies of the government and of census society were known to the workers. In this respect, the party's role in the first four months of the revolution was rather limited. The main issues and demands and organisational forms of the period did not have to be hatched in the Bolshevik Central Committee or at party conferences but arose directly out of the workers' own experience. Furthermore, all the mass actions of these months—the February, April and July Days—were initiated from below, catching the leadership off guard. It is true that this changed significantly after July, when the party's leadership role indeed became indispensable for the further development of the revolution. But it was the creativity, the independence and the initiative of the masses, and particularly of the skilled workers, the true vanguard of the working class and of the revolution, that left their mark on this first period.

The experiences that radicalised these workers were essentially political in nature (including the conflict over economic regulation). These were developments that unfolded in the public arena without yet having a direct impact on most factories. This in part explains their much more limited effect on the unskilled workers, who required something more personal and tangible to convince them of the need to re-evaluate their support for the coalition. The unskilled workers were also less integrated into the labour movement and generally lacked a firm commitment to the collective fate of the class and to its long-term aspirations. Soviet power was an unknown and risky business, and only immediate material necessity could move most of them to embrace it. But the more openly aggressive policies of the government and of capital towards the workers and the accelerated tempo of economic decline would soon provide this. After the initial negative reaction to the July Days had worn off, a swift and massive shift of unskilled workers to the Bolsheviks took place (in the capital as well as in Moscow and the provinces).

For the 'worker aristocracy', however, it was mostly a lack of faith in soviet power as a viable alternative that kept them attached to the coalition. For when it came down to it, they were not in basic disagreement with the majority of skilled workers in their evaluation of the politics of census society and of the government. But they found unacceptable the practical conclusions drawn by their radical counterparts. On the one hand, they could not envision the mass of workers, upon whom they tended to look condescendingly, as a governing class. On the other hand, and related to this, were their cultural and/or material ties to liberal society that exercised a restraining influence. The result was their silence in 1917. They too would eventually (though not very decisively) break with the coalition, but only when events appeared to force an immediate choice between that and counterrevolution.

For the workers who had participated in them, the July Days were a watershed that created a new and bewildering situation. A historian, if so inclined, could trace the roots of the civil war back to 1914, 1905 or even the Emancipation and beyond. But for these workers, it was the July Days that placed civil war on the agenda in all its terrifying concreteness.

Until now, they had been thinking almost exclusively in terms of revolutionary democracy and census society, and their perspective of the revolution had been one of an essentially peaceful development. The real significance of the July Days was to place in doubt the very validity of the concept of revolutionary democracy and to push to the fore a new one—proletarian dictatorship.

The workers, as we have seen, did not welcome this, and even their most radical elements reacted initially by clinging desperately to the old conception of the revolution. Lenin's post-July slogan, 'dictatorship of the proletariat and poorest peasantry', and its implications for action were not accepted wholeheartedly by most workers. Even into the autumn, when the extreme isolation of the Petrograd workers had been overcome through the swing of the provincial workers' and soldiers' soviets to the Bolsheviks, the growing radicalisation of the exhausted and embittered army, and, to some extent, by the outbreak of the peasant war, the lessons of July continued to haunt the workers and hold them back from taking the political initiative, as they had done repeatedly in the earlier phase of the revolution. Despite their growing alarm, they now waited for their leaders.

In the factories, parallel to these political developments and initially equally unrecognised by the workers, the social content of the revolution had been undergoing a transformation. Despite their insistence (not abandoned until after October) that workers' control did not mean socialism, this new demand of the revolution, by the very logic of events, was fast moving the workers beyond the bourgeois-democratic stage. Here, on the economic plane, the worker rank-and-file did not cede the initiative but continued to push their often reluctant leaders towards deeper and deeper involvement in the actual running of the factories.

This reversal of the relationship between masses and leaders in the political sphere was not a sign of indifference or quiescence. It was rather the result of the workers' realisation that the nature of the revolution had changed and with it the practical tasks that faced them. Before July, it had been a question of peacefully exerting pressure on the moderate leaders of the Soviet. After July, it could only be a question of armed struggle, and this required planning, organisation and leadership to have any chance of success.

But at least to an equal extent, the change stemmed from the workers' reluctance to accept the lessons of July. The soldiers wanted peace and the peasants land, but could they be counted upon to support a working-class initiative for soviet power directed against census society and, if it came to that, against the moderate socialists? Could the workers really manage the economy and the state against the opposition of all educated society? Even if the entire army and peasantry supported soviet power, experience had shown that these were scarcely active forces and for the most part they viewed the revolution almost exclusively in simplified terms of peace and land.

The July Days, thus, raised concretely before the workers the issue of proletarian dictatorship, not as a vision of a socialist paradise just around the corner, but as a practical, if extremely perilous, alternative to the defeat of the revolution. In this way, if February was very much a revolution of unbounded hopes, October would be one more of desperation (though, to be sure, not without its own indispensable measure of hope and enthusiasm), in the sense of the phrase that was heard with increasing frequency after July—that it is better to die standing than to live on one's knees.

Still, only a minority of workers, most notably from among the skilled metalworkers, who formed the backbone of the Bolshevik organisation in Petrograd, were able to contemplate this new perspective without flinching. It was to them that the initiative would fall in October. Once the affair was underway, the rest would rally. But this is the subject matter of another study to follow.

Notes and References

Chapter 1: Introduction

1. J. Keep, *The Russian Revolution* (New York: W. W. Norton and Co., 1976) p. xiv.
2. For an insightful critical review of the most recent work on the social history of the revolution, see R. Suny, 'Toward a Social History of the October Revolution,' *American Historical Review*, vol 88, no 1 (1983), pp. 31–52.
3. C. Johnson, *Revolutionary Change* (Boston: Little Brown and Co., 1966) p. 152.
4. Keep, *Russian Revolution*, pp. 77 and 68.
5. P. Avrich, *The Russian Anarchists* (London: Thames and Hudson, 1973) p. 142.
6. In L. H. Haimson (ed.), *The Mensheviks* (Chicago: University of Chicago Press, 1975) p. 7.
7. See, for example, S. P. Melgunov, *The Bolshevik Seizure of Power* (Santa Barbara: ABC:CAO, 1972) pp. 22–3.
8. See, for example, Johnson, *Revolutionary Change*, and S. Huntington, *Political Order in Changing Societies* (New Haven: Yale University Press, 1968).
9. See, for example G. L. Sobolev, *Revolyutsionnoe soznanie rabochikh i soldat Petrograda v 1917 g. Period dvoevlastiya* (L., 1973) p. 182.
10. A. Buzinov, *Za Nevskoi zastavoi* (M.-L., 1930) p. 103.
11. *Izvestiya* (3 Oct 1917); *Znamya truda* (4 October 1917).
12. A. L. Popov, *Oktyabr'skii perevorot* (Petrograd, 1919).

Chapter 2: Types of Political Culture in the Industrial Working Class of Petrograd

1. This section deals mainly with the metalworkers, who in 1917 accounted for 60 per cent of the industrial work force and the great majority of the skilled cadres. Apart from the printers (who are treated below in the section on the 'aristocracy'), the only other group with a relatively high skill profile were the woodworkers, who accounted for only 1.7 per cent of the industrial work force (see Table 3.1).
2. I. K. Naumov, *Zapiski vyborzhtsa* (L., 1933) p. 5.
3. See Table 3.4.
4. *Metallist*, no. 3 (1917) p. 3. The relationship between skill and type of production is confirmed by a comparison of the sex ratios of the work

182   *The Petrograd Workers and the Fall of the Old Regime*

force. In 1917, in the 31 European provinces of Russia, there were on average 28.4 women workers for every 100 males in metalworking, but only 17.4 per 100 in machine construction. Female labour was almost universally unskilled. A survey of the Petrograd metalworking industry found the average skill level among males to be 54.2 (on a scale of 1–100) and among females 12.1. *Ekonomicheskoe pololzhenie Rossii nakunune Velikoi Oktyabr'skoi Sotsialisticheskoi revolyutsii* (henceforth cited as Ek. Pol.) (M.-L., 1957) vol. I, pp. 43–4; D. A. Chugaev (ed.), *Rabochii klass sovetskoi Rossii v pervyi god diktatury proletariata* (M., 1967) p. 255.

5. E. A. Kabo, *Ocherki rabochego byta* (M., 1928) p. 19.
6. Buzinov, *Za. Nevskoi zastavoi*, pp. 27–8.
7. See, for example, V. S. Voitinskii, *Gody pobed i porazhenii* (Berlin, 1923) p. 283.
8. *Metallist*, nos. 1–2 (1917).
9. A. S. Shapovalov, *V bor'be za sotsializm* (M., 1934) p. 37.
10. H. Braverman, *Labor and Monopoly Capital* (New York and London: Monthly Review Press, 1974) pp. 110–11.
11. Ya. S. Rozenfel'd and K. I. Klimenko, *Istoriya mashinostroeniya SSR* (M., 1961) p. 54.
12. Shapovalov, *V bor'be za sotsializm*, p. 57.
13. Ibid., p. 74. 'Varshavka'—in workers' parlance, the Workshops of the N.W. Railroad linking Petrograd and Warsaw.
14. N. S-skii, *Psikhologiya russkogo rabochego voprosa* (St Petersburg, 1911) pp. 12–14.
15. A. Shlyapnikov, *Kanun semnadtsatogo goda* (M.-Petrograd, 1923) p. 5.
16. H. L. Haimson, mimeographed copy of paper delivered at meeting of the American Historical Association (1973), entitled 'The Workers' Movement on the Eve of the First World War', p. 36.
17. Shapovalov, *V bor'be za sotsializm*, p. 618.
18. This topic can only be touched upon here. However, the memoirs of Shapovalov offer a moving and vivid illustration of the process of the gradual awakening of new needs, and with them, a growing commitment to the revolutionary struggle. Buzinov, too, gives a good account of the awakening that occurred in the Nevskii District during the revolution of 1905–7. See also, B. Ivanov, *Zapiski proshlogo* (M., 1919) and L. M. Kleinbort, *Ocherki rabochei intelligentsii* (Petrograd, 1923).
19. Buzinov, *Za Nevskoi zastavoi*, pp. 101–3.
20. *V ogne revolyutsionnykh boev*, vol. I (M., 1967) p. 95.
21. Kleinbort, *Ocherki rabochei intelligentsii*, p. 16.
22. *Rabochii kontrol' i natsionalizatsiya promyshlennykh predpriyatii Petrograda v 1917–1919 gg.*, vol. I (L., 1949) p. 226 (henceforth cited as Rab. Kon.).
23. Ibid., pp. 100–1.
24. Cited in Sobolev, *Revolyutsionnoe soznanie*, p. 65.
25. Although I have tried to avoid the use of the term 'conscious' in my own writing on the workers because of the apparent value judgement it entails, one should note the strong consensus within the Russian labour movement, and, indeed, in society at large (S-skii also called the Peters-

burg workers 'the salt of the conscious working people' and singled out the skilled metalworkers for special mention) about which workers were the 'conscious' ones. Buzinov, an SR, contrasted the 'backward' unskilled textile and metalworkers to the 'conscious' skilled metalworkers. *Novaya zhizn*, the Menshevik–Internationalist paper, referred to the metalworkers as 'the most class conscious mass of Petrograd', and the Menshevik economist Bazarov noted that the unskilled labourers, as compared to the skilled workers, were not 'conscious or cultivated [*intelligentnye*]'. *Novaya zhizn*' (8 and 9 Dec 1917).

26. *Izvestiya* (20 June 1917).
27. V. Malakhovskii, *Iz istorii krasnoi gvardii* (L., 1925) p. 25.
28. M. G. Fleer, *Rabochee dvizhenie v gody voiny* (M.-L., 1925) pp. 222–3.
29. Buzinov, *Za Nevskoi zastavoi*, p. 126.
30. P. V. Volobuev, *Proletariat i burzhuaziya Rossii v 1917 g.* (M., 1964) p. 238.
31. I. Skorinko, 'Vospominanie rabochego ob Oktyabre', *Krasnaya letopis'*, no. 6 (1923) p. 145.
32. *Oktyabr'skaya revolyutsiya i fabzavkomy*, vol. I (M., 1927) p. 208 (henceforth cited as FZK).
33. E. Maevskii, *Kanun revolyutsii* (Petrograd, 1918) pp. 96–7.
34. Rab. Kon., pp. 152–3; *Velikaya Oktyabr'skaya sotsialisticheskaya revolyutsiya. Dokumenty i materialy. Nakanune Oktyabr'skogo vooruzhennogo vosstaniya 1–24 oktyabrya 1917 g.* (M., 1962) p. 311 (henceforth cited as Dok. Nak.).
35. Haimson (ed.), *The Mensheviks*, p. 13.
36. Shlyapnikov, *Kanun semnadtsatogo*, p. 11.
37. A. Buiko, *Put' rabochego* (M., 1934) pp. 94–5.
38. Z. V. Stepanov, *Rabochie Petrograda v period podgotovki i provedeniya Oktyabr'skogo vooruzhennogo vosstaniya* (L., 1973) p. 129.
39. According to the industrial census of August 1918, 84.2 per cent of the industrial working class of Petrograd was Russian. Poles constituted 5.8 per cent, Lithuanians and Letts 2.6 per cent, Finns 2.3 per cent, Germans 0.5 per cent and Jews 0.3 per cent. Ibid., p. 42.
40. Izrail' Moiseevich Kogan, for example, was elected by the workers of the Skorokhod Shoe Factory to the Petrograd Soviet on 17 December 1917. Leningradskii gosurdarstvennyi arkhiv Oktyabr'skoi revolyutsii i sotsialisticheskogo stroitel'stva, fond 7384, opis' 7, delo 21, list 80 (henceforth cited as LGAORSS).
41. Fleer, *Rabochee dvizhenie*, p. 209. In Moscow, by contrast, workers participated in a strike against firms with German ties. Shlyapnikov, *Kanun semnadtsatogo*, p. 184.
42. N. I. Potresov, *Posmertnyi sbornik proizvedenii*, pp. 230–42, cited in Haimson, *The Mensheviks*, p. 13.
43. V. Perazich, *Tekstily Leningrada v 1917 g.* (L., 1927) pp. 81–2, 86.
44. See, for example, T. Shatilova, *Ocherk istorii Leningradskogo soyuza khimikov 1907–1918* (L., 1927) p. 10.
45. *Istoriya Leningradskogo soyuza poligraficheskogo proizvodstva*, vol. 1 (L., 1925) p. 48.
46. S-skii, *Psikhologiya russkogo*, p. 14.

47. V ogne revolyutsionnykh boev, vol. II (M., 1971) pp. 34–5.
48. See, for example, A. E. Suknovalov et al., Fabrika 'Krasnoe znamya' (L., 1968) pp. 98–9; Rabotnitsa is replete with such accounts.
49. Suknovalov, Fabrika, pp. 58–80 passim.
50. Kabo, Ocherki rabochego byta, p. 127.
51. Rabotnitsa (19 April 1914).
52. Ibid. (16 March 1914), p. 2.
53. Ibid. (4 May 1914), pp. 12–13.
54. Kabo, o cherki rabochego byta, p. 132.
55. Rabotnitsa (16 March 1914).
56. Ibid. (16 March 1914) p. 10.
57. Ibid. (19 April 1914).
58. About one-half of Petrograd's 30 000–40 000 needleworkers worked in small workshops sewing underwear and uniforms for the army. The others worked at home in a putting-out system. See Table 3.2 and Velikaya oktyabr'skaya sotsialisticheskaya revolyutsiya. Dokumenty i materialy. Oktyabr'skoe vooruzhennoe vosstanie v Petrograde (M., 1957) p. 122 (henceforth cited as Dok. Okt.).
59. Rashin, Formirovanie rabochego, p. 601.
60. Kabo, Ocherki rabochego byta, pp. 30, 36, 39 and passim.
61. See, for example, K. Shelavin, Ocherki russkoi revolyutsii 1917 g., part I (Petrograd, 1923) p. 60 and Novaya zhizn' (8 Dec 1917), editorial by Bazarov.
62. Kleinbort, Ocherki rabochei intelligentsii, p. 84.
63. At the 20 March session of the Workers' Section of the Petrograd Soviet, one of the delegates from the Petrograd District stated:

> You know that there are two categories of workers at the factories: the lower—labourers and women, and the skilled workers, who receive rather decent remuneration corresponding to the high cost of living. It is not a question of those workers who receive a good wage; they are secure. But at yesterday's district meeting it turned out that at many plants they receive from 1.20 rubles to 1.30 rubles a day. In such conditions it is totally impossible to live in any human fashion. (LGAORSS, f.1000, op.73, d.12, 1.15.)

64. Shatilova, Ocherk istorii, p. 10.
65. S-skii, Psikhologiya russkogo, p. 41.
66. Novaya zhizn' (8 Dec 1917).
67. Kabo, Ocherki rabochego byta, pp. 132 and 223.
68. Novaya zhizn' (1 Aug 1917). See also ibid. (8 Dec 1917) for Bazarov's complaint that the unskilled masses, the war-time workers, failed to see the necessity of raising productivity, in contrast to the skilled workers, the 'genuine proletariat'. According to the August 1918 industrial census, 31.1 per cent of all factory workers in European Russia had owned land before the October revolution, with 20.9 per cent actually working it through members of their family in the village. In the more skilled printing and machine-construction industries, these figures were 17.4 and 9.8 and 24.1 and 13.9 respectively. In needlework too, they

were relatively low—23.8 and 17.1. In contrast, 29.3 per cent in metalworking owned land, with 19.6 working it.In cotton, the figures were even higher—33.6 and 20.4 respectively. Rashin, *Formirovanie rabochego*, p. 573.

69. C. W. Mills, *The Sociological Imagination* (New York: Oxford University Press, 1970) p. 6.
70. See, for example E. J. Hobsbawm, 'Peasants and Politics', *Journal of Peasant Studies*, vol. I (1973) p. 13; and B. Galeski, *Chlopi i zawod relnika* (Warsaw, 1963) p. 49, cited in T. Shanin (ed.), *Peasants and Peasant Society* (Harmondsworth: Penguin Books, 1971) p. 254. Galeskii has observed: 'Because the farmer's produce is essential and, at the lowest level, sufficient for human existence, the labour of the farmer is necessary for the existence of the society as a whole; but the existence of society is not to the same extent necessary for the existence of the farmer.' Ibid.
71. *Izvestiya* (3 Aug 1917).
72. Kleinbort, *Ocherki rabochei intelligentsii*, pp. 64, 67.
73. Ibid., p. 70.
74. Ibid.
75. Kabo, *Ocherki rabochego byta*, p. 222.
76. Sutti Ortiz, 'Reflections on the Concept of "Peasant Culture" and "Peasant Cognitive System"', in Shanin, *Peasants and Peasant Society*, p. 330.
77. According to one student of the Russian peasantry, periods of peasant unrest in the second half of the nineteenth and early twentieth centuries clustered around such external events as the tentative agrarian reforms of the late 1840s, the Crimean War, the Russo-Turkish War and the revolutions of 1905 and 1917. R. H. Scott, 'The Russian Peasantry in the First and Second Dumas', mimeographed seminar paper, Russian Institute, Columbia University (1973) pp. 10–11.
78. Buzinov, *Za Nevskoi zastavoi*, pp. 104–5.
79. Ivanov, *Zapiski proshlogo*, p. 63.
80. Ibid.
81. F. A. Bulkin, *Na zare profdvizheniya* (1924) p. 309.
82. *Izvestiya* (3 Aug 1917).
83. F. N. Samoilov, *Vospominaniya ob ivanovo-voznesenskom rabochem dvizhenii*, part II (M., 1924) pp. 65–88 passim.
84. Like the term 'conscious worker', 'worker aristocracy' was used by Bolsheviks and Mensheviks alike to denote the same type of worker. For example, the Menshevik–Internationalist, Osokin, referring to part of the printers, wrote of 'the worker aristocracy, to a significant degree detached from the masses, [that] has remained in the ranks of Menshevism'. *Novaya zhizn'* (7 Dec 1917).
85. This is especially true of the printer element of the 'aristocracy' which in Petrograd in 1912–14 was second only to the machine-construction workers in level of participation in the economic and political strike movement. See for example, *Byuleten' Obshchestva zavodchikov i fabrikantov Moskovskogo promyshlennogo raiona, Rabochee dvizhenie yanvar'–mai 1912*, pp. 13, 15, 22.

86. The printers were in fact not a homogeneous group, neither in terms of their material situation nor their political culture. For the present purposes 'printer' is used more or less synonymously with 'typesetters' (one-third of all Petrograd printing workers in 1905), as the numerically and ideologically dominant group that set the tone in the printing plants. *Istoriya Leningradskogo soyuza rabochikh poligraficheskogo proizvodstva* (L., 1925) p. 13. |

87. T. Shatilova, *Krasnaya letopis'*, no. 2 (1927) p. 187 and *Istoriya rabochikh Leningrada*, vol. I (L., 1972) p. 444.

88. In fact, by the start of the war, unemployment among printers reached 20–25 per cent, and between 1 Jan 1914 and 1 Jan 1917 their numbers in Petrograd declined from 23 000 to 19 000, while the proportion of women in the industry rose from 15.1 per cent to 33.7 per cent, indicating a serious decline in the overall level of skills. A. Tikhanov, 'Rabochie pechatniki v Petrograde (1904–1914)', in *Materialy po istorii professional'nogo dvizheniya v Rossii*, vol. III (M., 1925) p. 114, and Rashin, *Formirovanie rabochego*, p. 83.

89. *Istoriya Leningradskogo soyuza rabochikh poligraf*, p. 14.

90. Ibid., p. 17.

91. *Istoriya Leningradskogo soyuza rabochikh poligraf*, p. 13.

92. Ibid., p. 13.

93. *Materialy po statistike truda Severnoi oblasti*, vyp. I, p. 10. In fact two-thirds of all Petrograd industrial workers were employed in only 38 factories of over 2000 workers each. Stepanov, *Rabochie Petrograda*, p. 32.

94. *Istoriya Leningradskogo soyuza rabochikh poligraf*, p. 34.

95. Most larger factories in early March were in turmoil, the workers trying to win new economic demands. The eight-hour day, which was the major economic demand of the February revolution, had been instituted in the larger factories on the workers' own initiative as they returned following the general strike (see below, Chapter 4). Cited in R. J. Devlin, 'Petrograd Workers and Workers' Factory Committees 1917' (PhD Dissertation, SUNY Binghamton, 1976, mimeographed draft), Ch. II, p. 9 (emphasis my own).

96. Tikhanov, 'Rabochie pechatniki', p. 121.

97. *Istoriya Leningradskogo soyuza rabochikh poligraf*, p. 28; Tikhanov, 'Rabochie pechatniki', p. 117.

98. Tikhanov, ibid. pp. 113, 131.

99. *Pervyi legal'nyi Peterburgskii komitet RSDRP (b) v 1917 g.* (M.-L., 1927) p. 111 (henceforth cited as Peka).

100. Tikhanov, 'Rabochie pechatniki' pp. 115, 131–2.

101. *Doneseniya komissarov Petrogradskogo Voenno-revolyutsionnogo komiteta* (M., 1957) p. 205. Shotman similarly recalled a large number of workers at the Obukhovskii Factory living in state apartments with two rooms and a kitchen. A. Shotman, *Kak iz iskry vozgorelos' plamya* (L., 1935) p. 14. See also L. S. Ganichev, *Na Aptekarskom ostrove* (L., 1967) p. 143.

102. Ganichev, *Na Aptekarshom*, p. 128.

103. Tikhanov, 'Rabochie pechatniki', p. 122.
104. Shotman, *Kak iz iskry*, p. 14.
105. A. Buntilov, *Za pechatnym stolom* (M., 1923) pp. 8–9, 15. See also Stepanov, *Rabochie Petrograda*, p. 31, and *Rossiiskii proletariat. Oblik, bor'ba gegemoniya* (M., 1970) pp. 14–15, note 21.
106. *Izvestiya* (27 Oct 1917).
107. V. Kukushkin, *Sestroretskaya dinastiya* (L., 1959); and 'Na Sestroretskom zavode', in *Batsiony revolyutsii*, vol. I (L., 1967).
108. Shotman, *Kak iz iskry*, p. 14.
109. *Novaya zhizn'* (15 Dec 1917).
110. Samoilov, *Vospominaniya*, pp. 66, 89, 90.
111. Kleinbort, *Ocherki rabochei intelligentsii*, p. 81.
112. Ibid., p. 82.
113. Bulkin, *Na zare profdvizheniya*, p. 238.
114. See, for example, E. N. Burdzhalov, *Vtoraya russkaya revolyutsiya* (M., 1967) and A. Startsev, 'K voprosu o sostave rabochei krasnoi gvardii Petrograda', *Istoriya SSSR*, no. 1 (1962) p. 141.
115. P. F. Kudelli (ed.), *Leningradskie rabochie v bor'be za vlast' sovetov v 1917 g.* (L., 1924) p. 112.
116. See, for example, Suknovalov, *Fabrika 'Krasnoe znamya'*, pp. 63, 77, 85; S. Alliluev, 'V dni Oktyabrya na Elektricheskoi stantsii imeni 1886', *Krasnaya letopis'*, no. 6 (1923) p. 327; T. Shatilova, *Ocherk istorii soyuza khimikov 1909–1918* (L., 1927) p. 28; Perazich, *Tekstily Leningrada*, p. 91.
117. Stepanov, *Rabochie Petrograda*, p. 46.
118. L. V. Golovanova, 'Raionnye komitety RSDRP(b) Petrograda v 1917 g.' (Candidate's dissertation, Leningrad State University, 1974) Appendix, Table 7.
119. *V ogne revolyutsionnykh boev*, vol. II, p. 37.
120. Haimson, mimeographed draft of forthcoming study on Russian labour, first of four volume series, *Russian Society and Politics on the Eve of the First World War* (to be published by W. W. Norton), Ch. III. See also *Rech'* (3 May 1912), and *Pravda* (31 Aug 1912), cited in ibid., pp. 18 and 39.
121. Kleinbort, *Ocherki rabochei intelligentsii*, p. 30.
122. I. D. Levin, 'Rabochie kluby v Petrograde (1907–1914)', *Materialy po istorii professional'nogo dvizheniya v Rossii*, sbornik III (M., 1925) pp. 100–2.
123. Shapovalov, *V bor'be za sotsializm*, p. 121; A. K. Tsvetkov-Prosveshchenskii, *Mezhdu dvumya revolyutsiyamy* (M.-L., 1933) p. 87.
124. Dok. Nak., p. 306.
125. Scott, 'The Russian Peasantry', p. 20.
126. Kleinbort, *Ocherki rabochei intelligentsii*, p. 127.
127. D. Mandel, 'The Intelligentsia and the Working Class in 1917', *Critique*, no. 14 (1981), pp. 68–70.
128. Shlyapnikov, *Kanun semnadtsatogo*, p. 188.
129. Bulkin, *Na zare profdvizheniya*, p. 248.

Chapter 3: Social Composition of the Industrial Working Class of Petrograd and its Districts

1. *Materialy po statistike truda Severnoi oblasti*, vyp. I (1918) p. 18.
2. *Materialy po statistike Petrograda*, vyp. I (1920) p. 10.
3. *Materialy po statistike truda*, vyp. V, p. 43.
4. L. S. Gaponenko, 'Rabochii klass Rossii nakanune velikogo Oktyabrya', *Istoricheskie zapiski*, no. 73 (M., 1963) p. 51.
5. G. A. Trukan, *Oktyabr' v tsentral'noi Rossii* (M., 1967) pp. 16–17.
6. Stepanov, *Rabochie Petrograda*, p. 32.
7. Ibid.
8. The Bulletin of the Society of Industrialists of the Central Industrial Region noted in 1912 concerning Petrograd: 'That economic motives alone could not play a predominant role is clear if only from the fact that wages of metalworkers in Petrograd Guberniya are much higher than in other industrial *guberniyas*. The same can be said of the wages of workers in the printing industry. Nevertheless, the strike movement for this period was nowhere as intense in the Russian Empire as in Petrograd.' *Byuleten' obshchestva fabrikantov i zavodchikov Moskovskogo promyshlennogo raiona*, no. 16 (1912).
9. Stepanov, *Rabochie Petrograda*, pp. 31 and 42.
10. A. Anikst, *Organizatsiya raspredeleniya rabochei sily* (M., 1920) p. 51. cited in O. I. Shkaratan, 'Izmeneniya v sotsial'nom sostave rabochikh Leningrada 1917–1928', *Istoriya SSSR*, no. 5 (1959) p. 25.
11. N. Antonov, *Dva goda diktatury proletariata v metallopromyshlennosti Petrograda* (1920) p. 15, cited in Shkaratan, 'Izmeneniya v sostave'.
12. I. P. Leiberov and O. I. Shkaratan, 'K voprosu o sostave petrogradskikh promyshlennykh rabochikh v 1917 g.', *Voprosy istorii*, no. 1 (1961) p. 52 and pp. 42, 58, passim.
13. *Novaya zhizn'* (27 Dec, 1917).
14. V. A. Tsybul'skii, 'Rabochie Sestroretskogo zavoda v 1917', *Istoriya SSR*, no. 4 (1959) p. 143.
15. A. Smirnov, *Poslednie dni Utemanov* (M.-L., 1935) p. 8.
16. A. Arbuzova, 'Oktyabr' 1917 g. na Petrogradskom trubochnom zavode', *Krasnaya letopis'*, no. 6 (1923) p. 175.
17. Stepanov, *Rabochie Petrograda*, p. 42.
18. Rashin, *Formirovanie rabochego*, p. 575, Table 143.
19. Leiberov and Shkaratan, 'K voprosu', p. 51.
20. Stepanov, *Rabochie Petrograda*, p. 43 and Ek. Pol. vol. I, p. 43.
21. Leiberov and Shkaratan, 'K voprosu'.
22. *Krasnyi Treugol'nik na putyakh Oktyabrya* (L., 1927) p. 9.
23. Suknovalov *et al.*, *Fabrika 'Krasnoe znamya'*, p. 7.
24. I. M. Frantishev, *Leningradskie krasnostroiteli* (L., 1962) p. 59.
25. *Vyborgskaya storna* (L., 1957) p. 181.
26. Peka, p. 315.
27. *Znamya truda* (24 Aug 1917).
28. In common usage 'Vyborg District' usually also included Novaya derevnya and Polyustrovo. Some of the general sources for this section are: *Raionnye sovety Petrograda v 1917g.*, 3 vols (M.-L., 1966–8);

Golovanova, 'Raionnye komitety'; *V ogne revolyutsionnykh boev*; and Stepanov, *Rabochie Petrograda.*

29. *Iskra* (3 Oct 1917).
30. According to Golovanova, 51 one of the 56 (89.5 per cent) members of the Bolshevik Vyborg district committee between February and July 1917 were workers. The average for all districts was 74.1 per cent (Golovanova, 'Raionnye komitety', appendix, Table 7). A report by the Vyborg district committee in September 1917 on its first five months of legal activity noted that 'the esteemed task of being the initiator of the revolution fell upon the Vyborg District. But this task also carried many obligations: for lack of an organised central apparatus, the Petrograd Committee, it had to meet the very numerous requests for agitators and organisers not only in Petrograd but also in the provinces.' As for the role of the district committee itself, after the first few months of the revolution, 'many factories are managing on their own, and often a day will go by without a request [for speakers]. Only the army units totally rely on the agitational collegium. This ... speaks of the fact that here new capable workers have arisen who manage without outside help. And life required more than a few of them. We needed representatives to the local Soviets, central Soviet, local and central dumas. And the district was able to give.' *Revolyutsionnoe dvizhenie v Rossi v avguste 1917 g.* (M., 1967) pp. 94–6.
31. L. Leont'ev, 'V ryadakh "Mezhraionki"', *Krasnaya letopis'*, no. 11 (1924) p. 131.
32. *Raionnye sovety Petrograda v 1917 godu*, vol. II (L., 1967) p. 91 (henceforth cited as Raisovety).
33. *V ogne revolyutsionnykh boev*, vol. II, p. 102.
34. *Raisovety*, vol. I, p. 123.
35. Stepanov, *Rabochie Petrograda*, p. 33.
36. *Bol'sheviki Petrograda v Oktyabr'skoi revolyutsii* (L., 1957) p. 33.
37. *Moskovskaya zastava v 1917 godu* (L., 1957) p. 128.
38. Stepanov, *Rabochie Petrograda*, p. 35.
39. *V ogne revolyutsionnykh boev*, vol. II, p. 217.
40. *V boyakh za oktyabr'* (L., 1932) p. 27.
41. M. Rozanov, *Obukhovtsy* (L., 1938) p. 354.
42. Peka, p. 194.
43. Golovanova, 'Raionnye komitety', appendix, Table 1.
44. *Derevoobdelochnik*, no. 20 (Mar 1908).

Chapter 4: The Honeymoon Period—From the February to the April Days

1. Shlyapnikov, *Kanun semnadtsatogo goda*, vol. II, p. 104.
2. See, for example, ibid., vol. I, pp. 13–19.
3. I. P. Leiberov, 'O revolyutsionnykh vystupleniyakh petrogradskogo proletariata v gody pervoi mirovoi voiny i Fevral'skoi revolyutsii', *Voprosi istorii*, no. 2 (1964) p. 65.
4. E. N. Burdzhalov, *Vtoraya russkaya revolyutsiya* (M., 1967) pp. 32–3.

190 *The Petrograd Workers and the Fall of the Old Regime*

5. *Proletarskaya revolyutsiya*, no. 11 (13) (1923) pp. 265–6.
6. There are a number of useful general accounts of the February revolution written from different points of view: E. N. Burdzhalov, *Vtoraya russkaya revolyutsiya* (M., 1967); N. Sukhanov, *Zapiski o revolyutsii*, vol. I (Berlin–Petrograd, 1919); A. Shlyapnikov, *Semnadtsatyi god* (L., 1925); L. Trotsky, *The Russian Revolution*, vol. I, chs. 1–15, W. H. Chamberlin, *The Russian Revolution*, vol. I, chs. 1–4 (1935); S. Mstislavskii, *Sem' dnei* (Berlin–L.–M., 1932). Specific events will be mentioned here only in so far as they touch directly on the main issue: working-class attitudes.
7. Cited in Burdzhalov, *Vtoraya russkaya*, p. 117.
8. Ibid., p. 120.
9. Cited in ibid., p. 122.
10. 'Fevral'skaya revolyutsiya i Okhrannoe otdelenie', *Byloe*, nos. 7–8 (1918) p. 162. A more recent estimate based on more complete data sets the figure at 128 000. Leiberov, 'O revolyutsionnykh', p. 65.
11. Burdzhalov, *Vtoraya russkaya*, p. 143; Leiberov, ibid.
12. *Byloe*, nos 7–8 (1918) p. 173. One police official reported a hack driver saying: 'Tomorrow the cabbies will not be taking the general public but only the leaders of the disorders.' Ibid., p. 169. Cabbies were not noted for their radicalism.
13. Ibid., p. 174.
14. *Izvestiya Petrogradskogo soveta rabochikh i soldatskikh deputatov* (3 Mar 1917).
15. A. Shlyapnikov, *Semnadtsatyi god*, vol. I (M.-Petrograd, 1923) p. 240.
16. Peka, pp. x–xi. Emphasis my own.
17. *Revolyutsionnoe dvizhenie v Rossii posle sverzheniya samoderzhaviya* (henceforth: Dok. Feb) (M., 1957) p. 475. For similar resolutions, see *Pravda* (17 Mar 1917) (from Nobel', Vakuum and others); *Pravda* (23 Mar) (Sestroretsk Arms Factory); *Izvestiya* (4 Mar) (Petrograd Union of Woodworkers); (8 Mar) (meeting of printers).
18. *Pravda* (19 Mar 1917).
19. Ibid. For similar resolutions, see Dok. Feb., p. 478 (Sestroretsk Arms Factory); *Pravda*, no. 3 (1917) (tavern and hotel workers), Shlyapnikov, *Kanun semnadtsatogo*, vol. II, p. 292.
20. *Izvestiya* (4 Mar 1917).
21. N. Sukhanov, *Zapiski o revolyutsii*, vol. I, p. 210. See also W. G. Rosenburg, *The Liberals in the Russian Revolution* (Princeton: Princeton University Press, 1974) p. 178.
22. Although the Soviet EC had decided against direct Soviet representation in the government, Kerenskii, a member of the EC, entered the government on his own initiative. In a typically theatrical and emotionally charged speech before the 2 March plenum of the Soviet, he won approval 'by acclamation' (there was no discussion or vote) for his action. I have been unable to find any evidence of worker sentiment for or against Kerenskii on this. Apparently it made little difference.
23. M. Ferro, *La Révolution de 1917* (Paris, 1967) p. 178.
24. Dok. Feb., pp. 543–4; Rab. kon., p. 42.
25. LGAORSS, f. 24602, op. 7, d. 7, l. 68.
26. Ibid., f. 7384, op. 9, d. 293, l. 3.

27. Dok. Feb., p. 446.
28. LGAORSS, f. 4601, op. 1, d. 10, l. 9 ob.; Rab. kon., p. 57.
29. A. Tanyaev, *Ocherki po istorii zheleznodorozhnikov v revolyutsii 1917 g.* (M.-L., 1925) pp. 3–4.
30. *Izvestiya* (8 Mar 1917).
31. Ibid. (9 Mar 1917).
32. Tanyaev, *Ocherki po istorii*, p. 16.
33. F. Dingel'shtedt, *Krasnaya letopis'* (1925) no. 1 (12), p. 193.
34. *Pravda* (9 Mar 1917).
35. Burdzhalov, *Vtoraya russkaya*, p. 286.
36. *Rabochaya gazeta* (13 Mar 1907).
37. Ibid. (9 Apr 1917).
38. *Pravda* (8 Mar 1917).
39. Shlyapnikov, *Semnadtsatyi god*, vol. I, p. 225.
40. Burdzhalov, *Vtoraya russkaya*, p. 223.
41. Shlyapnikov, *Semnadtsatyi god*, vol. I, p. 222.
42. *Pravda* (7 Apr 1917).
43. *Izvestiya* (15 Apr 1917).
44. Ibid. (16 Apr 1917) and *Revolyutsionnoe dvizhenie v Rossii v aprele* (M., 1958) p. 393 (henceforth: Dok. Apr.).
45. Dok. Feb., p. 546.
46. Ibid., p. 554.
47. *Pervaya Petrogradksaya obshchegorodskaya konferenstiya RSDRP (b) v aprele 1917 g.* (M., 1925) pp. 16–17. See also M. Mitel'man, B. Glebov and A. Ul'yanskii, *Istoriya Putilovskogo zavoda 1801–1917 gg.*, 3rd edn (L., 1961) p. 574.
48. Shlyapnikov, *Semnadtsatyi god*, vol. II, p. 142.
49. M. Rafes, *Byloe*, no. 19 (1922) p. 194.
50. Sukhanov, *Zapiski o revolyutsii*, vol. I, p. 127.
51. Ibid., vol. III, pp. 217, 223, 310, 313.
52. *Pravda* (11 Apr 1917).
53. V. Perazich, *Tekstili Leningrada v 1917 g.* (L., 1927) p. 28.
54. A Smirnov, *Poslednie dni Utemanov, 1917 god na fabrike 'Skorokhod'* (M.-L., 1935) pp. 39–40.
55. Sukhanov, *Zapiski o revolyutsii*, vol. I, pp. 22 and 96.
56. *Byloe*, nos. 7–8 (1918) p. 171.
57. Shlyapnikov, *Kanun semnadtsatogo goda*, pp. 103–4.
58. Ibid., p. 115.
59. E. Maevskii, *Kanun revolyutsii—iz istorii rabochego dvizheniya nakanune revolyutsii 1917 goda* (Petrograd, 1918) p. 5.
60. Shlyapnikov, *Kanun semnadtsatogo*, vol. I, pp. 116–19.
61. Ibid., pp. 119–20.
62. In a sense, the Mensheviks were driven to insist on the existence of a progressive, potentially revolutionary segment of census society, since they were convinced that the working class alone could never succeed in carrying through the democratic revolution. As for the peasants, whom the Bolsheviks counted on as allies of the workers, they were not to be trusted. In fact, to the Mensheviks, they represented a benighted mass that was a potentially counterrevolutionary force.
63. Maevskii, *Kanun revolyutsii*, p. 4.

64. Shlyapnikov, op cit., p. 126.
65. One should note that strikes, in contrast to the tactics advocated by the Workers' Group, represented an *independent* working-class tactic. Maevskii, *Kanun revolyutsii*, pp. 7–8.
66. Sukhanov, *Zapiski o revolyutsii*, vol. I, p. 18.
67. Even now, however, the census opposition dared call only for a 'government of confidence' and not a 'responsible government'. As for any action, that was entirely out of the question. R. Pearson, *The Russian Moderates and the Crisis of Tsarism* (London and Basingstoke: Macmillan, 1977) p. 114.
68. Maevskii, *Kanun revolyutsii*, p. 10. Not that the Kadets were grateful for this help. *Rech'*, the organ of their party, labelled as a provocation the rumours of a demonstration. B. B. Grave, *Burzhuaziya nakanune Fevral'skoi revolyutsii* (M.-L., 1927) p. 181; Maevskii, *Kanun revolyutsii*, p. 11.
69. Grave, *Burzhuaziya nakanune*, p. 184.
70. *Byloe*, p. 160.
71. Maevskii, *Kanun revolyutsii*, p. 12.
72. L. Trotsky, *History of the Russian Revolution*, vol. I (London: Sphere Books, 1965) pp. 134–5; Sukhanov, *Zapiski o revolyutsii*, p. 63.
73. Burdzhalov, *Vtoraya russkaya*, vol. I, p. 203.
74. Ibid., p. 68.
75. Maevskii, *Kanun revolyutsii*, p. 12.
76. Shlyapnikov, *Semnadtsatyi god*, vol. I, p. 203.
77. Ibid.
78. *Znamya truda* (17 Nov 1917).
79. Stankevich, an SR, put this phenomenon into perhaps clearer perspective in his memoirs: 'Officially, they celebrated, blessed the revolution, shouted "hurrah" for the fighters for freedom, decorated themselves with ribbons and walked around with red banners. All said "we," "our" revolution, "our" victory, "our" freedom. But in their hearts, in intimate conversation, they were horrified, shuddered, and felt themselves captives of a hostile elemental milieu travelling along an unknown path.' Cited in Sobolev, *Revolyutsionnoe soznanie*, p. 111.
80. Dok. Feb., p. 420.
81. Shlyapnikov, *Semnadtsatyi god*, vol. I, p. 224.
82. Burdzhalov, *Vtoraya russkaya*, pp. 380–1.
83. B. Shabalin, 'Ot fevralya k oktyabryu—iz istorii zavoda "Krasnyi Treugol'nik"', in *Bastiony revolyutsii*, vol. I, p. 269.
84. Cited in Sobolev, *Revolyutsionnoe soznanie*, p. 237.
85. S. Mstislavskii, *Sem' dnei* (Berlin–Petersburg–M., 1922) p. 65.
86. Burdzhalov, *Vtoraya russkaya*, pp. 244–5.
87. Rafes, *Byloe* (1922) p. 187. Here one can also see the strange coexistence of anxiety and elation.
88. Perazich, *Tekstili Leningrada*, p. 23.
89. Ibid., p. 19.
90. Ibid., p. 22. See also A. Smirnov, *Poslednie dni Utemanov*, p. 29.
91. Cited in Burdzhalov, *Vtoraya russkaya*, pp. 203–4.
92. *Pervaya Petrogradskaya*, pp. 13, 19.

93. *Rabochaya gazeta* (7 Mar 1917). See also 12 Mar and *Izvestiya* (2 Mar 1917).

94. Zalezhskii tried to explain the PC's endorsement of the PG in these terms—it could not go against the will of the Soviet. But in fact, this was the main motivation of only the left minority in February. V. N. Zalezhskii, 'Penvyi legal'nyi Peka', *Proletarskaya revolyutsia*, no. 13 (1923) p. 145. As Lenin stated in April: 'Even our Bolsheviks showed a trusting attitude towards the government, and one can explain this only by the intoxication with the revolution.' V. I. Lenin, *Polnoe sobranie sochinenii*, 5th edn (M., 1962) vol. XXXI, p. 106.

95. Lenin, *Polnoe Sobranie*, pp. 106–7.

Chapter 5: The February Revolution in the Factories

1. Cited in Sobolev, *Revolutsionnoe soznanie*, p. 58.
2. Cited in Mitel'man *et al.*, *Istoriya Putilovskogo*, p. 487.
3. *Rech'* (29 Mar 1917).
4. *Rabochaya gazeta* (7 Mar 1917).
5. A. Ya. Grunt, *Pobeda Oktyabr'skoi revolyutsii v Moskve* (M., 1961) p. 38.
6. LGAORSS, f. 4591, op. 1, d. 1, l. 26. (Conference of Factories of the Artillery Authority).
7. *Izvestiya* (6 Mar 1917).
8. Sobolev, *Revolutsionnoe soznanie*, p. 58.
9. *Pravda*, no. 11 (1917).
10. LGAORSS, f. 7384, op. 9, d. 293, l. 5. (6 Mar 1917).
11. Dok. Feb., p. 230.
12. Perazich, *Tekstili Leningrada*, p. 31 (Maxwell Mill).
13. Dok. Feb., pp. 569–77.
14. Ibid., p. 39.
15. *Pravda* (9 Mar 1917).
16. Thus, in the Moscow District, an SR stronghold well into August and September, the workers were extremely hostile to the Soviet's decision. See for example, the very strongly worded resolution of the Dinamo Electrical Factory (43 per cent female) (Ek. Pol., vol. I, p. 42), roundly condemning the Soviet and flatly refusing to return to work. LGAORSS, f. 7384, op. 9, d. 293, l. 11.
17. Dok. Feb., p. 231.
18. *Izvestiya* (10 Mar 1917).
19. Sobolev, *Revolutsionnoe soznanie*, p. 61.
20. *Torgovo-promyshlennaya gazeta* (17 Mar 1917).
21. Peka, pp. 27–8.
22. Cited in P. V. Volobuev, *Proletariat i burzhuaziya v 1917 g.* (M., 1964) p. 64.
23. Cited in V. I. Selitskii in *Istoriya rabochikh Leningrada*, vypusk II (L., 1963) p. 17.
24. Volobuev, *Proletariat i burzhuaziya*, p. 126.
25. Ibid., p. 90.
26. Ibid., p. 91.

27. Ibid., pp. 90–1.
28. Ek. Pol., vol. I, p. 45.
29. LGAORSS, f. 1000, op. 73, d. 6, l. 4.
30. Ibid., ll. 9–10.
31. Ibid., ll. 26–8.
32. Ibid., l. 11. One might note in passing that the formulation of this demand, at least from a Marxist perspective, is strictly 'reformist'.
33. Ek. Pol., vol. I, p. 41.
34. Suknovalov and Fomenkov, *Fabrika 'Krasnoe znamya'*, p. 63.
35. Smirnov, *Poslednie dni Utemanov*, pp. 24–6.
36. LGAORSS, ll. 14–15.
37. *Izvestiya* (24 Mar 1917). In the last week in March the paper was full of such resolutions.
38. Dok. Feb., p. 570.
39. *Izvestiya* (31 Mar 1917).
40. *Izvestiya*, organ of the Petrograd Soviet, in an editorial on 11 April on this 'campaign of the bourgeois press', declared: 'You try to frighten us with the spectre of civil war, but it is you who have begun it.'
41. Volobuev, *Proletariat i burzhuaziya*, p. 157.
42. LGAORSS, f. 4601, op. 1, d. 10, l. 33.
43. Volobuev, *Proletariat i burzhuaziya*, p. 157.
44. Dok. Apr., p. 468.
45. *Rabochaya gazeta* (7 and 16 Apr 1917).
46. M. G. Fleer, *Rabochee dvizhenie v gody voiny* (M., 1925) pp. 298–304.
47. In many state enterprises, however, where the administrators were literally servants of the old regime, the right of 'control' over management was immediately asserted. This issue will be treated below.
48. LGAORSS, f. 4602, op. 7, d. 7, l. 68. Similar purges occurred in Portugal after the democratic revolution of April 1974. See, for example, *The New York Times* (14 May 1974).
49. Mitel'man *et al.*, *Istoriya Putilovskogo*, p. 567. See also N. S. Sergeev, *Metallisty–Istoriya Leningradskogo Metallicheskogo zavoda im. XXII s'ezda KPSS* (L., 1967) p. 374.
50. Perazich, *Tekstili Leningrada*, p. 20.
51. See Sergeev, *Metallisty*, p. 374; and M. Mikhailov, *Krasnaya letopis'*, nos 50–1 (1932) p. 189.
52. GIALO, f. 416, op. 25, d. 5, ll. 2–3.
53. See, for example, Sergeev, *Metallisty*; and LGAORSS, f. 4601, op. 1, d. 10, l. 33.
54. GIALO, l. 12. Also cited in Sobolev, *Revolutsionnoe soznanie*, p. 72.
55. Shlyapnikov, *Kanun semnadtsatogo goda*, vol. I, p. 11.
56. See Sergeev, *Metallisty*, p. 379; and Rab. Kon., p. 45.
57. GIALO, f. 416, op. 5, d. 30, l. 19.
58. Ibid., f. 416, op. 25, d. 5, l. 6.
59. Ibid., f. 416, op. 5, d. 30, l. 64.
60. Ibid.
61. Ibid., l. 155.
62. Rab. Kon., p. 42.
63. Shlyapnikov, *Kanun semnadtsatogo*, vol. I, p. 167.

64. *Izvestiya* (11 Mar 1917). In passing, one should note the political functions assigned to the factory committees, as described in the second point. In fact, the committees regularly called meetings on political questions, organised the workers' militia and led the workers in their political actions.
65. Maevskii, *Kanun revolyutsii*, p. 34.
66. Dok. Feb., pp. 491–2.
67. G. Borisov and S. Vasil'ev, *Stankostroiteli imeni Sverdlova* (L., 1962) p. 80.
68. Sobolev, *Revolutsionnoe soznanie*, p. 82.
69. Dok. Feb., p. 484.
70. M. Balabanov, *Rabochee dvizhenie v Rossii v gody pod'ema 1912–1914 gg.* (L., 1927) p. 31.
71. *Pravda* (8 Apr 1917).
72. LGAORSS, f. 1000, op. 73, d. 16, l. 6.
73. Ibid., l. 30.
74. Rab. Kon., p. 57.
75. Ibid., pp. 58 and 53.
76. Dok. Feb., pp. 575–7. For the provisional constitution of the factory committee, see Dok. Apr., pp. 358–60.
77. Cited in Sobolev, *Revolutsionnoe soznanie*, p. 66.
78. Rab. Kon., p. 179.
79. LGAORSS, f. 9391, op. 7, d. 8, ll. 7 and 12.
80. Ibid., l. 30.
81. Ibid., f. 9391, op. 1, d. 11, l. 4.
82. Tanyaev, *Ocherki po istorii*, p. 53.
83. K. Bazilevich, *Professional'noe dvizhenie rabotnikov svyazi* (M., 1927) p. 40.
84. Dok. Apr., pp. 383–5.
85. Balabanov, *Rabochee dvizhenie*, p. 38.
86. Dok. Feb., pp. 479–80.

Chapter 6: From the April to the July Days

1. Sukhanov, *Zapiski o revolyutsii*, vol. III, p. 244.
2. *Novaya zhizn'* (20 Apr 1917).
3. *Vestnik Vremennogo pravitel'stva* (7 Mar 1917).
4. *Rabochaya gazeta* (14 Mar 1917).
5. Dok. Feb., p. 465.
6. *Rabochaya gazeta* (21 Mar 1917).
7. In May, Milyukov stated publicly that this declaration was worded so that its true content would be in total contradiction to what it appeared to say. Ibid. (6 May 1917).
8. Ibid. (12 Apr 1917); *Pravda* (13 Apr 1917).
9. *Rabochaya gazeta* (15 Apr 1917).
10. A group of left Bolsheviks of the Petrograd Committee led by a certain Bagdat'ev published a leaflet calling for full power to the soviets. They

were taken to task by Lenin and the CC and accused of adventurism. V. I. Lenin, *Polnoe sobranie sochinenii*, vol. XXXI, pp. 319–20. Apparently these Bolsheviks were largely from the Vyborg District. At the 22 April session of the First Petrograd City Conference of Bolsheviks, one speaker noted: 'Yesterday we did not take into account the circumstances of the situation and put forth unsuitable slogans. The Vyborg comrades understand this especially keenly.' *Pervaya petrogradskaya obshchegorodskaya konferentsiya RSDRP (b)* (M.-L., 1925) p. 59.

11. *Rabochaya gazeta* (21 Apr 1917).
12. Ibid. (22 Apr 1917).
13. Sobolev, *Revolutsionnoe soznanie*, pp. 223–30.
14. Dok. Apr., pp. 740–50.
15. Hats, as opposed to kerchiefs, symbolised 'society'.
16. Perazich, *Tekstili Leningrada*, p. 42.
17. P. F. Kudelli, *Leningradskie rabochie v bor'be za vlast' sovetov v 1917 g.* (L., 1924) p. 15.
18. *Delo naroda* (25 Apr 1917).
19. Kudelli, *Leningradskie rabochie*, p. 23.
20. Dok. Apr., p. 167.
21. Startsev, 'K voprosu', p. 11.
22. Dok. Apr., p. 438.
23. Ibid., p. 438; Startsev, 'K voprosu', pp. 116–22.
24. *Rabochaya gazeta* (22 Apr 1917).
25. V. V. Grebach, *Rabochie Baltiitsy v trekh revolyutsiakh* (L., 1959) p. 115; Dok. Apr., p. 733.
26. *Izvestiya* (27 Apr 1917).
27. Dok. Apr., p. 773.
28. *Rabochaya gazeta* (22 Apr 1917).
29. Among these were: Rozenkrants Copper Foundry (*Pravda* (28 Apr 1917)); Old Parviainen (Kudelli, *Leningradskie rabochie*, p. 24); Russkii Renault, Langezipen Machine-construction Factory, Puzyrev Auto Factory, New Lessner Machine-construction Factory, Russko-Baltiiskii Wagon-construction (Dok. Apr., pp. 732–68, passim); Sestroretsk Arms Factory (*Bastiony revolyutsii*, vol. I, p. 236); and others.
30. *Pravda* (22 Apr 1917).
31. *Soldatskaya pravda* (26 Apr 1917), cited in Sobolev, *Revolutsionnoe soznanie*, p. 237.
32. Ibid.
33. *Pravda* (26 Apr 1917).
34. Dok. Apr., p. 733.
35. Ibid., p. 748.
36. *Rabochaya gazeta* (14 Apr 1917).
37. Sukhanov, *Zapiski o revolyutsii*, vol. III, p. 276.
38. Ibid., pp. 275–6.
39. *Rabochaya gazeta* (25 Apr 1917).
40. *Novaya zhizn'* (2 May 1917).
41. Ibid. (14 May 1917).
42. *Izvestiya* (3 May 1917).
43. *Rabochaya gazeta* (9 May 1917).

44. Ibid. (12 May 1917).
45. Ibid.
46. Ibid. (25 Apr 1917).
47. Among the factories calling for soviet power that were not heard from were: United Cable (Dok. Apr., p. 895); Voennopodkovnyi (ibid., p. 844); 1250 workers of the new mechanical shop of the Putilov Works (*Pravda* (9 May 1917)); Tseitlin (ibid. (18 May, 1917)); and also two textile mills—Nevka and Nevskaya Nitochnaya (Perazich, *Tekstili Leningrada*, p. 42).
48. *Rabochaya gazeta* (3 May 1917).
49. *Vtoraya i tret'ya obshchegorodskie konferentsii bol'shevikov v iyule i sentyabre 1917 g.* (M.-L., 1927) p. 26.
50. *Novaya zhizn'* (4 July 1917).
51. *Raisovety Petrograda v 1917 g.* (henceforth: Raisovety) (M.-L., 1966) vol. I, pp. 71, 123.
52. *Bastiony revolyutsii*, vol. I, p. 131.
53. *Stankostroiteli imeni Sverdlova* (L., 1962) p. 76.
54. Ek. Pol., vol. I, p. 42.
55. *Pravda* (16 June 1917).
56. *Putilovtsy v trekh revolyutsiakh* (L., 1933) p. 338.
57. *Pravda* (27 June 1917).
58. *Literaturnoe nasledstvo* (M., 1971) no. 8, p. 341.
59. M. Bortik, 'Na Trubochnom zavode' in *Professional'noe dvizhenie Petrograda v 1917 g.* (L., 1928) p. 296.
60. A. Arbuzova, *Krasnaya letopis'*, no. 6 (1923) p. 175.
61. Bortik, 'Na Trubochnom', p. 272.
62. Perazich, *Tekstili Leningrada*, p. 42.
63. Suknovalov and Fomenkov, *Fabrika 'Krasnoe znamya'*, pp. 62, 79; Ek. Pol, vol. I, Table 7.
64. Shabalin, 'Ot fevralya k oktyabryu', pp. 278–9.
65. I. M. Frantishev, *Leningradskie Krasnostroiteli* (L., 1962) p. 67. See also *Vtoraya i tret'ya*, p. 63.
66. Ibid., p. 94.
67. As noted, the principal exception were the printers. At their All-Russian Congress in December 1917, of 95 delegates, there were 48 Mensheviks and 6 Menshevik sympathisers, 15 Bolsheviks and 4 sympathisers, and only 5 SRs and 5 Left SRs (*Znamya truda* (19 Dec 1917)). Thus, although generally rejecting the Bolsheviks (in Petrograd itself, the Bolsheviks briefly controlled the Printers' Union in the October period), the printers, as urbanised skilled workers, supported the SDs overwhelmingly and even gave the Bolsheviks twice as much support as the populists.
68. V. S. Voitinskii, *Gody pobed i porazhenii*, vol. I (Berlin, 1923) p. 185. Unlike the SDs, the SRs had been advocates of individual terror. The renown of their exploits had been a factor in the early weeks of the revolution in attracting to their party the mass of politically illiterate workers who had arrived during the war. On the other hand, the work of the SDs, and the Bolsheviks in particular, had been largely underground and anonymous during the war.
69. Cited in *Novaya zhizn'* (28 June 1917).

198   *The Petrograd Workers and the Fall of the Old Regime*

70. The campaign was run on national as well as municipal issues.
71. Some heavily working-class districts such as Petergof, Nevskii and Novaya derevnya were not incorporated into the city until the summer.
72. *Revolyutsionnoe dvizhenie v Rossii v mae-iyune* (henceforth: Dok. May) (M., 1959) p. 293.
73. FZK, vol. I, p. 107.
74. *Rabochaya gazeta* (20 Apr); *Pravda* (20 Apr); *Novaya zhizn'* (20 Apr); *Izvestiya* (20 Apr 1917). See also Chamberlin, *History of the Russian Revolution*, p. 162.
75. Sukhanov, *Zapiski o revolyutsii*, vol. III, pp. 339–40.
76. *Rabochaya gazeta* (20 Apr 1917).
77. *Pravda* (20 June 1917).
78. This TsIK was elected at the All-Russian Congress of Soviets in June and took over from the old EC that had consisted of the Petrograd EC plus some provincial delegates.
79. *Izvestiya* (29 June 1917).
80. *Pravda* (1 July 1917).
81. Dok. May, p. 492.
82. Ibid., pp. 489–90.
83. Sukhanov, *Zapiski o revolyutsii*, vol. III, pp. 347–8; *Novaya zhizn'* (28 Apr 1917); *Rabochaya gazeta* (29 Apr 1917).
84. Sukhanov, loc. cit.
85. *Novaya zhizn'* (9 June 1917).
86. Dok. May, p. 186.
87. Ibid., p. 311.
88. *Izvestiya* (20 June 1917).
89. *Rabochaya gazeta* (10 May 1917); *Novaya zhizn'* (11 May); *Rech'* (14 May).
90. *Novaya zhizn'*.
91. N. S. Sergeev, *Istoriya Leningradskogo Metallicheskogo zavoda imeni XXII S"ezda KPSS* (L., 1967) pp. 391, 398; Dok. May, p. 493; *Novaya zhizn'* (9 June); *Izvestiya* (19 June 1917).
92. Latsis, *Proletarskaya revolyutsiya*, no. 5 (1923) p. 107.
93. Sukhanov, *Zapiski o revolyutsii*, vol. III, pp. 357–8.
94. Resolution of the general assembly of 19 June. Note how these very 'leftist' workers rejected anarchism out of hand. It was not among this element that the anarchists found the very limited support they did before October. *Pravda* (24 June 1917).
95. Dok. May, p. 567. In Kronstadt power was effectively in the hands of the local soviet.
96. To mention one counter-argument: a major cause of the economic crisis was the disorganisation of transport. Yet, according to one estimate, 200 000 railroad cars were needed to move the factories. Surely it made better sense to use them to move the raw materials to the factories, rather than tie up so many badly needed cars. Moreover, the owners refused to commit themselves to a date for resuming production, some saying it was impossible before January 1919. Petrograd was the main centre of war production! FZK, vol. II, p. 31, and Sukhanov, *Zapiski o revolyutsii*, vol. VI, p. 64.
97. *Novaya zhizn'* (1 July 1917). *Novaya zhizn'* correctly pointed out to the

Prince that, to the degree that such chaos did exist in Russia—pogroms, lynching and other 'anarchistic acts'—it was found almost exclusively in the provinces.

98. Rab. Kon., p. 43.
99. *Rabochaya gazeta* (26 May 1917). See also ibid., 28 May and Dok. May, pp. 280–1.
100. *Izvestiya* (2 June 1917).
101. Dok. May, p. 301.
102. L. Kochan, *Russia in Revolution* (London: Paladin, 1970) pp. 218–20.
103. *Rabochaya gazeta* (25 May 1917).
104. Ibid. (28 May 1917).
105. *Rabochaya gazeta* (18 June 1917). See also the Vulkan resolution in *Pravda* (7 June).
106. P. Kudelli, *Leningradskie rabochie v bor'be za vlast' sovetov v 1917 g.* (L., 1924) pp. 34–5.
107. *Izvestiya* (23 June 1917).
108. Dok. May, p. 567. See also, ibid., pp. 564–9 passim.
109. *Novaya zhizn'* (10 May 1917).
110. *Novoe vremya* (20 June 1917).
111. Perazich, *Tekstili Leningrada*, p. 85.
112. *Rabochaya gazeta* (14 May 1917); Sukhanov, *Zapiski o revolyutsii*, vol. III, p. 109.
113. *Rech'* (13 May 1917).
114. *Novaya zhizn'* (20 May 1917).
115. Ibid. (19 May 1917).
116. Ibid. (21 May 1917).
117. Ibid. (2 June 1917); Dok. May, p. 197.
118. *Izvestiya Moskovskogo Voenno-promyshlennogo komiteta*, no. 13 (1917) p. 15. cited in P. V. Volobuev, *Ekonomicheskaya politika Vremennogo pravitel'stva* (M., 1962) p. 35.
119. *Rabochaya gazeta* (20 May 1917). This analysis could easily have appeared in *Pravda*, only the practical conclusions would have been very different. While *Pravda* called for soviet power, *Rabochaya gazeta* counselled restraint and caution in the choice of means of struggle. Only thus, it argued, could the working class avoid a repeat of November 1905 when the Petersburg industrialists responded to a general strike for the eight-hour day with a general lockout that was a prologue to total defeat. For the Mensheviks, the revolution was doomed to defeat if it could not retain the support of the liberal elements of census society. (Who these were in the late spring of 1917 was a different question.) For the Bolsheviks, the revolution could not succeed unless revolutionary democracy, led by the working class, took power on its own, removing census society, whose interests were opposed irreconcilably to those of revolutionary democracy. The only way to retain the alliance with census society that the Mensheviks so valued was to sit by and watch the revolution go down the drain.
120. FZK, vol. I, pp. 105–6.
121. Ibid., p. 123.
122. Ibid., p. 100.
123. Sukhanov, *Zapiski o revolyutsii*, vol. IV, p. 110.

123. Sukhanov, *Zapiski o revolyutsii*, vol. IV, p. 110.
124. See, e.g. Bogdanov's reaction to the plan in the EC, ibid., p. 113.
125. This point is worth emphasising because of the long-standing tendency in the Western historiography to argue that the Bolsheviks merely 'used' the factory committees to gain a political foothold on their way to seizing power, only to discard them once they had secured a majority in the soviets. The above discussion should make clear that Bolshevik success in the factory committees was not a matter of demagoguery or manipulation. In the workers' minds, state economic regulations, workers' control and soviet power were inseparably intertwined.
126. 'Petrogradskie rabochie ob iyul'skikh dynakh', *Krasnaya letopis'*, no. 9 (1924) p. 33.
127. Perazich, *Tekstili Leningrada*, p. 81.
128. Dok. May, p. 481.
129. See also the case of the Kenig Sugar Refinery, *Izvestiya* (10 May and 10 June 1917) and Peka, p. 185.
130. *Putilovtsy v trekh revolyutsiyakh*, p. 236.
131. Ibid., p. 291.
132. E. E. Kruze, *Petrogradskie rabochie v 1912–14 godakh* (M.-L., 1961) p. 72; Stepanov *Rabochie Petrograda*, p. 27; Mitel'man *et al.*, *Istoriya Putilovskogo*, p. 631.
133. *Putilovtsy v trekh revolyutsiyakh*, p. 236.
134. Mitel'man *et al.*, *Istoriya Putilovskogo*, p. 577.
135. Ibid., p. 590.
136. Ibid., pp. 614–23. In August at the Second Factory Committee Conference, Ivanov, a Putilov worker, told the assembly that 'when you discuss the current moment you must say loudly to the entire people how the bourgeoisie wants to saddle and ride us. Take note how for five months they have led us Putilovtsy by the nose, not letting us work calmly and then they place the whole blame on us. If the masses are agitated, it is because they are half hungry, and as toilers yourselves . . . you will raise your voice for all of Russia to hear what sort of deception has been committed in regard to the foremost fighters of the working class, the Putilov workers.' FZK, vol. I, p. 210.
137. Dok. May, p. 558.
138. According to *Novaya zhizn'* (16 May 1917), prices rose more in the first two and a half months of the revolution than in the entire preceding two and a half years. For a lower estimate of the rate of inflation, see *Istoriya SSSR*, no. 3 (1959) p. 224.
139. Perazich, *Tekstili Leningrada*, pp. 69–73; *Rabochaya Gazeta* (6 June 1917).
140. FZK, vol. I, pp. 102–3.
141. *Novaya zhizn'* (28 May 1917).
142. *Rabochaya gazeta* (18 June 1917). See also the resolutions of the printers of Kibbel (ibid., 5 July 1917); the general assembly of delegates of Petrograd printing plants (ibid., 8 July 1917); Leont'ev Textile Mills (ibid., 14 Apr 1917).
143. Compare *Rabochaya gazeta*'s pre-election editorials: 'Who votes for the Leninists votes against the Soviet of Deputies for fratricidal struggle

within revolutionary democracy for the disintegration and ruin of the revolution . . . Who can vote for a party that calls for anarchistic demonstrations, a party on whose conscience lies the responsibility for introducing a split into the Russian Revolution?' (ibid., 26 and 18 May 1917).

144. Dok. May, pp. 563–4.
145. Lenin, *Polnoe Sobranie*, vol. XXV, pp. 91–3.
146. *Izvestiya* (20 June 1917).

Chapter 7: The Struggle for Power in the Factories in April–June

1. Dok. Apr., p. 444.
2. FZK, vol. I, p. 148; *Izvestiya* (17 June 1917); *Novaya zhizn'* (19 June 1917).
3. Rab. Kon., p. 104.
4. Ibid., p. 111.
5. *Izvestiya* (17 June 1917).
6. Rab. Kon., p. 75.
7. Cited in Ferro, *La Révolution*, p. 400.
8. *Den'* (17 June), cited in ibid., p. 401.
9. See, for example, the cases of the Soikin Printing Press (*Rabochii put'*, 7 Sept 1917); Russkaya Univernil' (*Rabochaya gazeta*, 2 July 1917); unnamed (ibid., 18 May 1917); Brenner Factory (*Novaya zhizn'*, 22 July 1917; FZK, vol. I, p. 147; *Revolyutsionnoe dvizhenie v Rossii v iyule 1917 g.* (henceforth: Dok. July) (M., 1959) p. 341); Aerowheel Factory (Rab. Kon., pp. 112–14); Petichev Cable Factory (FZK, vol. II, pp. 54–5); Nevskii Shoe Factory (ibid., p. 57); Promet Pipe Factory (*Izvestiya*, 17 June 1917; *Novaya zhizn'*, 19 June 1917). These are only a sample of such cases.
10. V. I. Selitskii, *Petrogradskie massy v bor'be za rabochii kontrol'*, p. 200, cited in Sobolev, *Revolutsionnoe soznanie*, pp. 260–1.
11. FZK, vol. I, p. 112. Lenin's 'April Theses' did state: 'Not the "introduction of socialism" as our direct task, but the transition to *control* on the part of the Soviet of WD of the social production and distribution of goods' (Dok, Apr., p. 5). But this was a question of regulation by a soviet state. Workers' control involved the immediate establishment of direct control at the plant level, although it by no means excluded state control. In fact, the opposite was true.
12. *Pravda* (24 May 1917).
13. *Putilovtsy v trekh revolyutsiyakh*, p. 431.
14. FZK, vol. I, p. 122. See also the speeches of Fokht, Vakkhanen and Tseitlin, ibid., pp. 123–4.
15. Ibid., p. 67.
16. Ibid., p. 183.
17. Rab. Kon., p. 75.
18. Ibid., pp. 70, 80; *Putilovtsy v trekh revolyutsiyakh*, p. 337.
19. *Nakanune Oktyabr'skogo vooruzhennogo vosstaniya, 1–24 oktyabrya* (henceforth: Dok. Nak.) (M., 1962) p. 288.
20. FZK, vol. I, p. 113.

21. *Izvestiya* (17 June 1917).
22. See also the case of the Brenner factory. *Novaya zhizn'* (22 July 1917); FZK, vol. I, p. 147; Dok. July, p. 342.
23. FZK, vol. I, p. 181.
24. Dok. April, p. 445; FZK, vol. I, p. 93.
25. See note 22.
26. FZK, vol. I, p. 171.
27. *Novaya zhizn'* (13 May 1917). See also Perazich, *Tekstili Leningrada*, p. 80.
28. *Rabochaya gazeta* (6 June 1917).
29. FZK, vol. I, p. 126.
30. *Putilovtsy v trekh revolyutsiyakh*, p. 333.

Chapter 8: The July Days

1. Dok. May, p. 500.
2. *Novaya zhizn'* (10 June 1917).
3. Dok. May, p. 501. *Rabochaya gazeta* claimed that these 300 workers were in fact Bolsheviks, and undoubtedly many were. But they were at the same Putilov workers and most, if party members, had joined only since February. (The first meeting of the factory party collective was attended by only 56 workers (Mitel'man *et al.*, *Istoriya Putilovskogo*, p. 562).) If they did not represent the mood of the entire factory, then at least of a very significant segment.
4. *Pravda* (1 June 1917).
5. Dok. May, p. 560.
6. M. Mikhailov, *Krasnaya letopis'*, no. 50 (1932) p. 108.
7. A week earlier, a representative of the Soviet complained that the factory had stopped making contributions to that body. Ibid., p. 200.
8. Dok. May, pp. 558–61.
9. M. I. Latsis, *Proletarskaya revolyutsiya*, no. 5 (1923) p. 106.
10. Dok. May, pp. 559–60.
11. Among the historical monographs on the July Days, one should mention especially A. Rabinowitch's *Prelude to Revolution* (1968) and O. A. Znamenskii's *Iyul'skii krizis v 1917 g.* (1967).
12. 'We see', one worker told the Soviet Congress, 'that the government of capitalists desires from time to time to let some workers' blood flow.' Znamenskii, *Iyul'skii*, p. 22.
13. *Rabochaya gazeta* (28 June 1917).
14. Ibid. (2 July 1917).
15. 'Petrogradskie rabochie ob iyul'skikh dnyakh', *Krasnaya letopis'*, no. 9 (1924) pp. 19–41 passim.
16. Latsis, *Proletarskaya revolyutsiya*, no. 5 (1923) p. 111.
17. Znamenskii, *Iyul'skii Krizis*, pp. 16–17.
18. A. Metelev, *Proletarskaya revolyutsiya*, no. 6 (1922) pp. 159–61.
19. They resigned ostensibly in protest over concessions made by the socialist ministers to the Ukrainian Rada, which was demanding autonomy.
20. Bolshevik policy was to keep the workers from demonstrating at this time.

21. *Krasnaya letopis'*, no. 9 (1924) p. 19.
22. Znamenskii, *Iyul'skii Krizis*, p. 55.
23. Ibid., pp. 84, 106; *Rabochaya gazeta* (6 July 1917); Perazich, *Tekstili Leningrada*, p. 81, *Krasnaya letopis'*, no. 9 (1924) p. 31.
24. P. Milyukov, *History of the Second Russian Revolution*, vol. I, p. 244. Cited in Chamberlin, *History of the Russian Revolution*, vol. I, p. 171.
25. Dok. July, p. 21.
26. Sukhanov, *Zapiski o revolyutsii*, vol. IV, p. 430.
27. It is true that Chernov was arrested by a group of sailors and narrowly rescued by Trotsky. But Trotsky implies that these sailors were in fact provocateurs. At any rate, maximalist and anarchist influence was considerably stronger among the Kronstadt sailors than in the Petrograd working class.
28. Metelev, *Proletarskaya revolyutsiya*, no. 6 (1922) p. 171.
29. Sukhanov, *Zapiski o revolyutsii*, p. 440.
30. Chamberlin, *History of the Russian Revolution*, p. 177.
31. *Krasnaya letopis'*, no. 9 (1924) pp. 25, 34.
32. Ibid., pp. 30–1.
33. I. G. Tomkevich, *'Znamya oktyabrya' – ocherki istorii zavoda* (L., 1972) p. 40. See also Perazich, *Tekstili Leningrada*, p. 86 on beatings and arrests of Textile Union activists.
34. *Vtoraya i tret'ya obshchegorodskie konferenstsii bol'shevikov v iyule i sentyabre 1917 g.* (henceforth: *Vtoraya*) (M.-L., 1927) p. 83.
35. Sukhanov, *Zapiski o revolyutsii*, vol. V, p. 20.
36. See, for example, Dok. July, pp. 161–4; Peka, pp. 211–14; *Istoriya Leningradskogo ordena Lenina i ordena Krasnogo znameni obuvnoi fabriki imeni Ya. Kalinina* (L., 1968) p. 171.
37. *Krasnaya letopis'*, pp. 38–41.
38. *Novaya zhizn'* (18 July 1917); Sukhanov, *Zapiski o revolyutsii*, vol. IV, p. 501. It was later learned that Kerenskii had ordered these ships sunk in the event they proved 'undependable'.
39. Ibid., p. 486.
40. *Rabochaya gazeta* (11 July, 1917).
41. Sukhanov, *Zapiski o revolyutsii*, p. 506. It should be noted that in this Tsereteli was acting independently of the Menshevik CC where Dan's position had won out, viz. that the major threat to the revolution was from the right.
42. Ibid., vol. V, p. 115.
43. Ibid., vol. IV, p. 474; Tomkevich, *'Znamya oktyabrya'*, p. 20.
44. Metelev, *Proletarskaya revolyutsiya*, no. 6 (1922) p. 172.
45. Latsis, *Proletarskaya revolyutsiya*, no. 5 (1923) p. 114; Rabinowitch, *Prelude to Revolution*, p. 211.
46. *Izvestiya* (6 July 1917).
47. *Vtoraya*, p. 60.
48. Metelev, p. 171. See also *Novaya zhizn'* (7 July 1917).
49. I. Naumov, *Zapiski vyborzhtsa*, p. 32.
50. Peka, p. 211.
51. FZK, vol. I, p. 191.
52. *Vtoraya*, p. 61. The same was noted by several Bolshevik and non-Bolshevik observers. Ibid., p. 68; *Novaya zhizn'* (11 July 1917).

53. *Vtoraya*, pp. 61–2; Peka, p. 210; *Novaya zhizn'* (13, 19, 20 July 1917).
54. Sukhanov, *Zapiski o revolyutsii*, vol. v, pp. 20–2.
55. Ibid., p. 23.
56. *Izvestiya* (14 July 1917). See also, e.g., Tomkevich, *'Znamya oktyabrya'*, p. 40.
57. *Krasnaya letopis'*, no. 9 (1927) p. 35. See also Ya. Temkin, *U nas na Galernom ostrovke* (L., 1958) p. 12.
58. Few workers from this district participated in the demonstrations. See below, p. 175.
59. Dok. July, p. 103.
60. Dok. July, pp. 162–3; *Vtoraya*, p. 63.
61. *Vtoraya*, pp. 61–4, 92; B. Shabalin, 'Ot fevralya k oktyabryu', in *Bastiony revolyutsii*, vol. i, p. 293.
62. *Vtoraya*, p. 57.
63. The reference is apparently to a revolutionary committee set up in the factory to fight counterrevolution.
64. Dok. July, p. 71.
65. *Izvestiya* (5 July 1917). The TsIK expelled Lenin and Kamenev pending the results of an investigation into the charges that the Bolsheviks had taken German gold.
66. Ibid.(12 July 1917).
67. Peka, p. 212.
68. *Novaya zhizn'* (7 July 1917).
69. Peka, p. 213.
70. Perazich, *Tekstili Leningrada*, p. 86.
71. Ibid.
72. *Novaya zhizn'* (8 July 1917).
73. *Vtoraya*, p. 95.
74. *Krasnaya letopis'*, no. 9 (1927) p. 32.
75. To take one measure, in the 20 August duma elections, the Bolsheviks received one-third of the vote, as compared to 20 per cent in the May district duma elections. The SRs gathered only 37 per cent of the vote this time and the Mensheviks 4 per cent, a drastic decline from the 56 per cent received by the moderate socialists in May (*Delo naroda*, 23 Aug). Moreover, among the Mensheviks and SRs the left wings, which stood closer to the Bolshevik position, were gaining steadily.

Selected Bibliography

I Archives

Leningradskii gosudarstvennyi arkhiv Oktyabr'skoi revolyutsii i sotsialisticheskogo stroitel'stva (LGAORSS)
    fond 171, opis' 1, delo 1 (Kolpino District Soviet protocols)
    1000/73/12 (Petrograd Soviet, Soldiers' Section protocols, 12 Mar 1917)
    1000/73/16 (Petrograd Soviet, Workers' Section protocols, 20 Mar 1917)
    4591/1/1 (general factory assemblies and conferences of the Petrograd
        Metalworkers' Union, protocols, Mar–Dec 1917)
    4601/1/10 (Arsenal Factory committee protocols, 7 Mar–30 Dec 1917)
    4602/7/7 (Patronnyi Factory general assembly protocols, 3 Mar–11 Nov
        1917)
    7384/7/21 (Mandate Committee of EC of Petrograd Soviet)
    7384/9/293 (Petrograd Soviet, factory resolutions on return to work,
        6–16 Mar 1917)
    9391/1/11 (Admiralty Shipyard general assembly protocols, 12 Apr
        1917–9 Dec 1918)
Gosudarstvennyi istoricheskii arkhiv leningradskoi oblasti (GIALO)
    416/25/5 (Baltic Shipyard administration—conciliation chamber)
    416/5/30 (Baltic Shipyard administration—conciliation chamber pro-
        tocols, 1917)

II Published Documents and Statistics

Chugaev, D. A. ed. *Rabochii klass Sovetskoi Rossii v pervyi god diktatury
    proletariata* (M., 1967)
Doneseniya komissarov Petrogradskogo Voenno-revolyutsionnogo komiteta,
    2 vols (M., 1957)
*Ekonomicheskoe polozhenie Rossii nakanune Velikoi Oktyabr'skoi sotsialis-
    ticheskoi revolyutsii*, 3 vols (M.-L., 1957) (Ek. Pol.)
'Fevral'skaya revolyutsiya i Okhrannoe otdelenie', *Byloe*, nos 7–8 (1918)
Fleer, M. G. ed. *Rabochee dvizhenie v gody voiny* (M., 1925)
Grave, B. B. ed. *Burzhuaziya nakanune Fevral'skoi revolyutsii* (M.-L.,
    1927)
Lenin, V. I., *Polnoe sobranie sochinenii*, 5th edn (M., 1958–67)
Materialy po statistike Petrograda, vypusk I (1920)
Materialy po statistike truda, vypusk V
Materialy po statistike truda severnoi oblasti, vypusk I (1918)
Mikhoilov, M., 'Rabochie zavoda Baranovskogo v bor'be za Oktyabr',
    Krasnaya letopis', no. 50–1 (1932)
Oktyabr'skaya revolyutsiya i fabzavkomy, 2 vols (M., 1927–8) (FZK)

205

Pervaya Petrogradskaya obshchegorodskaya konferentsiya RSDRP(b) v aprele 1917 g. (M., 1925)
Pervyi legal'nyi Peterburgskii komitet RSDRP(b) v 1917 g. (M.-L., 1927) (Peka)
Popov, A. L. ed. *Oktyabr'skii perevorot* (Petrograd, 1919)
Putilovtsy v trekh revolyutsiyakh (L., 1933)
Rabochii kontrol' i natsionalizatsiya promyshlennykh predpriyatii Petrograda v 1917–1919 gg., vol. I (L., 1949) (Rab. Kon.)
Raionnye sovety Petrograda v 1917 g., 3 vols (M.-L., 1966–8)
Velikaya Oktyabr'skaya sotsialisticheskaya revolyutsiya. Dokumenty i materialy
 Revolyutsionnoe dvizhenie v Rossii posle sverzheniya samoderzhaviya (M., 1957) (Dok. Feb.)
 Revolyutsionnoe dvizhenie v Rossii v aprele 1917 g. (M., 1958) (Dok. Apr.)
 Revolyutsionnoe dvizhenie v Rossii v mae–iyune 1917 g. (M., 1959) (Dok. May)
 Revolyutsionnoe dvizhenie v Rossii v iyule 1917 g. (M., 1959) (Dok. July)
 Revolyutsionnoe duizhenie v Rossii v avguste 1917 g. (M., 1947) (Dok. Aug.)
 Nakanune Oktyabr'skogo vooruzhennogo vosstaniya, 1–24 oktyabrya 1917 g. (M., 1962) (Dok. Nak.)
 Oktyabr'skoe vooruzhennoe vosstanie v Petrograde (M., 1957) (Dok. Okt.)
Vserossiiskaya promyshlennaya i professionel'naya perepis' 1918 g. Trudy Ts SU vol. XXVI, vypusk 1 and 2 (M., 1926)
Vtoraya i tret'ya obshchegorodskie konferentsii bol'shevikov v iyule i sentyabre 1917 g. (M.-L., 1927) (Vtoraya)

III Workers' Memoirs

Alliluev, S., 'V dni Oktyabrya na Elektricheskoi stantsii imeni 1886', *Krasnaya letopis'*, no. 6 (1923)
Arbuzova, A., 'Oktyabr' 1917 na Trubochnom zavode', *Krasnaya letopis'*, no. 6 (1923)
Buiko, A., *Put' rabochego* (M., 1934)
Buntilov, A., *Za pechatnym stolom* (M., 1923)
Buzinov, A., *Za Nevskoi zastavoi* (M.-L., 1930)
Ivanov, B., *Zapiski proshlogo* (M., 1919)
Kudelli, P. F., ed., *Leningradskie rabochie v bor'be za vlast' sovetov v 1917 g.* (L., 1924)
Metelev, A., 'Iul'skoe vosstanie v Petrograde', *Proletorskaya revolyutsiya*, no. 6 (1922)
Naumov, I. K., *Zapiski vyborzhtsa* (L., 1933)
'Petrogradskie rabochie ob iyul'skikh dnyakh', *Krasnaya letopis'*, no. 9 (1924)
Samoilov, F. N., *Vospominaniya ob ivanovo-voznesenskom rabochem dvizhenii*, part II (M., 1924)

Shapovalov, A. S., *V bor'be za sotsialism* (M., 1934)

Shlyapnikov, A. S., *Kanun semnadtsatogo goda* (M.–Petrograd, 1923)

Shotman, A., *Kak iz iskry vozgorelos' plamya* (L., 1935)

Skorinko, I., 'Vospominaniya rabochego ob Oktyabre 1917 g.', *Krasnaya letopis'*, no. 6 (1923)

Tikhanov, A., 'Rabochie pechatniki v Petrograde, 1907–1914', in *Materialy po istorii professional'nogo dvizheniya v Rossii*, sbornik III (M., 1925)

V boyakh za Oktyabr' (L., 1932)

V ogne revolyutsionnykh boev, 2 vols (M., 1967 and 1971)

Vyborgskaya storona (L., 1957)

Zalezhskii, V. N., 'Peryyi legal'nyi Peka', *Proletarskaya revolyutsiya*, no. 13 (1923)

IV Memoirs of Non-workers

Bulkin, F. A., *Na zare profdvizheniya* (L., 1924)

Dingel'shtedt, F., 'Vesna proletarskoi revolyutsii', *Krasnaya letopis'*, no. 1(12) (1925)

Latsis, M. I., 'Iyul'skie dni v Petrograde', *Proletarskaya revolyutsiya*, no. 5 (1923)

Leont'ev, L., 'V ryadakh "Mezhraionki"', *Krasnaya letopis'*, no. 11 (1924)

Maevskii, E., *Kanun revolyutsii* (Petrograd, 1918)

Malakhovskii, V., *Iz istorii krasnoi gvardii* (L., 1925)

Mstislavskii, S., *Sem' dnei* (Berlin–Petersburg–M., 1922)

Rafes, M., 'Moi vospominaniya', *Byloe*, no. 19 (1922)

Sukhanov, N., *Zapiski o revolyutsii*, 7 vols (Berlin–Peterburg–M., 1919–23)

Tsvetkov-Prosveshchenskii, A. K., *Mezhdu dvumya revolyutsiyamy* (M.-L., 1933)

Voitinskii, V. S., *Gody pobed i porazhenii*, 2 vols (Berlin, 1923)

V Contemporary Press and Periodicals

Byuleten' obshchestva fabrikantov i zavodchikov Moskovskogo promyshlennogo raiona. (Moscow area industrialists' bulletin)

Delo naroda (SR)

Derevoobdelochnik (Petersburg Union of Woodworkers)

Iskra (Menshevik–Internationalist)

Izvestiya (Organ of Petrograd Soviet EC and later also of TsIK)

Metallist (Petrograd Union of Metalworkers)

Novaya zhizn' (Menshevik–Internationalist, Gorky's paper)

Pravda (Bolshevik)

Rabochaya gazeta (Menshevik–Defencist)

Rabotnitsa (Bolshevik, women workers' bi-monthly)

Rech' (Kadet)

Torgovo-promyshlennaya gazeta (commerce and industry)

Znamya truda (Left SR)

208   *The Petrograd Workers and the Fall of the Old Regime*

VI Secondary Sources: Histories of Factories, Unions, Industries, etc.

Bastiony revolyutsii sbornik materialov po istorii leningradskikh zavodov v
    1917 g. (L., 1957)
Bazilevich, K., *Professional'noe dvizhenie rabotnikov svyazi* (M., 1927)
Borisov, G. and Vasil'ev, S., *Stankostroiteli imeni Sverdlova* (L., 1962)
Bortyk, M., 'Na Trubochnom zavode' in *Professional'noe dvizhenie v Petrog-
    rade v 1917 g.* (L., 1928)
Frantishev, I. M., *Leningradskie krasnostroiteli* (L., 1962)
Ganichev, L. S., *Na Aptekarskom ostrove* (L., 1967)
Grebach, V. V., Kuznedsov, K. A., et al., *Rabochie baltiitsy v trekh revolyut-
    siyakh* (L., 1959).
*Istoriya Leningradskogo ordena Lenina i ordena krasnogo znameni obuvnoi
    fabriki im. ya. kalinina* (L., 1968)
Istoriya Leningradskogo soyuza rabochikh poligraficheskogo proizvodstva
    (L., 1925)
Krasnyi Treugol'nik na putyakh Oktybrya (L., 1927)
Kabo, E. A., *Ocherki rabochego byta* (M., 1928)
Kukushkin, V., *Sestroretskaya dinastiya* (L., 1959)
Mitel'man, M., Glebov, B. and Ul'yanskii, A., *Istoriya Putilovskogo zavoda*,
    3rd edn (L., 1961)
Notman, K. V., 'Trubochnyi zavod na Oktyabr'skikh putyakh', *Krasnaya
    letopis'*, nos 50–1 (1932)
*Ocherk istorii Leningradskogo soyuza rabochikh derevoobdelochnikov za
    1917–18 gg.* (L., 1927)
Perazich, V., *Tekstili Leningrada v 1917 g.* (L., 1927)
Rozanov, M., *Obukhovtsy* (L., 1938)
Rozenfel'd, Ya. S. and Klimenko, K. I., *Istoriya mashinostroeniya SSSR*
    (M., 1961)
Sergeev, N. S., *Metallisty—Istoriya Leningradskogo metallicheskogo zavoda
    imeni XXII s"ezda KPSS* (L., 1967)
Shatilova, T., 'Professional'nye soyuzy i Oktyabr'', *Krasnaya letopis'*, no. 2
    (1927)
Shatilova, T., *Ocherki istorii leningradskogo soyuza khimikov v 1907–1918
    gg.* (L., 1927)
Smirnov, A., *Poslednie dni Utemanov—1917 na fabrike 'Skorokhod'* (M.-
    L., 1925)
Suknovalov, A. E. and Fomenkov, I. N., *Fabrika 'Krasnoe znamya'* (L.,
    1968)
Tanyaev, A., *Ocherki po istorii zheleznodorozhnikov v revolyutsii 1917-go
    goda* (M.-L., 1925)
Temkin, Ya., *U nas na Galernom ostrove* (L., 1958)
Tomkevich, I. G., *'Znamya Oktybrya'—ocherki istorii zavoda* (L., 1972)
Tsybul'skii, V. A., 'Rabochie Sestroretskogo zavoda v 1917 g.', *Istoriya
    SSR*, no. 7 (1959)
Vasil'eva, M. V., *Rabochie fabriki Svetoch v trekh revolyutsiyakh* (L., 1968)

VII Secondary Sources—General

Avrich, P., *The Russian Anarchists* (London: Thames and Hudson, 1973)
Avrich, P., 'The Bolshevik Revolution and Workers' Control in Russian Industry', *Slavic Review*, vol. XXII, no. 1 (1973)
Balabanov, M. S., *Ot 1905 k 1917 g.* (M.-L., 1927)
Balabanov, M. S., *Rabochee dvizhenie v Rossii v gody pod"ema 1912–14 gg.* (L., 1927)
Braverman, H., *Labor and Monopoly Capital* (New York: Monthly Review Press, 1974)
Burdzhalov, E. N., *Vtoraya russkaya revolyutsiya* (M., 1967)
Chamberlin, W. H., *History of the Russian Revolution* (New York: Universal Library, 1965)
Devlin, R., 'Petrograd Workers and Workers' Factory Committees in 1917' (PhD dissertation, SUNY Binghamton, 1976)
Ferro, M., *La Révolution de 1917* (Paris: Aubier, 1967)
Gaponenko, L. S., 'Rabochii klass Rossii na kanune velikogo Oktyabrya', *Istoricheskie zapiski*, no. 73 (M., 1963)
Golovanova, L. V., 'Raionnye komitety RSDRP (b) Petrograda v 1917 g.' (Candidate's dissertation, Leningrad State University, 1974)
Haimson, L. H., ed., *The Mensheviks* (Chicago: University of Chicago Press, 1975)
Haimson, L. H., *Russian Society and Politics on the Eve of the First World War*, vol. I (New York: W. W. Norton, forthcoming)
Hasegawa, T., *The February Revolution: Petrograd, 1917* (Seattle, 1980)
Hobsbawm, E. J., 'Peasants and Politics', *Journal of Peasant Studies*, vol. I (1973)
Istoriya rabochikh Leningrada, vol. I (L., 1972)
Johnson, C., *Revolutionary Change* (Boston: Little Brown, 1966)
Keep, J., *The Russian Revolution—A Study in Mass Mobilization* (New York: W. W. Norton, 1976)
Kleinbort, L. M., *Ocherki rabochei intelligentsii* (Petrograd, 1923)
Kochan, L., *Russia in Revolution* (London: Paladin, 1966)
Koenker, D., *Moscow Workers and the 1917 Revolution* (Princeton: Princeton University Press, 1981)
Kruze, E. E., *Petrogradskii rabochie v 1912–14 gg.* (M.-L., 1961)
Leiberov, I. P., 'O revolyutsionnykh vystupleniyakh petrogradskikh rabochikh v gody pervoi mirovoi voiny i Fevral'skoi revolyutsii', *Voprosy istorii*, no. 2 (1964)
Levin, I. D., 'Rabochie kluby v Petrograde (1907–14)' in *Materialy po istorii professional'nogo dvizheniya v Rossi*, sbornik III (M., 1925)
Mandel, D., 'The Intelligentsia and the Working Class in 1917', *Critique*, no. 14 (1981)
Melgunov, S. P., *The Bolshevik Seizure of Power* (Santa Barbara: ABC-CAO, 1972)
Pearson, R., *The Russian Moderates and the Crisis of Tsarism* (London and Basingstoke: Macmillan, 1977)
Rabinowitch, A., *Prelude to Revolution—The Petrograd Bolsheviks and the July 1917 Uprising* (Bloomington: Indiana University Press, 1968)

Rashin, A. G., *Formirovanie rabochego klassa Rossii* (M., 1958)
Rosenburg, W. G., *The Liberals in the Russian Revolution* (Princeton: Princeton University Press, 1974)
Rossiiskii proletariat: Oblik, bor'ba, gegemoniya (M., 1970)
Scott, R. H., 'The Russian Peasantry in the First and Second Dumas', mimeographed seminar paper (Russian Institute, Columbia University, 1973)
T. Shanin, ed., *Peasants and Peasant Society* (Harmondsworth: Penguin, 1971)
Shelavin, K., *Ocherki russkoi revolyutsii 1917 goda, fevral'-iyul'*, part I (Petrograd, 1923)
Shkaratan, O. I., 'Izmeneniya v sotsial'nom sostave rabochikh Leningrada 1917–28', *Istoriya SSSR*, no. 5 (1959)
Shkaratan, O. I. and Leiberov, I. P., 'K voprosu o sostave petrogradskikh promyshlennykh rabochikh v 1917 g.', *Voprosy istorii*, no. 1 (1961)
Shlyapnikov, A., *Semnadtsatyi god* (M.–Petrograd, 1923)
Smith, S. A., *Red Petrograd: Revolution and the Factories – 1917–18* (Cambridge: Cambridge University Press, forthcoming 1983)
S-skii, S., *Psikhologiya russkogo rabochego voprosa* (St Petersburg, 1923)
Sobolev, G. L., *Revolyutsionnoe soznanie rabochikh i soldat Petrograda v 1917 g. Period dvoevlastiya* (L., 1973)
Startsev, A., 'K voprosu o sostave petrogradskoi krasnoi gvardii', *Istoriya SSSR*, no. 1 (1962)
Stepanov, Z. V., *Rabochie Petrograda v period podgotovki i provedeniya Oktyabr'skogo vooruzhennogo vosstaniya, avgust'-oktyabr' 1917 g.* (L., 1965)
Suny, R. G., 'Toward a Social History of the October Revolution', *American Historical Review*, vol. 88, no. 1 (1983)
Tilly, C., 'Revolutions and Collective Violence', in Greenstein, F. and Polsby, W. W., eds, *Handbook of Political Science*, vol. V (Reading Mass: Addison-Wesley, 1975)
Trotsky, L., *History of the Russian Revolution*, 3 vols (London: Sphere Books, 1965)
Trukan, A. G., *Oktyabr' v tsentral'noi Rossii* (M., 1967)
Volobuev, P. V., *Proletariat i burzhuaziya v 1917 g.* (M., 1964)
Volobuev, P. V., *Ekonomicheskaya politika Vremennogo pravitel'stva* (M., 1962)
Znamenskii, O. A., *Iyul'skii krizis v 1917 g.* (M.-L., 1964)

Index

Admiralty Shipbuilding Factory, 172
Admiralty (sub) District, 58, 126
Aerowheel Factory, 201 n9
Afanas'ev, D., 167–8
Aivaz Machine-construction Factory,
    132–3, 159–60
Aleksandr-Nevskaya Textile Mill, 59
Aleksandr-Nevskii (sub) District, 59, 126
Aleksandrovskii Locomotive Factory, 57
anarchism, 2, 18, 36, 103, 107, 146
    154–5, 203 n27
anarchists, 127, 132–3, 154, 198 n94
Anikst, A., 47
Antipov, N. K., 154
Antonov, A., 37, 47
April crisis, 4, 69, 111–20
Arsenal Factory, 36
Artur Koppel' Wagon-construction
    Factory, 57
Avilov, N. P., 138

Babytsyn, A. A., 16
bakers, 31
Balabanov, M., 29
Baltic Shipbuilding Factory, 55, 98–100,
    117
Baltic Wagon-construction Factory, 154
Baranovskii Machine-construction and
    Pipe Factory, 123, 160, 202 n7
Bazarov, V., 28, 66, 183 n25, 184 nn61
    and 68
Benois Machine-construction Factory,
    152
Bol'shaya Sampsion'evskaya
    Manufaktura, 64
Bolshevik party
    in April crisis, 195–6 n10
    Central Committee of, 67, 74, 127,
        158–9, 163–4, 168
    and civil war, 119, 168
    and coalition, 120
    and dual power, 66–7, 79
    and eight-hour day, 89
    in February Revolution, 63, 74, 80–1

First Petrograd Conference of, 72,
    83–4, 196 n10
in July Days, 6, 163–4, 202 n20
after Juy, 7, 166–76 *passim*
and June demonstration, 127–30
and liberal bourgeoisie, 74–9, 199
    n119
Petersburg Committee of, 41, 49, 63,
    67, 69, 130, 152, 160–1, 168, 170
Second Petrograd Conference of, 123,
    125, 173
social composition of, 40–1, 55–6, 189
    n30
and Soviet majority, 160–1
in State Duma, 33, 67
support for, 3, 19, 40, 52, 55, 58, 73, 75,
    113, 123–8, 144–5, 158–9,
    172–3, 179, 204 n75
view of unskilled workers, 28
and war, 71–2, 113
and War-Industry Committees, 74–5
and workers' control, 104, 152
in Workers' Section of Soviet, 122–3,
    134
bourgeoisie, *see* census society
Brenner Machine-construction Factory,
    201 nn9, 12
Buiko, A., 22, 32
Bulkin, F., 40, 43
Burdzhalov, E. N., 79
Buzinov, A., 7, 11, 15–19, 30–2, 50, 182
    n18, 183 n25

Cable Factory, 67
census society
    in April crisis, 114–16
    in central city districts, 48–60 *passim*
    and coalition, 120
    definition of, 4
    and economic regulation, 31, 138–9,
        141
    in February Revolution, 61, 66, 80, 192
        n79
    hostility to soviet of, 114, 130–1